The Authors

Geoff Berry is the former head of the Centre for Public Services Management and Research (CPSMR) which is based at Staffordshire University Business School. He now runs a consultancy business, specialising in policing and crime risk management.

Jim Izat has extensive experience both as a practitioner in industry at the top management level and in teaching management within Staffordshire University Business School. He specialises in strategic and human resource management.

Rob Mawby is the Senior Research Fellow at CPSMR. He holds a Masters degree in Computing Science and specialises in communication and strategic image management.

Lynne Walley is a senior lecturer at Staffordshire University Business School. She holds a Masters degree in Criminology and specialises in criminal justice matters. She is an Associate and former deputy head of CPSMR.

Alan Wright is senior lecturer at The Institute of Police and Criminological Studies, Portsmouth University. He served in the Metropolitan Police (mainly in CID) from 1960 until 1985, reaching the rank of Chief Superintendent. He holds a PhD in Political Theory. He has extensive experience in police related research and specialises in corporate governance, business ethics and strategic management.

Practical Police Management

Geoff Berry   Jim Izat   Rob Mawby

Lynne Walley   Alan Wright

© Police Review Publishing Co 1998

First edition 1995

Second edition 1998

ISBN 0 85164 0931

**Police Review
Publishing Co
Celcon House
289-293 High Holborn
London WC1V 7HU**

Printed and bound by The Lavenham Press
Sudbury, Suffolk

Preface to First Edition

Key national objectives, local policing plans and local financial management were unlikely to have been considered by many of today's police managers when they joined the service some years ago. Indeed, the idea that management practices and techniques rooted firmly in the private sector could and should have a place in the police service was, until relatively recently, given little credence.

However, since 1979 and the advent of the Conservative government, there has been increasing emphasis on effective management in the police service in England and Wales. Home Office circulars, legislation and the studies of a range of organisations, most notably by the Audit Commission, have presented managers in the police service with new challenges. These, together with the provisions of the Police and Magistrates' Courts Act 1994 mean that now, more than ever, senior police officers have to manage effectively (even finance) as well as be effective in their role as police officers. Even civilians, who may have worked within a police environment for some years, now find themselves faced with management situations which they could not have envisaged when they first took up their positions.

The available literature on police management has however been relatively sparse until now. With the exception of Dr Tony Butler's worthy text on strategic management, there has been almost a complete lack of literature which addresses the practical problems of managing in the modern police service.

There is a pressing need for officers and civilian staff to carry out managerial tasks, both simple and complex, across the organisation. It is not just senior and ACPO officers, shift inspectors or divisional superintendents who need to be effective managers. Senior and tutor constables have some responsibility for managing resources (especially information); detective constables and detective sergeants have management responsibilities in their investigations and civilians across the service in a variety of roles have to fulfil management tasks.

There is a need for a text book which helps officers and civilian staff to deal with these responsibilities and this book meets that need. It is the first to consider the practical management issues facing the police service in the 1990s in the UK and offer possible solutions to the challenging issues facing managers in the service.

Chapters one and two outline in more detail why there is a need to give greater consideration to the principles of effective management and the trends in management structures within the service.

Each subsequent chapter broadly takes as its focus a particular resource area, namely, finance, people, information, technology, projects, image and specific issues surrounding the role and management of civilians in the service. The issues and principles relating to the management of these resources are then explored within a police context to give a practical guide to managers, both police and civilian, in the service. There is also a chapter which introduces the concepts of strategic management and how they have been applied to the police service. The book concludes with a brief review of the future of management in the police service and a full bibliography is provided.

As such, the book considers generic management skills and how they relate to the situation within the police. The wide ranging experience of the authors ensures that the concepts introduced are related at all times to the policing context. The result is a text which is of value across the whole of the service, no matter what your management position may be or the department or functional area in which you work. If you are fulfilling any management role in the service, or have ambitions to climb the ladder of promotion, it is our intention that you should be able to gain something from the book.

We have prepared the material by calling on our work across the police service over recent years. As such, we would like to thank a large number of officers, too numerous to mention for their advice and assistance in preparing this volume. It is only by asking those doing the job that we can identify the nature and requirements of the job to be done.

In conclusion, we extend our thanks to Glenys Spraggett, who painstakingly proof read the manuscript. We must also thank our respective families. They had to endure and accommodate our late nights, early mornings and 'moods' in the preparation of this volume. Hopefully, it was worth it.

Geoff Berry, Jim Izat, Rob Mawby, Lynne Walley
June 1995

Preface to Second Edition

The requirement for a Second Edition of Practical Police Management has been brought about by the success of the first. All copies of the first printing have now been sold, yet the demand for copies continues. Rather than simply reprint the first edition, the publishers asked the authors to update the text to take account of the developments in policing which have taken place since the first edition was published.

Although the structure of the book remains the same, additional material has been added to take account of the very constructive comments which the authors have had from readers. This edition includes a totally new chapter on managing professional conduct, extra information on environmental scanning in the chapter on strategic management, an enlarged bibliography and extensive updating elsewhere. As before, we owe our thanks to the large number of police officers and others who have given advice and assistance.

Geoff Berry, Jim Izat, Rob Mawby, Lynne Walley, Alan Wright
August 1997

Contents

Chapter 1: The need to consider management · 1

Chapter 2: Management structures in the police service · 15

Chapter 3: Strategic management and planning · 39

Chapter 4: Managing finance   **61**

Chapter 5: Managing people   **77**

Chapter 6: Managing professional conduct   **101**

Chapter 7: Managing change and development   121

Chapter 8: Managing information   141

Chapter 12: Managing civilians   229

Chapter 13: Managing the future:
whither police management?   245

Chapter 1

The Need to Consider Management

Introduction

It is intended in this opening chapter to examine the development of management within the police service. This development runs parallel with increasing pressures, both within the service and outside it, for greater accountability and the effective use of manpower and resources.

The development will be set against the historical background and will chart the success in terms of moving from the historical, simplistic, beginnings to the present-day sophisticated managerial structures as adopted in many large corporations.

Having established the background and the emergence of a non-managerial culture, the instruments which have underpinned the evolution of management structures will be examined in the light of the quest for effectiveness and efficiency *(the details of which will be addressed in chapter 2).*

Historical Perspective

> *'E'ry member of the force
> has a watch and chain, of course;
> If you want to know the time,
> ask a P'liceman.'*
>
> E.W.Rogers

Community policing, the buzz words of the 1990s, existed in the middle ages in the form of a constable assisted by a watchman. The practice of 'hue and cry' whereby the fugitive would be pursued by the whole community meant that every citizen had a responsibility for law and order. This recurring theme is presently enjoying a hearty revival. There was an underlying social ethos that everyone had a duty to maintain the King's Peace and was therefore able to perform a citizen's arrest on his offending contemporaries.

The notion of a constable and a local man of authority, namely a justice of the peace, together with the tenet of collective responsibility, formed the first police system.

In 1552, Sir Edward Coke then Lord Chief Justice stated that the desirable qualifications for the office of constable were honesty, knowledge and the ability to perform certain duties within the community. This role began, over the following years to encompass administrative functions.

The office of constable was viewed in a somewhat detached way with the hierarchical and seemingly totally separate judicial positions of the magistracy and the crown.

The fact that the office of constable was imposed rather than chosen meant that many men suffered extreme financial hardship during their tenure of office. It was not unusual for the more financially able to pay someone to deputise for them. This often led to the role of constable being filled by a dishonest idiot often more corrupt than those he was attempting to police (Critchley 1978).

The thread of corruption ran boldly through the middle of the criminal justice system in the 17th and 18th centuries when cries of profligacy came from all quarters and could be found at all levels. Constables were easily corruptible, as were justices of the peace who were financially rewarded in proportion to the amount of convictions they made.

To stem this deterioration of the system, with its foundation of corruption and personal avarice, clearly needed a strong and influential character who eschewed greed and had high altruistic principles. That person was found in London in 1748 in the form of Henry Fielding, best known today as the author of *Tom Jones*. Fielding with the help of his brother and a secret government grant, was able to stabilise the office of chief metropolitan magistrate and was in a position to pioneer policing reforms for London which eventually became adopted nationally.

During the office of Henry Fielding and his brother John at Bow Street there were few calls for police reform. However, Henry did form a group headed by the chief constable of Holborn. This was the early Bow Street Runners, who wore no uniform and were only distinguishable by the staff that they carried.

The dichotomy remained that whilst English people were reluctant to accept any form of social constraint, there were continual incidents of public uprising, and the watchmen of the day could only observe such disturbances passing by and *'calling the hour as if in a time of profound tranquillity'*.

Movements Towards the Metropolitan Police Act 1829

During this time Pitt's government sought to establish a formal system of policing to cover the London metropolitan area. It was to consist of a board of three salaried justices of the peace who were to act as commissioners of police. They were to have ultimate authority over constables and a chief constable. Constables were forbidden to take bribes and were required to patrol both on foot and on horseback. These reforms were seen as radical in the extreme and Pitt, after facing fierce opposition was forced to withdraw the bill. However Ireland sought to embrace many of these proposals and from them came the formation of the Royal Irish Constabulary.

It was as a direct consequence of Sir Robert Peel serving as chief secretary for Ireland between 1812 and 1818, and his being instrumental in the implementation of the reforms there that, on his return, they came to be imported to England, when he was ultimately appointed home secretary.

Sir Robert Peel's ultimate objective was the creation of a national police system, but he firstly had to address the policing arrangements in London. He examined the use of volunteer personnel as instruments in performing policing tasks and raised the question:

> *'Should we entrust a grocer, or other tradesman,*
> *however respectable, with the direction and*
> *management of 5,000 or 6,000 inhabitants?'*

The timing of Peel's proposals for reform coincided with a number of events. Firstly due to their corruption and ineptitude, public confidence in parish constables and local watchmen was waning. Secondly the government of the day preferred law enforcement to be carried out by professionals and thirdly legal philosophers such as Bentham and Colquoun had, to some extent, educated the public in the form of publications and lectures, as to attitudes on crime and punishment.

Sir Robert Peel's reforms allowed him under The Metropolitan Police Act to appoint two commissioners, who, together with Peel, were instrumental in forming the police structure as we know it today. Within a very short period the Metropolitan force was 3,300 uniformed officers with an intense and structured recruitment programme and accommodation in the form of station houses. 'Three thousand unarmed policemen, cautiously feeling their way against a hostile public brought peace and security to London in place of the turmoil and lawlessness of centuries' (Critchley 1978).

Establishing a National Police Force

During the next twenty years the embryonic forces already established in towns such as Bristol, Manchester and Liverpool began to take the same shape as the metropolitan force in London. Regular police forces were established with the implementation of the Municipal Corporations Act 1835, and from 1856 the first inspectorate of police was appointed, its main objective was to formulate consistency between the forces and to establish their official accountability. However from their inception the inspectors dealt with the chief constables and propagated an independence from the Home Office. Nevertheless their reports were forwarded to the home secretary who was then able to formulate a common policy and pay structure, but there were, at that time, 237 separate forces in England and Wales and this was not an easy task. They ranged in size to those similar to the Metropolitan force to a small borough force consisting of one man.

It is easy to see, given certain circumstances, that influential men were able to manipulate the policing practices of their small towns. Unlike today the approval of the home secretary was not required for the appointment of a chief constable. This led in many situations to corrupt and dubious activities. To alleviate such practices the inspectorate was able to recommend reforms to the home secretary to standardise such issues as pay, disciplinary matters and appointments (Brogden 1982).

As an instrument of understanding the climate of the day with regards to the character of police officers, it is amusing to read Thos. Marriott's book *A Constables Duty and How to Do It.* which was published in 1894. This book gives a marvellous insight into policing at that time and highlights perfectly that offences such as those committed whilst under the influence of drugs and joyriding are not new. He refers to it being 'a felony to administer chloroform, laudanum or any other stupefying drug to assist in the commission of an offence' and the 'furious driving of a bicycle or carriage in the street'. Nor, would it seem that the image of the hard drinking policeman as portrayed by 1970s genre of television police drama is a new one. Marriott points out that it is an offence for anyone to knowingly 'harbour a Constable during any part of the time appointed for duty, unless for the purposes of keeping or restoring order'.

The image of the morally correct, upright officer was perpetuated during evidence given, some twenty years later, to the Desborough Committee (1919) who were examining the pay and conditions of the service.

'Nowadays a policeman must be as brave as a lion as patient as Job, as wise as Solomon, as cunning as a fox must be learned in law and local bye-laws, must be of strong character, resist all temptations, and be prepared to act as a Doctor, support to the weak, terror to evil-doers, a friend and counsellor to all classes and a walking encyclopedia.'

This Committee's recommendations resulted in improved terms of pay and conditions in a standardised form, but it ruled out any form of nationalising the service as a whole. Among its main recommendations was the creation of a separate department within the Home Office to deal solely with issues pertaining to the police. Such a department would act as a 'clearing house' for information regarding criminals and more organised crime. Desborough also led to the formation of the Police Federation committees were formed for each rank level and as policy, the Home Secretary opened the annual conference, a practice that still survives today.

A Quest for Efficiency

Having looked, rather briefly, at the establishment of the police generally, the quest for refinement and efficiency begins. As has already been implied, the critical relationship is between the policy makers and those that implement that policy. It is essential therefore that non-police decision makers are aware of the impact of their policies. *(These elements will be considered more fully in Chapter 2.)*

Because of the nature of the police culture, and its practical approach, the notion of management is thought, within the service, to divorce itself from the realities of policing. The existence of such a sub culture merely entrenches group solidarity and re-enforces patterns that have existed forever.

However, significant changes in the organisation and tactics of the police service, and, the fact that being bound to a flexible and dynamic criminal justice system, mean that it cannot operate in isolation. Often that notion of isolation has led to a separate managerial style which has entrenched the idea that the police can behave in a cavalier manner within the organisation; commands are obeyed because of rank and not because of rationale and policy. It is true to say that few organisations are placed under such scrutiny as the police and few are operating on a foundation of quicksand as they are. This makes long term strategies difficult to plan.

Moving the Goal Posts – External Pressure for Change

Sir Robert Mark said in 1977 'the politicians make the laws the police enforce them, the lawyers man the trials and the prison or probation service deal with the convicted offenders'. This simplistic view is set purely in terms of policing as law enforcement.

External pressure continues concerning whether society wants the police to be detectors or preventors, and this situation is not always aided by government policy in the way that it swings from being punitive to welfarist. Any questions regarding police management cannot be divorced from the political arena or policing culture.

A further intrinsic factor is that long term strategic planning is constantly being threatened by short term cost cutting exercises influenced largely by 'fire-fighting' style management and when public outcry and media sensationalism require a sudden change of priority.

If external controls are forced upon a hostile police they are likely to prove counter-productive (Reiner 1981). This homily was to prove particularly true in 1993 when Sir Patrick Sheehy's proposals were announced. What then, have been the most recent major external influences of change on the police service? It is intended to look at some of the major reports and reviews that have had a significant effect on the management and efficacy of the service as a whole and not to list the corollary of such reports up to the present time.

The Conservative party had ridden on the law and order ticket for a number of years. Its overt policy whilst in government from 1979 to 1997 had been one of tackling crime as a team event with the public playing a major role. Thatcherism proved to be the basis for the theory and the massive amount of legislation that was passed during Margaret Thatcher's premiership in the 1980s bears testament to this, for example, the Prosecution of Offences Act, the Public Order Act, the Sexual Offences Act and several Criminal Justice Acts to name but a few.

A great deal of this legislation embraced control and was often a reactive, rather than proactive response to public concerns. One notable area was that of juvenile offending which put simplistically had the agenda of care and welfare in the 1970s and early 1980s, but of fear and panic in the late 1980s and early 1990s. Hence the large amount of 'controlling' legislation regarding juveniles and young people.

The post-Thatcher era dawned, bringing with it good and bad news for the police; the good news being the return to consensus about policing and the bad news being the view that the police were failing on almost all fronts and in need of reform (Reiner 1992).

Twin themes arose from the plethora of reports and legislation of the late 1980s. Firstly, the police alone could not address the whole problem of crime and crime management, and secondly, and inextricably bound to this, was the notion that the police should participate in community partnerships.

All the major political parties put forward a strong emphasis on law and order during the 1997 general election campaign. However whilst Michael Howard, soon to be the ex Home Secretary, addressed the issue of juvenile offending by implementing a programme to build secure units to house persistent recidivists. Jack Straw his shadow, and soon to be Home Secretary, sought, once in office, to address the root causes of juvenile offending, whilst retaining many of the more punitive measures of the former government, i.e. night time curfews for juveniles and the continuation of the 'boot camp' experiment (*Daily Telegraph* 10.6.97).

The increased community involvement exposed the police as a cultural organisation even more and highlighted both their good and bad management practices. Moving 'into the community' laid their management structures and styles open to wider scrutiny. Community liaison was further entrenched by S.96 Police Act 1996.

Whilst there was a continual process of managerial and resource development within the service, which continues today, certain reports have been landmarks in that development process.

Home Office Circulars 114/83 and 106/88

Home Office circulars serve as guidelines for forces who are expected to adhere to them, and so whilst they do not have the force of law it is customary that they are followed. Circular 114/83 *'Manpower, Effectiveness and Efficiency in the Police Service'* focused the minds of those involved in both resource allocation and management. It stated that police resources would no longer be funded from a 'bottomless pit'. It went on to say that forces needed to demonstrate that they were using their resources as effectively and efficiently as possible before any further applications for extra funding would be considered. This included the utilisation of civilians set against the cost effectiveness of using police officers.

The circular stated that forces would be subject to HMIC inspection and review and were therefore more accountable than before. *(The actual practice of inspection is dealt with in chapter 2.)*

The message of circular 114/83 was further re-iterated in circular 106/88 *'Applications for Increases in Police Force Establishments'* which made further suggestions on resource allocation:

> *'Precise duties and locations envisaged for additional manpower must be specified. The Home Secretary commends the practice in many forces of supporting their applications with a thorough review of the way in which existing resources are being directed.'*

The implication was that many forces were not being managed effectively, that many systems were flawed and that there were gross inconsistencies within forces. Equally that they should use allocation models to target resources effectively.

These arguments continued and were given a further emphasis in a paper published three years later.

The Audit Commission – Reviewing the Organisation of Provisional Police Forces

In 1991 the Audit Commission published its ninth paper. This addressed the managerial reforms of the 1980s, as chronicled earlier, and sought to restructure local sub-units, Basic Command Units, to aim for more rapid and flexible response. The review, intended as a long term strategy, aimed to address pragmatic problems and be productive in reducing management overheads, matching resources and increasing accountability. Specialist units as favoured during the 1980s can be manpower intensive, and can develop in an ad hoc manner, with little or no management structure. Therefore, it has been argued that inflated management activity does not add any real value to core policing.

The review observed that resource allocation to forces remains a lottery where, despite a Home Office formula being used to assess bids, a truer representation would be achieved by giving line managers discretion and flexibility in the use of their resources.

Counter arguments for Basic Command Unit's state that buying-in specialist resources, whilst seeming to be effective, can have a number of disadvantages, not least the fact that specialist resources may be required for more than one incident in a command area at the same time. Equally the flatter managerial style does not always take into account the unavailability of senior officers as a result of sickness, holidays, promotion, leave or attending courses.

Critics of the Audit Commission say that the agenda of total uniformity in management on-costs aimed for by the Home Office is unrealistic given the size of forces sizes and areas of expertise. This seems to be a perfectly valid criticism based on the rationale that police officers are locally appointed individuals policing by consent and that not all initiatives can be measured with the value for money ruler. Most internal reforms, as will be seen, have often been initiated by the forces themselves.

The whole tenor of this report was one of encouraging flatter management structures which set the scene for later, more radical, reviews of the service.

Many of these themes were echoed in the police reform White Paper *A police service for the 21st Century* in 1993. Estimates stated that only 40% of police time is spent dealing directly with crime, and this percentage neither matches the Home Office objectives, nor the ethos that has existed for hundreds of years.

The public, when surveyed, consistently state that it would like to see more officers on the street and the police service is constantly under pressure to respond directly to the public's priorities. Michael Howard, when Home Secretary, significantly increased the establishment numbers in 1996, with forces being allocated phased in higher recruitment numbers over a 3 year period. (Extra £247 million allocated, with each force receiving a fair share of the funding for 5,000 police constables over 3 years – David Maclean – Home Office Minister – Home Office press release 29.1.97.)

The White Paper suggested that forces should have a greater flexibility to decide on their own numbers, both of officer and civilian status. In terms of direct management, the paper recommended that there should be a fuller and more devolved operational management responsibility. Some forces had already devolved their management structure before either this white paper or the Audit Commission Paper 9 recommended such practice.

The Morgan Report

Published in 1991, this report, *'Safer Communities – The Local Delivery of Crime Prevention Through the Partnership Approach'*, popularised the idea of multi-agency partnerships and acknowledged that the police did not represent the panacea to all society's evils. Accordingly the push for co-operation became apparent from a number of government agencies e.g. the Department of Trade and Industry, the Department of the Environment, and via the extension of such schemes as Neighbourhood Watch and local crime prevention panels. The report comprehensively covers the chronology of the key Home Office initiatives leading up to this partnership approach.

The main problem, at that time, was that in practice crime prevention issues were very high on the public agenda and yet in reality marginalised and given minimal priority on the police agenda.

It is recognised that the police are safekeepers of vast amounts of data regarding the community, but the utilisation of that data must be done in an effectively managed and controlled way. *(This issue will be dealt with in chapter 8.)* Today, as more emphasis is put on the police to have an effective management structure, information management is an integral part of the whole organisation.

On the basis of reports reviewed, the Morgan Report determined that within the area of crime prevention they could highlight five different models. They were the Independent model, the Local Authority model, the Police Centred model, the Police Centred Headquarters model and the Indeterminate model. However in addressing these different models, the underlying factor was that the police must have some input into **all** of these. Equally any new multi-agency partnerships must not **conflict** with the statutory duties of the police but be taken on board **as well**.

The report recommended that chief officers should nominate a senior officer to ensure that any geographical responsibilities were similar to local authority boundaries. The Structural and Boundary Changes orders of 1995/6 affected some fourteen forces.

The Sheehy Report 1993

'When constabulary duty's to be done
the Policeman's lot is not a happy one.'

W S Gilbert

Sir Patrick Sheehy started the review procedure at a disadvantage, it will be argued, because even on his appointment as chair of the review, critics said that as a businessman he would attempt to bring commercial practices to the police service. His main opponents argued that the service could not be run like a business enterprise. That statement is true in that some police work cannot be quantified. However the application of business practices in **certain** areas could be realistically achieved.

Entire texts have been produced looking at this report, analysing it, criticising it, evaluating it, looking at its hidden agenda, protesting against it and, dare it be said, a few praising it.

As a piece of independent work no other single report has caused such a furore within the police force for decades. It sought to build on the foundations laid by the Audit Commission Paper 9 and the White Paper – *A police service for the 21st Century*. However the positive, gentle approach that had formerly been adopted was laid aside and many areas of the policing arena were exposed and subjected to scrutiny. Many would say that this can only be a good thing, however this report stirred such intense feelings that many officers, both senior and junior, felt betrayed.

In terms of management the whole tenor of the report was a continuation of the path towards a leaner, more effective management style.

> *'There is little encouragement for the police to manage their resources, the detailed system of central and local external controls over financial, management and managerial matters provide significant barriers, provides no financial or other incentive to buy in or adopt best practice from other forces and organisation, to make improvements of an organisational nature or to seek other efficiency savings. Where the will to make managerial changes and improve efficiency exists the fact that pay and conditions of service are enshrined in statutory regulation, deters and prevents the sensible exercise of local discretion and the introduction of change.'*

Comments from officers that the present managerial structure was 'like an up-side down pyramid' and that there was 'institutional acceptance of seniority and superiority of senior officers' and that 'elaborate management structures are not substitutes for leadership' only seek to reinforce the growing need to address management issues.

The Sheehy framework aimed not only to reduce the management tier of responsibility but to extend that responsibility to encompass areas of administration and information management along with resource management, change management and accountability within the rank structure. To that end the report outlined, in detail, the proposed core functions for all ranks taking into account these proposals.

Reactions of the report were extreme and varied. On one hand the Police Federation said that the suggested proposals would strike at the very heart of policing. This sentiment was echoed by the Superintendents Association who commented on the effect such proposals would have on recruitment, retention and morale. On the other hand reaction from the commerical world supported the financial and structural reoganisation of the police (Newburn 1995).

Whilst it has to be said that the furore following the report successfully resulted in the defeat of many of the proposals, suggestions on rank and management as flatter structures were implemented.

Posen and Cassels

Hot on the heels of Sheehy came yet another review of policing functions, namely the Home Office **Posen Inquiry** into 'core' and 'ancillary' tasks (Home Office 1994). The aim of the review was to list 85 tasks and divide them into 'core' and 'ancillary' roles, their categorisation then determining whether they should be carried out by the police or some other body. This prompted the then Vice Chairman of ACPO, John Hoddinot, to ask 'why on earth do we need another inquiry?' Equally, he contended that such inquiries have lacked the objectives and terms of reference to achieve that magic answer to the question, 'what should the police do?'

The Posen Inquiry coincided with the independent Cassels inquiry commissioned by the Policy Studies Institute and the Police Foundation (1996).

This review aimed to refresh the parts that other reviews failed to reach by taking a holistic view of policing through addressing police key activities, 85 in total, public demands for assistance and safety measures. The questions that the committee asked included:

- What are the central tasks of the police?
- How and by whom should those tasks be defined?
- What are the roles of other agencies?
- Should the emphasis be on prevention?

They concluded that no major police roles should be transferred either to the public sector or to local authorities. Whilst both reviews are pivotal to understanding the symbolic nature of policing and the division of activities neither impacted on the management role within the service.

Change from Within

> *'Change is inevitable. In a progressive country change is constant.'*
>
> Benjamin Disraeli

The service, in many respects faces up to, and realises, the need for change. There has clearly been a cultural change within the service stemming largely from incidents that have exposed individual officers or forces for their malpractice. Over the years many examples abound of police deviance and, when highlighted, forces have been more than keen to correct internal practices and policies. It is unfortunate that often such incidents have to occur before management address such issues. However the wind of change seems to be upon us.

The urgency for change gathered speed in the early 1980s when Britain saw serious public order riots and many criminal justice observers have referred to the 1980s as the 'decade of trouble'. This decade of trouble is perfectly chronicled in his book *Talking Blues*, which lists the major events from the January 1980 to the end of November 1989 (Graef, 1989).

Notable events from that chronology have had significant impact on both the change of culture and of policies. For example, they include the arrest in 1980 of Peter Sutcliffe for the 'Yorkshire Ripper' murders, which generated intense criticism of the police handling of the case. The Byford Report (1982) reviewed the catalogue of mistakes made during the investigation, and as a result, the major incident procedure was completely changed and many incident rooms computerised in the attempt to eradicate duplicity and missed opportunities. The report was so critical of management decisions that it still remains on restricted access and is considered too sensitive for either police officer or public perusal.

Following a 'fly on the wall' documentary in 1982, filmed in Thames Valley, which exposed the appalling way in which rape victims were dealt with, many forces addressed their treatment of such victims by using female officers and specialised rooms in which women could be examined and interviewed.

Specific incidents, already well documented, have led to forces restructuring certain units and sharply changing lines of management and policy. Reading the commentators of the day, (Reiner, 1991: Holdaway, 1983: Morgan 1989) it is easier to correlate the massive amounts of legislation during the 1980s with the equally swift moving tide of internal change. The notion of accountability had dawned and due, in part, to the errors of judgment of forces, their mystique had fallen away.

With many good management practices established, forces are now able to communicate with each other and share common experience through the various committees, the format of which will be examined in the next chapter. Officers from different forces are able to meet regularly and they know that they are operating within a system that has some parity in terms of pay and conditions.

ACPO in 1993 embarked on a new trail under the heading 'Getting Things Right'. This initiative aimed to 'do the right things' as well as 'doing things right' and set out its objectives to cover six main areas:

- Leading and managing people, embracing the principles of total quality management which have been pioneered in the business sector. Aims in this area included the promotion of teamwork, trust, openness, empowerment, and the value of employees in their own progression through the service.

- The second area concerned communication and the most effective use of the wealth of data and information circulated within forces. *(This topic is dealt with in detail in chapter 8.)*

- The third area addressed simplifying internal organisation to ensure local control.

- Managing resources was the fourth area and was aimed at the process of devolved budgets and resource availability. It concerns the auditing and re-evaluating of existing systems of work and re-focusing lost objectives.

- Area five sought to empower officers to act with authority in areas in which they had some say, to make decisions and not only act on them, but also to see that others act on them.

- The final area addresses strategies for future action and re-iterates that change can and will be brought about by the officer on the 'front line'.

Are these objectives realistic? Many forces have already put systems into place to measure such aims. Notably, Staffordshire undertook a staff perception survey, in 1994, which sought to gain the views of all employees, both officers and civilians. The survey revealed that quality of service was the main priority for most staff and further promoted the view that management needed to take a flatter, more consultative approach to all aspects of the organisation.

Quality of Service

A great deal of evidence is available to support internal striving for quality of service, not least in the forces' annual reports. In reviewing these reports, the commitment to addressing force quality of service is instantly recognisable. The reports, as a whole, can be categorised as focusing on eight broad areas:

- Quality of service
- Public contact
- Cracking crime
- Safer roads
- Patrolling
- Partnerships
- Cost
- Force commitment

All forces are employed in these elements to a greater or lesser extent.

Within these categories, forces are circulating booklets on their corporate plans and informing the public of their response times and procedures, both on the telephone and in writing. Forces are keen to prove their commitment to the public and to be seen to be addressing public needs and fears, and so, have prioritised in areas such as car crime, burglaries and public order events. Specific operations have also sought to combat car thieves, rural crime and drink driver amongst others.

Where there have been localised concerns on single issues, these have often been subject to partnership initiatives and concentrated police resources, notably rural watches including 'horse watch' schemes, 'elderly watch' and 'pub watch' programmes. Problems raised here concern the sustainability of police resources given the intensity of such operations and the raised public awareness.

Forces are now looking not only to the national quality standards such as the Citizens Charter Mark and Investors in People Award, but also to European standards of quality management in the form of the European Foundation of Quality Management. The EFQM was founded in 1988 by a consortium of European businesses, in 1991 the European Quality Award was established. Institutions are assessed on seven criterion, their leadership, policy and strategy, people management, resources, processes and system management, customer satisfaction and last, but not least people satisfaction, that is how the organisation is meeting the needs of its employees. The first UK police service to achieve this award were South Yorkshire.

Whilst recognising the dichotomy of the role of policing, the controllers versus partners scenario, it is apparent that the police are often the forerunners in community partnerships. Their evolution is therefore remarkable in that not only has the ethos of policing changed, but the structure is unrecognisable from that first envisaged. The current structure including Home Office involvement, the role of leading actors such as the HMIC, chief constables, ACPO and the Federation together with the legislative effects on the service are discussed in the next chapter.

Chapter Summary

- Policing has developed in a disparate way within the criminal justice system and concepts of management are new to the service, both internally and externally.

- The quest for efficiency within the service is a comparatively new idea, notions of resource allocations and effective management are impacting to a service that has previously not had to count the cost.

- External calls for the service to be accountable and cost effective have projected management theories into a previously lavish culture which pursued criminals without counting the cost.

- The open, flatter management styles which have evolved in the last ten years together with the massive media exposure and public thirst for accountability have produced a service that is, itself, eager to improve and introduce effective management.

- Internally, forces are striving to prove that they are effective and not only doing an excellent job but being seen to do an excellent job

- The service is looking not only to localised and national co-operation and standards but also with a view to complying with, and setting, standards for their European counterparts.

Chapter 2

Management Structures in the Police Service

Introduction

'The depository of power is always unpopular.'

Disraeli

A structure is defined as the way in which something is constructed. It is a supporting framework or it is essential elements. Within an organisational structure, particularly the police service, employees know that their work must be contained within that rigid and inherent structure. That formal structure encompasses set tasks and divisions of labour, although they can be in a hybrid form, a hierarchical line management with defined promotion prospects and the employees' (officers') co-operation and participation.

All these elements, together with the ability to delegate, a recognised appraisal system, and effective methods of communication, when teamed with specified offices, selection processes and individual rights and responsibilities form what we would all recognise as a bureaucratic working organisation.

This chapter will examine the management structures within the police service and those which govern it. It will explore the role of the chief officer and his/her interaction with the Home Office, police authority and the local community. Within the evolutionary process of management structures, it is intended to look at instruments which play a major role in policy making and accountability, namely ACPO, HMI and the police authorities.

A Structured Framework

It has been argued by some that the police management structure is unique. This is plainly not true and the many reforms recommended by Sir Patrick Sheehy sought to align policing managerial functions with those in the commercial world. The police framework, one which is quasi-military, is regarded as being sacred and those who oppose it, or wish to radically reform, are labeled iconoclasts.

The pyramid rank system, as illustrated in fig. 2.1 *(the historical roots of which were discussed in chapter 1)* means that often the most important job, that of beat officer, is seen as the least valued, in terms of pay and career achievement, whilst middle managers steadily climb the career ladder.

Promotion procedures entrench the notion of 'winners' and 'losers' within the hierarchy. Within the service the perception is that beat officers are devalued and 'career misfits' whilst the public perception is totally the reverse. This illustrates that the management structures are not addressing public needs. It was interesting to note that a small Welsh community clubbed together to 'buy' a beat officer. (*Daily Telegraph* 15th January 1995). It is a strong reminder that the public are demanding a more visible police service.

Continually, in public surveys of recent years, including many of those undertaken by the Centre for Public Service Management and Research, the public have put as their highest priority a stronger police presence on the streets. Market Opinion Research International (MORI) conducted a survey in 1994 which

Fig 2.1: The pyramid rank system
(including numbers of officers for provincial forces)

ACPO	194	
Superintend	1,310	
Chief inspector	1,720	
Inspector	6,280	
Sergeant	18,776	
Constable	96,531	

Source: HMIC data, June 1997, but relating to the financial year 1995/6.

revealed that 87% of the public wanted more officers on the beat. However this indicator of public expectation has to be balanced against rapid responses (999 calls) and other operational responses (*see Figure 2.2 overleaf*).

The Established Structure

In order to discuss the structures of today we need to examine how they have evolved. To do that we have to go back some thirty five years to the Royal Commission on Police 1962, from which evolved the single most significant piece of legislation which was to form the basis of our modern police service, the Police Act 1964, repealed by the Police Act 1996.

The Royal Commission examined in detail the role of the chief officer and placed his responsibilities and powers on a statutory footing in relation to the Home Office and his local police authority. They took evidence on the independent status of the chief officer and made recommendations for the provision of greater accountability, particularly in the arena of police complaints. These two elements continue to give cause for concern and will therefore be dealt with in some detail in this chapter.

The terms of reference for the Royal Commission were extremely wide. They were to review the constitution and functions of local police authorities, to review the status and accountability of forces and to examine the relationship with the public and complaints procedures, as well as looking at the principles of remuneration and setting a suitable level and number on qualified recruits. This all pervasive review was an early Sheehy, Posen and Cassels rolled into one!

The Commission took as its starting point the local character of the office of constable, the common law origin of the office, the subordination of constables to justices of the peace, the embodiment of constables into forces and the subjection of forces to some local democratic supervision (Oliver 1987).

The Royal Commission inquired into the creation of a national police force, an issue that has been raised almost continually since, and the bulk of the Commission's recommendations were given statutory weight in the form of the Police Act 1964.

Fig 2.2

Force	Police strength	Civilians force strength including women from 1996	Traffic wardens	Total staff	Special constable strength	All staff including Specials	Population of force area (1000s)	Population per police officer
Avon and Somerset	2,981.00	1,213.17	113.64	4,307.81	688.00	4,995.81	1,456.17	488.48
Bedfordshire	1,126.00	472.91	33.00	1,631.91	189.00	1,820.91	543.20	482.41
Cambridgeshire	1,238.10	529.71	43.00	1,810.81	275.00	2,085.81	687.83	555.55
Cheshire	1,997.93	632.04	35.00	2,664.97	274.00	2,938.97	975.67	488.34
City of London	869.18	324.09	0.00	1,193.27	77.00	1,270.27	270.00	310.64
Cleveland	1,420.34	553.31	24.00	1,997.65	195.00	2,192.65	560.14	394.37
Cumbria	1,115.00	407.81	20.00	1,542.81	201.00	1,743.81	490.20	439.64
Derbyshire	1,764.10	654.90	51.00	2,470.00	413.00	2,883.00	954.09	540.84
Devon and Cornwall	2,898.90	1,120.88	124.34	4,144.12	1,102.00	5,246.12	1,530.14	527.83
Dorset	1,263.00	616.50	57.00	1,936.50	254.00	2,190.50	672.32	532.32
Durham	1,400.95	526.50	20.00	1,947.45	187.00	2,134.45	607.87	433.90
Dyfed-Powys	991.00	309.50	20.00	1,320.50	314.00	1,634.50	472.53	467.82
Essex	2,884.30	1,129.55	137.50	4,151.35	608.00	4,759.35	1,497.21	519.09
Gloucestershire	1,132.70	401.71	34.00	1,568.41	333.00	1,901.41	549.61	485.22
Greater Manchester	6,938.00	2,601.07	195.50	9,734.57	746.00	10,480.57	2,578.01	371.58
Gwent	1,043.50	377.50	29.00	1,450.00	136.00	1,586.00	452.27	433.42
Hampshire	3,347.10	1,323.00	80.40	4,750.50	539.00	5,289.50	1,730.44	517.00
Hertfordshire	1,712.00	753.68	67.50	2,533.18	315.00	2,848.18	853.20	489.37
Humberside	2,041.00	682.72	58.42	2,782.14	391.00	3,173.14	889.52	435.82
Kent	3,120.10	1,140.90	73.00	4,334.00	555.00	4,889.00	1,545.88	495.46
Lancashire	3,174.05	1,115.30	115.00	4,404.35	531.00	4,935.35	1,424.05	448.65
Leicestershire	1,908.50	667.00	72.00	2,647.50	360.00	3,007.50	916.93	480.45

Lincolnshire	1,144.60	446.30	24.00	1,614.90	299.00	1,913.90	605.80	529.27
Merseyside	4,407.00	1,549.39	135.50	6,091.89	343.00	6,434.89	1,434.41	325.48
Metropolitan Police	27,305.50	14,311.40	1,550.00	43,166.90	1,841.00	45,007.90	7,455.42	273.04
Norfolk	1,401.00	532.20	43.00	1,976.20	319.00	2,295.20	768.51	548.54
North Wales	1,377.50	513.00	20.00	1,910.50	332.00	2,242.50	657.81	477.54
North Yorkshire	1,324.40	520.08	23.61	1,868.09	360.00	2,228.09	726.93	548.87
Northamptonshire	1,152.50	511.00	27.00	1,690.50	289.00	1,979.50	594.81	516.10
Northumbria	3,668.30	1,399.30	117.00	5,184.60	471.00	5,655.60	1,441.73	393.02
Nottinghamshire	2,318.65	979.10	69.00	3,366.75	537.00	3,903.75	1,030.91	444.62
South Wales	3,027.00	1,187.03	110.00	4,324.03	461.00	4,785.03	1,330.44	439.52
South Yorkshire	3,078.20	1,268.00	79.00	4,425.20	381.00	4,806.20	1,305.43	424.09
Staffordshire	2,208.80	753.50	37.00	2,999.30	702.00	3,701.30	1,054.49	477.40
Suffolk	1,137.80	485.16	31.00	1,653.96	407.00	2,060.96	649.29	570.66
Surrey	1,643.81	754.00	38.39	2,436.20	260.00	2,696.20	774.28	471.03
Sussex	3,073.50	1,131.46	141.00	4,345.96	511.00	4,856.96	1,448.61	471.32
Thames Valley	3,674.00	1,738.00	125.00	5,537.00	744.00	6,281.00	2,017.16	549.04
Warwickshire	979.00	376.05	14.00	1,369.05	344.00	1,713.05	496.30	506.95
Wast Mercia	2,016.75	969.71	47.00	3,033.46	613.00	3,646.46	1,116.39	553.56
West Midlands	7,145.06	2,780.00	220.50	10,145.56	897.00	11,042.56	2,627.83	367.78
West Yorkshire	5,142.00	2,036.50	123.50	7,302.00	709.00	8,011.00	2,103.97	409.17
Wiltshire	1,218.45	452.58	21.00	1,692.03	233.00	1,925.03	587.51	482.18
Provincial Total	97,505.07	37,936.11	2,849.80	138,291.00	17,895.00	156,186.00	44,429.86	455.67
England and Wales Total	124,810.60	52,247.51	4,399.80	181,457.90	19,736.00	201,193.90	51,885.28	415.71

Source: HMIC, supplied June 1997, but relating to the financial year 1995/6.

Section 48 of the Act stated that a chief officer would be vicariously liable for the torts or wrongful acts committed by his officers whilst 'under his direction and in the performance of their duty'.

The Act also introduced changes to the disciplinary procedures and provided the Home Secretary with the power to compulsorily amalgamate forces where he thought fit. The Act also extended the discretionary power to the Home Secretary to set up local inquires regarding policing matters and stated that when asked to do so, the chief officer should provide the Home Secretary with a full report on any issue of policing in that area. The force amalgamations, foreseen at the time of the 1962 Commission, when there were 125 separate police forces in England and Wales, took place after the 1974 Local Government Act, which reorganised force strength to the present day forty three, and gave rise to criticism that local influence had been lost.

The Act stated that the police force 'shall be under the direction and control of the chief officer' and whilst the commission's recommendation that the Home Secretary should have a statutory duty to ensure the efficiency of the police was not enshrined in the subsequent Act, it did state that he had an 'overall statutory duty to exercise powers in such a manner and to such an extend as appears to him best calculated to promote the efficiency of the force.'

The Police Act 1996 consolidated the 1964 Act, with the exceptions of SS.37, 60-65 and schedules 5 and 9, together with Part IX of the Police and Criminal Evidence Act 1984 and Part I of the Police and Magistrates' Courts Act 1994. The main provisions of the Act deal with the composition and maintenance of police authorities, the functions of the Secretary of State and the handling of police complaints. It does not substantially change the provisions of the 1964 Act or the 1994 PMC Act.

In terms of management structures, the service as a whole is managed by a tripartite framework of control. That consists of the chief officer, central government and the police authority and a balance has long been weighed to ensure co-operation and parity between the three offices. It is intended to look at the roles of these three to determine their evolution and compatibility.

The Role of the Chief Constable

*'My friend was of the opinion that when a man
of rank appeared in that character he deserved
to have his merit handsomely allowed.'*
Samuel Johnson

The Royal Commission pondered the legal status of chief officers as indeed have the law courts in a number of cases. Of course in common law an officer may be personally liable to be sued for damages in relation to unlawful acts committed whilst he is on duty. Any costs awarded are paid out of the local police fund. Where an officer has committed an offence and his chief officer has decided not to prefer charges then the police authority can recommend that he ought to. Any chief officer that is in regular conflict with this authority over force disciplinary matters would be subject to censure from the Home Secretary.

However, with regard to the chief officer himself, the two single most important words that are constantly repeated by all commentators are 'independence' and 'discretion'. With regard to these two elements, the Commission entrenched the statement made in the report of the Royal Commission of Conditions of Police Service in 1949, that the police authority had no right to give the chief officer orders regarding the way in which police duties were carried out. However he could not 'divest himself of responsibility by turning to them for guidance or instruction on the matter of police duty'.

Lord Denning, the former Master of the Rolls, commenting in the famous case of *R v Metropolitan Police Commissioner ex. p. Blackburn 1968* further entrenched chief officers' independent nature by stating that they were answerable to 'the law and to the law alone'. In the same case Lord Justice Salmon stated that 'constitutionally it is clearly impermissible for the Home Secretary to issue any order to the police in respect of law enforcement' More recently in *R v Oxford ex. p. Levey 1986*, the Master of the Rolls, Sir John Donaldson stated that 'chief constables have the widest possible discretion'.

Accordingly we can draw the inference from the wealth of case law that a chief constable cannot be told how to enforce the law, but given present and increasing future financial constraints will there become a covert method of control?

In terms of the appointment and dismissal of a chief officer, the police authority has this within its remit but it is with the consent of the Home Secretary, who can veto their selection and may also initiate the dismissal of a chief officer or speed his retirement in the interests of efficiency (S.11 the Police Act 1996). There have always been calls for chief constables to be more 'cosmopolitan' (Merton, 1957) and there does seem to be more evidence of chief officers moving around and younger blood appearing. At the time of writing (July 1997) there are 2 female chief officers, one in Lancashire and one in Wiltshire.

Reiner (1991) noted that the average age for appointment to the post was 50 years of age. With the youngest appointment at 42, is it a sign of old age when **chief** constables start looking younger and wearing lipstick?

Positive moves to select the correct calibre of officer was addressed by an ACPO working party *Providing Future Officers of Police 1990*. It recommended that some young officers should be targeted and monitored by the HMI during their career progression; they would receive intensive training in the form of courses at Bramshill and within a framework of 'extended interviews'. They also recommended the expansion of the graduate entry scheme, however this seems to have become a hollow suggestion as some 7 years later many forces are re-evaluating the scheme because of its cost.

The appointment of chief constables has been chronicled by Critchley (1978) and more recently by Robert Reiner (1991) in his book *Chief Constables*, which examined the social, educational and philosophies of the chief officers of the early '90s.

With regard to the tenure of chief officers, something that is within the present debating arena, Reiner (1991) noted that only 17% had been in office for 11 years or more whilst 62% had been in office between 1 and 5 years. The bulk of chief officers have been deputies in other forces and ACPO promotes plural force experience by stating that an officer is prohibited from occupying three ACPO roles in the same force.

Reiner asked chief officers about their primary concerns and by far the highest priority was the area of budgeting and finance with 57% saying that more of their time was being occupied 'balancing the books'. Comments made by some chief constables have highlighted the general concerns in managing a fixed budget within a fluid criminal justice system requiring resources to be spread more and more thinly. Peter Bensley, chief constable of Lincolnshire (*Police Review* 4.11.94) argued that giving local commanders their own budgets was wasted when it would later be taken back to cover Headquarters deficits. The authors would argue that this exercise is also pointless when policing managers who joined the force to uphold the law find themselves acting as accountants.

Arguments have been extrapolated, both within the service and outside it, that the solution to this financial dichotomy, lies in the role of the chief officer being split into two, with a chief operational manager responsible for purely policing issues and a chief executive who is responsible for the financial corporate management. The Audit Commission *Cheques and Balances* papers 13 and 14, (dealt with in greater depth in chapter 4), recommend that devolved budgeting enables forces to delegate spending to a local level. Financial and management training is currently undertaken at the National Police Training College (Bramshill) within the 'Police Management Programme', this programme is aimed at the ranks of Inspectors and Chief Inspectors. Further modules on finance are contained in other senior management programmes at the College. The authors worked with the Home Office in formulating a local policing plans framework which sought to link financial needs with local policing priorities. An illustration of which is given in Figure 2.3 *(opposite)*.

What happens when forces have unprecedented numbers of major incidents in one financial year and allocated funding is spent? Can a realistic figure be put on the spending in Gloucester incurred by the Fred and Rosemary West case?

From April 1st 1995, when cash limited budgets came into effect under the 1994 Police and Magistrates' Courts Act (PMC Act) and police authorities became independent, to whom should chief officers turn when emergency funding is required to cover temporary crime spates or unforeseen environmental protests?

A recent case on the use of police resources and a chief constable's decision not to apply to the Home Office for special assistance was *R v Chief Constable of Sussex ex parte International Trader's Ferry Ltd 1997 (2 All ER 65)*. This case centred on the exportation of livestock by ITF and questioned not only the relationship between a chief constable, his police authority and the Home Office but also raised the contentious issues of free movement of goods within the EU and civil liberties.

At the height of this protest some 1,125 officers were deployed in escort duties. The Home Secretary was informed by the chief constable and a representative of the police authority that a request for special payments may be made. The Home Secretary stated that the force must show that expenditure was "unforeseen, exceptional and threatened the efficiency of the force" (quoted in the Divisional court). The level of protest subsequently dropped and the police strength was reduced to 315 officers, this situation prevailed for some four months. The chief constable then wrote to ITF stating that the police presence would be reduced to 2 days per week or 4 days per fortnight, which would still enable the company to continue their business.

Fig 2.3: Local policing plans – Framework

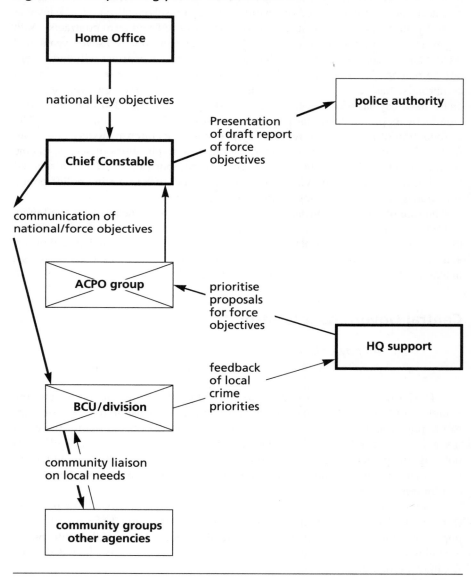

ITF claimed that the chief constable was in breach of his duty to "keep the peace" and that his actions contravened Art. 34 of the EC Treaty as being "qualitative restrictions on exports, prohibited by the member states". It was held that the chief constable's finances were finite given the expectations of local people to receive effective policing and that the limitation of police protection to 2 days per week did not amount to an unlawful restriction on exports.

The issue of performance related pay and fixed term contracts, a major recommendation of the Sheehy Report which struck at the heart of policing and produced the most determined opposition, has been resolved at senior rank level at least, by an ACPO settlement which addresses future fixed term contracts. With regard to chief officers, their contracts will run between four and seven years, and ACPO has secured the assurance that no senior officer's contract will end before he/she reaches 50 or before he/she has 25 years' pensionable service. Equally a compromise has been reached regarding 'appraisal related pay', the proposed 10% on the basic pay has been reduced to 7.5%. A study was conducted in 1995 comparing chief officers pay with similar positions in industry (*Police Review* 20.1.95). The introduction of performance related pay per se arouses intense anxiety and, from figures that have been discussed so far, the financial implications of such a scheme would far outweigh any tangible gain. The new composition of ACPO, discussed later, has meant that the previously perceived conflict of formulating police policy and strategy whilst negotiating senior officers pay will no longer arise.

The role of the chief constable is a complex one which encapsulates the fetters of tradition with the uncertainty of taking forces into the 21st century. As officers they are financially liable, operationally liable and accountable to police authorities and they are operating within a political climate that wants them to act more as a managing director rather than an upholder of the law.

Central Government Control

'All power is not to all.'

Virgil

The 1962 Royal Commission recommended that the Home Secretary and the Secretary of State for Scotland should be statutorily responsible for the efficiency of the police and take on the following duties – the power to appoint the chief inspector of constabulary, the power to introduce schemes to promote efficient policing, the power to amalgamate forces, and the power to call for annual reports from chief officers, (extended under the Police and Magistrates' Courts Act 1994 to call for reports from the newly constituted police authorities).

It is still fairly true to say that the constitutional structure of our policing framework in Britain gives little opportunity for overt political control, although opponents of the 1994 Criminal Justice and Public Order Act argued that the police are being used as an instrument in a class war with travellers being hounded while fox hunters roam free.

The Home Secretary takes on a number of roles, i.e. he may order an inquiry or lay before Parliament an annual report that he has received from a chief officer. However he will not inform Parliament of any police work that he considers should not be publicly disclosed, for example a large, sensitive operation dealing with drugs or organised crime.

Home Office circulars serve as an additional instrument of governmental control. In reality they have little legal effect but terms such as advise, guidance and directions are used liberally. Regulatory circulars inform forces of administrative changes, whilst directive circulars are generally treated as being mandatory.

Notable recent circulars on juvenile cautioning have imposed a degree of conformity. Equally the Home Office is seen as a clearing house for disseminating views, which have often been ascertained during lengthy consultative periods.

Anyone viewing the conclusions of the first stage of the Home Office Police Research Group 'Police Operations Against Crime' research will note that a number of external bodies, both academic and management/financial consultants, have contributed significantly and have made a number of detailed recommendations in specific areas.

The 1964 Police Act, now S.11 Police Act 1996, bestowed powers on the Home Secretary enabling him to retire a chief officer whom he considered incompetent; there have been no recent cases, but one in the 1980s led to an officer retiring following a bout of imprudent spending – this case had a number of vitiating factors interwoven with a local political struggle.

Many academic commentators have questioned the real sanctions available to the Home Secretary to address the inefficiency of an errant chief officer given that the judicial control, as mentioned above, appears to grant them carte blanche operationally.

The issue of operational accountability was tested in the case of *Hill v Chief Constable of West Yorkshire 1987 (2 WLR 1126)*. Issues arose following the arrest of the Yorkshire Ripper, Peter Sutcliffe. Mrs. Hill was the mother of Jacqueline Hill who was murdered by Sutcliffe. She claimed damages in tort for negligence relating to the conduct of the police investigations and claimed that the arrest of Sutcliffe, his questioning and subsequent release had failed to prevent the murder, by him, of her daughter. She was able to show that the police had made an investigative hash of the inquiry by spending an inordinate amount of time on hoax calls and letters. They had also interviewed Sutcliffe on two separate occasions and accepted his uncorroborated alibi, provided by his wife. Mrs. Hill alleged that the police owed her a duty of care and that that duty had been breached.

The Court of Appeal was unwilling to push the boundaries of duty of care, stating that because of limited resources the police could not enforce all of the law all of the time, and that by merely undertaking the investigation they did not create a special (legal) relationship with Sutcliffe.

However in the case of *Swinney and another v Chief Constable of Northumbria 1996 (3 All ER 449)* it was held that a special relationship did exist between an informant and the police. Here an informant gave information as to the identity of a person implicated in the murder of a police officer. The person identified was known to be a violent man and the informant requested that no contact be made which would enable her to be traced. However the information was recorded and subsequently stolen from an unattended police car. The identity of the informant became known and both her and her husband were subjected to violent threats resulting in their suffering psychiatric damage.

In *Savage v Chief Constable of Hampshire Constabulary 1997 (2 All ER 631)* it was held that a police informant was not precluded from voluntarily stating in open court that he was an informant and entitled to recover payments promised under an oral agreement in exchange for information.

The Police Authority – A Changing Role

'The first of earthly blessings – Independence...'
Gibbon

One element of the management structure experiencing increasing importance is that of the police authority.

As early as 1949 it was established that police authorities had no right to give a chief officer orders about the disposition of the force. Whilst he is always responsible to his authority and should turn to them for guidance or instruction on matters of policing, he is not operationally responsible to the authority (Royal Commission on Conditions of Police Service 1949).

The Royal Commission in 1962 went further to define the duties of police authorities and they focused on four main areas. Firstly that police authorities should be responsible for the provision of an 'adequate' police force, secondly that they should constitute a body of local citizens to secure the maintenance of law and order and give the chief officers advice on local issues. Thirdly to appoint, discipline and remove chief officers, and lastly, to act as an effective liaison agent between the police and the public.

Their responsibilities include the provision and maintenance of buildings. This has been a rather difficult area in relation to the renewal of equipment and the investment in new and innovative hardware for the police. This provision has become blurred over the years and was often construed as being the actual provision of adequate and efficient policing.

Whilst many of the functions of the police authority were accepted, the membership was often queried as to its impartiality, given the political slant in their constitution.

Prior to the 1994 PMC Act, 49% of police finance came from the local authority and 51% from the Chancery. The authority was made up of 2/3 county councillors and 1/3 magistrates. They had enormous control over finances and were responsible for the appointment of the chief officer and his discipline, subject to the approval of the Home Secretary.

The balance of power is a delicate one, a balance that has not always been maintained. Some particularly outspoken chief officers have clashed with their authorities, who have in turn accused chief officers of being too autocratic and not engaging in any form of consultation. A notable judgment was that of *R v Secretary of State for the Home department ex. parte Northumbria Police Authority 1988 (2 WLR 590)*. This case examined the tripartite situation and held inter alia that in order to keep the Queen's peace the Home Secretary could, seemingly, over ride the authority's opinion of what they considered to be necessary equipment.

The confusion of the tripartite roles have for some time led to calls for reform. These calls have arisen from the lack of sanctions available for errant forces other than their not been granting their certificate of efficiency by the inspectorate. This has been witnessed most critically in Derbyshire where the force has been refused its certificate twice. What implication does that have on the effective policing of Derbyshire if the police authority, with their 2/3 council control, are responsible for the allocation of funding? The authors would argue that that situation leaves the police with little control over their own destiny. However many present commentators have said that that particular force operates more effectively than many with comparatively unlimited resources. In fact, whilst force equipment often leaves a lot to be desired, the managerial styles and operational structures readily take on new ideas and appear to outsiders to be organisationally very competent.

The PMC Act, as the most important piece of police legislation since the 1964 Act, sought to address many of the criticisms of the composition and powers of the police authorities, and takes the whole service one step nearer towards a national force with centralised objectives being set by government. Whilst the 1996 Police Act has repealed large sections of the PMC there have been few significant changes with regard to police authorities.

Due to the many criticisms of abuse of power and the political imbalance, as mentioned earlier, the Act set out to modify local authority involvement in the service. However due to the House of Lords' opposition and tabling amendments, the Home Secretary was forced in February 1994 to do a U turn to avoid defeat of the Bill. He was further compromised in March of that year when the Lords' actions again threatened to defeat the Bill.

As illustrated in Figure 2.4 *(overleaf)*, the Act brings a strong emphasis of 'partnership' rather than the previously witnessed dominant authority or chief officer. By recognising a function the Act then divides part of the function responsibility into the tripartite, for example, with regard to local policing plans, the chief officer having complete operational freedom is able to determine local needs and prioritise his/her resources and staffing. He is then able to draft his local policing plan and issue those plans in consultation with the authority. These plans include a 'statement of the authority's priorities for the year of the financial resources expected to be available and the proposed allocation of those resources...' The Act makes provision for the Secretary of State to 'loan' or 'grant' to a police authority any sum which it may require to meet its expenditure, this is now covered by S.94 of the 1996 Police Act. The exact sum of money must be determined by the Secretary of State and be repaid before the end of the authorities first precepting year.

Section 3 of the Act, as amended by SS.4/5 of the 1996 Police Act, provided for the reduction of the size of police authorities and specified membership not to exceed seventeen. Schedule 1B sets out the constitution of the members to contain nine members of the relevant council, five appointed independent members and three magistrates. Critics have stated that instead of increasing the number of magistrates with the emphasis on their independence, the Act has drastically reduced them. This has resulted in some large petty sessional divisions who have previously had one or two magistrates on the authority now having no representation at all.

The appointment of the chairman of the authority received some comment as to the 'independence' of an elected local businessman. The Home Secretary had not envisaged that his original plan to have the power to elect the chairman would arouse such opposition. This fierce opposition proved effective and the chairman is now to be elected at the annual meeting from among the members. However ministerial involvement in selection has been questioned as has the fact that the chairman is not locally accountable.

Fig 2.4: The balance of power

Police Authority	Chief Constable	Home Office
Maintain efficient force	Responsible for direction and control of force	Promotes efficiency of police service
Agrees budget, main responsibility for expenditure	Prepares draft budget Financial management	Determines grant
Employs civilians Appoints CC	Control and direction of officers and civilians	Approves appointment of CC
Sets local objectives Procures local views	Adhere to local and national objectives and targets	Sets national objectives directs levels of performance levels
Issues local policing plans	Draft local policing plans	Receives copy of local policing plan
Control finances for extra resources	Operational and resource allocation control	Can determine levels of performance

The underlying intention as to the workings of the authorities is that they should mirror commercial enterprises, this theme echoes Baroness Thatcher's entrepreneurial worship.

Local business men have actively been targeted and greater store is now placed on their experience, background and suitability. However, only future evaluation of their efficacy will decide whether the reform of policing authorities has been achieved (Loveday 1994).

It will be particularly interesting to witness a tripartite clash whereby the chief officer is opposed to the authority local policing plan. In these circumstances how can set objectives and targets be reached and would this compromise the operational functioning of the force? We stand as a society on the ethics of 'policing by consent', operational policing cannot be bought. Whether this entrepreneurial spirit of fixed term contracts, performance related pay and business strategies fits easily with our traditional police culture, only time and future case law will tell.

The Police Complaints System

> 'To complain of the age we live in to murmur
> at the present possessors of power...'
>
> Edmund Burke

The Royal Commission looked at measures to provide greater accountability, particularly within the arena of police complaints, whilst leaving operational independence unfettered.

The 1964 Police Act introduced changes to the disciplinary procedures and left the handling of complaints entirely to the senior officer, and proposals put forward in 1974 and 1976 led to the formation of the Police Complaints Board, which enabled proceedings to be taken against an officer and further investigations to be made. However critics still argued that the police were able to control and contain the complaints made against them by having an internal investigative process. Despite attempts to introduce degrees of independence none appeared to placate the critics.

It would seem fair to state that the main catalyst in the police complaints procedure was the Scarman Report in 1981 which resulted from the Brixton disturbances. In concluding his report on the riots he stated 'consultation and accountability are the mechanisms – in part administrative and in part legal – upon which we rely to ensure that the police in their policies and operations keep in touch with and are responsible to the community that they police'(para. 5.57).

Many facets of the community were extremely critical of the complaints procedure and apparent lack of visible accountability. This was highlighted by a series of incidents in the late seventies and early eighties in which alleged attacks by the police were not seen to have been investigated thoroughly. No-one was more aware of this than the police themselves who had called for the introduction of an independent body to prove impartiality.

During the Brixton riots inquiry Lord Scarman examined the police complaints process and stated that often complaints, in the main, consisted of an aggrieved member of the public complaining about the actions of a single officer. The procedures for investigations available at that time appeared to further entrench public mistrust when complaints were investigated internally and the complainant was rarely informed of the outcome.

As there were no consultative procedures in place, Lord Scarman recommended that a statutory duty should be imposed on police authorities and on the chief constable to establish local liaison committees in order to alleviate the public misgivings in allegations against the police.

Many of Lord Scarman's proposals were acted upon and together with an all round review of procedures backed by calls for reconciliation procedures and independent supervision, the Home Affairs Committee 1981 and the Police Complaints and Discipline Procedures Cmnd. 9072, led to a legislative format in the form of the Police and Criminal Evidence Act 1984.

This Act created the Police Complaints Authority (PCA) which established a three tiered framework for dealing with complaints against the police. Encapsulated in S.85 of PACE, they briefly consisted of tier one allegations which resulted in death or serious injury to be investigated under the direction of the police complaints authority. Tier two allegations of varying seriousness would require the chief officer to inform the PCA, such formal investigations could be undertaken by either the chief officer's force or another force. The last and final tier established was one of informal resolution, this only applied where the complainant agreed to this method of inquiry and an officer would be assigned to deal with this matter.

The Police Complaints Authority acts in a supervisory capacity and does not have an investigative role. They must supervise investigations into allegations of death or serious injury and may supervise any other investigation where they consider it pertinent, for example allegations of police corruption or criminal activity. Resource implications require the authority to consult with the chief officer before committing any of his resources to an investigation. The loss, to a major investigation, of a senior officer can have massive resource implications for a chief officer. Such investigations can be complex and lengthy and may mean that a chief officer loses an experienced senior investigating officer leaving his operational strength much reduced.

Home Office sponsored research (Maguire and Corbett, 1991) identified four goals that the system should aim to achieve:

- The maintenance of police discipline
- Satisfaction of complainants
- The maintenance of public confidence in the police
- The provision of feedback to disseminate good practice

The Police and Magistrates' Courts Act 1994 amended parts of the Police and Criminal Evidence Act 1984 with regard to matters of police disciplinary procedure. The Act updated the wording of many sections relating to issues which should be brought to the attention of the police complaints authority by another authority, for example, the chief officer or the police authority. This serves to widen the area of accountability when referring to an officer who has 'behaved in a manner which would justify disciplinary proceedings' rather than the reference ten years earlier to 'an offence against discipline'.

It would appear that disciplinary matters are being viewed in a more open forum with all parties being required to be increasingly accountable. In December 1994 a person who made a complaint under the complaints procedure which resulted in the dismissal of an officer had no right to have copies of documents from the subsequent appeal *(R v Secretary of State for Home Department ex parte Goswell)*.

Calls for the reconstruction of the complaints procedure, making it a totally independent body have not been addressed. There has been no independent assessment of the costs of either the present system or the formation of a new one. An annual estimate of costs incurred by one force, West Midlands, have been put at £1.5 million *(The Guardian* 12.6.96).

The PCA has called for additional powers to enable it to appoint non police investigation teams in exceptional circumstances *(New Law Journal* 30.5.97). However the current practices remain further entrenched by the 1996 Police Act, whose provisions appear to indicate that few significant changes will take place with regard to investigative procedures.

Proactively, the Met. have announced that a special squad concentrating on corruption will be created within the Complaints Investigation Bureau.

Regional Crime Squads have often been criticised with regard to their management of investigations. One main criticism has been that officers are often too long in post and that this "failure to rotate officers can lead to corruption". However current debate is divided as to the standard of proof required in allegations of corruption. ACPO believe that a civil standard of proof, that is a balance of probabilities, should be applied to all misconduct cases whilst the Superintendents Association and the Police Federation believe that the criminal standard of proof, beyond reasonable doubt, should remain *(Police Review* 13.6.97).

In concluding this section on the police complaints system, controversy currently surrounds the Director of Public Prosecutions regarding her failure to instigate proceedings against police officers involved in two deaths whilst in custody. deaths. The leadership and the organisation of the Crown Prosecution Service (CPS) have been called into disrepute by the deaths, in 1994, and the subsequent failure to proceed. In July 1997 the High Court quashed decisions by the CPS not to prosecute the police officers involved (*Daily Telegraph* 27.7.97).

Such high profile cases, when not thoroughly investigated, merely serve to discredit the entire complaints system, both internally and the, perceived, external safeguards.

The Role of ACPO

> *'The rank is but the guineas stamp,*
> *the mans the gawd for a' that.'*
>
> Robert Burns

The Association of Chief Police Officers was formed in 1948 as an amalgamation of county and borough chief officers. The Committee on Police Conditions and Service taking evidence on structure and remuneration would only hear from a single representative body, and ACPO was formed for this purpose. It was, and still remains, an informal body with no statutory definition (Reiner, 1991). However it has developed into a highly organised and respected policy forming instrument. It is able to negotiate pay deals and formulate police strategies in all areas of operational policing.

This duality of approach led, in April 1996, to a dramatic reconstruction, splitting the Association into two separate bodies, one promoting the professional interests of the service and the other looking after the interests of senior officers as a staff association, to be known as Chief Police Officers Staff Association (CPOSA). The former, newly constituted body will keep the name, use of the crown and the logo, but differs in a variety of ways (*Policing Today*, April 1996).

One significant difference is the decision to broaden the membership base to include an associate membership of senior civilian staff.

The structure of ACPO is illustrated in Figure 2.5 which clearly shows the commitment to operational policing matters with all contemporary issues being addressed by one or other principle committee.

Until 1996 all chief officers were members of ACPO and the principal officers are elected at the annual conference. Now after appointment to chief officer, an invitation is extended to join the association, it may or may not be accepted.

The officers of the association will consist of the president, who has to be a chief constable, who holds office for one year, the vice president, the immediate past president, the commissioner of the Met. the general secretary, the honorary treasurer and representatives from the assistant chief officers.

The hierarchy of ACPO consists of the principal officers, the steering committee which is made up of officers of the associations, and which can act in times of emergency. CPOSA acts for senior officers on all matters relating to pay and conditions, an illustration of this was mentioned earlier in relation to the negotiation of fixed term contracts for chief officers. They will also be responsible for securing

Fig 2.5: Summarised structure of the Association of Chief Police Officers for England, Wales and Northern Ireland

PRESIDENT
(post held for one year)

First Vice President   Second Vice President   Immediate Past President

General secretary

CHIEF CONSTABLES' COUNCIL
(Chief constable ranking officers of the 43 forces)

CO-ORDINATING COMMITTEES OF ACPO

International Affairs	Finance	Quality of service
Chairman	Chairman	Chairman
Secretary	Secretary	Secretary

PRINCIPAL COMMITTEES OF ACPO
(two ACPO members, a CC and a DCC/ACC ranking officer from each of eight ACPO regions)

Crime Committee	General Purpose Committee	Personnel and Training
Chairman	Chairman	Chairman
Hon Secretary	Hon Secretary	Hon Secretary
Standing Sub-committees **Ad Hoc Working Parties**	**Standing Sub-committees** **Ad Hoc Working Parties**	**Standing Sub-committees** **Ad Hoc Working Parties**
Technical and Research	Technical and Research	Technical and Research
Chairman	Chairman	Chairman
Hon Secretary	Hon Secretary	Hon Secretary
Standing Sub-committees **Ad Hoc Working Parties**	**Standing Sub-committees** **Ad Hoc Working Parties**	**Standing Sub-committees** **Ad Hoc Working Parties**

ACPO Representatives on over 60 Groups chaired by Government Departments and more than 100 other groups and Committees

Amended from *Policing Today 1996*

satisfactory arrangements for existing and future chief officers with regard to their contracts, performance related pay and bonuses.

The Council of Association plays a major role in policy making, this council acts for senior officers within the technical and professional arena. For the purposes of administration, ACPO divides regionally into eight regions, the north west, the north east, the midlands, the east, the south east, the south west, Wales and the metropolitan region. Each area organises conferences, discusses local issues and is able to directly refer a matter to ACPO nationally and ask for local priorities to be referred to the Home Office.

As illustrated by figure 2.5, there are a number of principal ACPO committees, these are chaired, usually, by a chief officer and they consider matters within their field of expertise, this structure will remain under the new format. In the past, for example, in 1993 the Quality of Service committee, in consultation with the Police

Staff Association, UNISON and with the backing of the Home Office, formed a working party aimed at ensuring that the management, leadership, communications and internal systems of police forces are of the right quality, and that the quality of service provided both to external customers of the police and internal customers within forces, was of the highest possible standard. This initiative *'Getting Things Right'* aimed to concentrate on *doing the right things* in addition to the previous emphasis of *doing things right*. The main objectives of this initiative were discussed in chapter one.

A previous ACPO policy document issued in 1990 concentrated on common purposes and values within the service. The whole tenor of the document was one of customer care, dealing with ways in which the police could improve their attitudes and behaviour towards the public. It formed the basis of many internal initiatives to address the handling of victims of crime, the expectations of the public regarding the police response to crime, and the commitment displayed by forces through contact with the public via station visits, letters and telephone communication.

The policy document paralleled recommendations from a study commissioned by the Joint Consultative Committee which comprises representatives from ACPO, the Police Federation and the Superintendents' Association. This committee aims to facilitate liaison between the staff associations and this policy review proved to be unique in that it drew together all the staff associations in order to highlight 'the dull ache that the service had long experienced in relation to resources was changing to an acute pain'.

Each of the 43 forces provided information for this substantial review and six were involved in the major collation of research material. The review examined seven of the most salient issues concerning a service moving towards the 21st century. These included:

- Demands and resources
- Efficiency and effectiveness
- The Home Office circulars 105/88 and 106/88 (relating to civilian staff and establishment compliment)
- Public surveys and consultative committees
- A policing survey (dealing with all aspects of public and police contact) and the policing of the 1990s.

This review was hailed by many as being a holistic one and its many recommendations have subsequently been acted upon. Some of the recommendations have become enshrined in legislation and many have been adopted as good practice. They also highlighted the need for the service to continue and expand research areas to ascertain the efficacy of the many initiatives in operation.

The Police Federation

Whilst the Federation is not officially a trade union they act in a similar capacity. Many observers are critical of their influence, but the Federation represents the rank and file officer, and they carry as their standard their role of independence. In addition they have for some time called for police complaints to be investigated by a wholly separate and independent body. SS.59/60 of the 1996 Police Act determined the continuation of the Federation as a representative body for rank and file officers except in questions of promotion and some areas of discipline. The Federation acts through local and central representative bodies.

At their annual conference in 1997 the Federation discussed a wide range of issues, including the use of body armour, the uniformity of police training and the proposed changes in the disciplinary regulations. Areas of major concern to the service are discussed as well as calls for changes in the political arena.

The Police Superintendents' Association

The Police Superintendents' Association is the sole representative body of members of police forces in England and Wales maintained under S.1 of the Police Act 1964 in the rank of superintendent. The Association is divided into five districts that cover all forces, with each district having elected officials. From these officials are elected representative members of the associations' National Executive Committee. The association has three full time posts, the National President, National Secretary and the National Assistant Secretary.

The Association meets at district and national conferences. There are established advisory committees within which each district is represented. These advisory committees mirror the ACPO thematic committees.

The objects of the Association are to maintain and improve upon the professional status of superintendents and to consult, negotiate and participate on matters relating to duties, responsibilities and welfare of members and the efficiency of the police service.

Due largely, as a result of the falling numbers of officers at Superintendent rank, 30% in the last five years, the Association has commissioned research to *"evaluate the impact on the reduction in posts, at both superintendent and inspector ranks, on command resilience; and to create a strategy to safeguard the appropriate level of command and management posts"*. The research will be undertaken by Cardiff Business School and basic findings will be presented at the Association's annual conference.

The Role of Her Majesty's Inspectorate

'Mens sibi conscia recti – A mind conscious of right.'
Virgil

The Inspectorate was established in 1856 and originally acted in a purely cosmetic role rather than one of operational review. It was more concerned with 'the quality of saluting and the cleanliness of station floors than operational policing' (Geoffrey Dear HMI). Inspectors are constitutionally independent and are appointed under S.38 Police Act 1964, as amended by the Police and Magistrates' Courts Act 1994. Traditionally they have themselves been appointed from the ranks of chief officers, although in 1993 two lay Inspectors were appointed.

Historically, the Inspectorate operated, in a seemingly artificial and dignified role having little real efficacy in terms of sanctions for errant forces. Inspections were often limited to observable organisational procedures with a bias towards administrational practices. Criticisms that any sanctions that the Inspectorate had were totally defunct (Brogden, 1982) rang somewhat hollow when Derbyshire's certificate was suspended in 1992 and later refused in 1993/4. It became clear that the Inspectorate were acting in a more interventionist manner.

As discussed in chapter 1 the Home Office circular 114/83 changed the way in which forces would be reviewed financially and much greater emphasis was placed on the importance of effective resource utilisation. This emphasis has, in part, changed the role of the HMI. However it would be wrong to assume that the sole and primary role of the inspectorate is that of inspecting forces. The practise of granting or declining certificates of efficiency ceased in 1996. Inspections now take three forms. Primary (triennial), Performance Review (annual) and Thematic (ad hoc).

The regions for which the eight inspectorate are responsible have been rationalised to five. Time spent in the region is used to foster co-operation and work with local projects.

Their overall role, as they perceive it, is that of advisor/facilitator to chief officers. They are a semi-independent body, whose members, usually having been chief constables, can empathise with the chief officer. At the time of writing there is one lay Inspector and 2 lay assistant Inspectors.

Their role is balanced between the Home Office, as their employer, and their empathy with their ex-fellow officers. They are invited to become an inspector by the Queen on the recommendation of the Home Secretary, and their role is becoming increasingly co-ordinated as they act as facilitators for encouraging standardisation.

The advisory role of the Inspectorate is twofold, firstly they have act in some advisory capacity to the Home Office. This does not take the form of professional advice on policing policy, but they contribute advice with regards to determining criteria on policing plans, key objectives and performance indicators.

With regards to police authorities the inspectorates function was determined by the Police and Magistrates' Courts Act 1994 which laid down duties and responsibilities, the Act sought to give the public more information regarding force performance and the more open management structure.

Within the HMI role certain issues are becoming more pertinent, i.e. there are issues relating to the media and how forces deal with high profile cases and topics. Current issues relate to performance indicators and the pressures on the service to provide value for money. This ethos has underpinned all the recent legislation pertaining to the police service and within their role as advisor/facilitator, HMI's financial guidance will become very relevant, as will their role in providing a 'national oversight of policing standards' (Reiner, 1992) with their enhanced status. However, this enhanced status must show impartiality and not merely represent ex chief officers purporting to work for the Home Office.

Having mentioned the 1996 Police Act and the most recent case law relating to police resources, this chapter could not conclude without reference to the Criminal Procedure and Investigations Act 1996, the Police Act 1997, the Police Act (Health and Safety) Act 1997 all of which will impact on various elements of police management.

The Criminal Procedure and Investigations Act 1996

The main tenet of the Act formulates the rules on disclosure of material in criminal investigations and will undoubtably impact on the way in which investigations are processed and managed. It's main provisions deal with primary disclosure by the prosecutor, compulsory disclosure and voluntary disclosure by the accused. Confidentiality of material and time limits for preparation of material are all prescribed.

The Act introduces a two stage process for prosecution, introduces compulsory disclosure about the defence case in Crown court cases and is supplemented by a Code of Practice.

In preparation for the changes, extensive training has been undertaken jointly by the Crown Prosecution Service (CPS) and the police service. A national training package augmented by seminars was delivered and was hoped to be completed by mid 1997.

The Codes of Practice deal not only with disclosure but also with the regime which must be adhered to and any subsequent disciplinary matters (*Police Review* 7.2.97).

The Police Act 1997

The main provisions relate to the National Criminal Intelligence Service (NCIS) and the National Crime Squad and their respective functions. The general functions of NCIS are to:

> *'Gather, store and analyse information in order to provide criminal intelligence, to provide criminal intelligence to police forces in Great Britain, the Royal Ulster Constabulary (RUC), the National Crime Squad and other law enforcement agencies, and to act in support of such police forces carrying out their criminal intelligence activities.' (S.2 The Police Act 1997)*

The Service will be headed by a Director General, who holds the rank of chief constable in Great Britain, or the RUC, is at commissioner level in the Metropolitan service or the City of London. The appointment will be made by the NCIS Service Authority and will be approved by the Secretary of State who will also be responsible for setting objectives and issuing codes of practice.

The National Crime Squad (NCS) whose function will be to "prevent and detect serious crime which is of relevance to more than one police area in England and Wales". Their other functions will include the support of individual forces, at the chief officers request, the support of NCIS, at the Director General's request. They will also be able to institute criminal proceedings and act in support of other law enforcement agencies.

The other significant provision of the Act was the formation of the Police Information Technology Organisation whose main function would be to carry out activities relating to information technology and systems used by police forces and authorities, this function would also include research pertaining to information technology.

The Police (Health and Safety) Act 1997

The Health and Safety at Work etc Act 1974 has previously excluded police officers under the premise that they are not 'employees' but 'office holders'. However chief officers have applied the objectives – *"to secure and improve the health, safety and welfare of people at work"* and *"to protect the health and safety of others affected by work activities"* on a voluntary basis.

A European directive changed the wording in 1989 to 'workers' rather than 'employees' this, together with other directives aimed at risk assessment of police activities rather than work environments meant that pressure has been applied to include the police service and its activities in statutory regulations.

Under this new Act, which comes into effect in April 1998, officers will have access to industrial tribunals on matters relating to health and safety issues. When enacted, duties will exist under criminal law.

Chapter Summary

- The management structure within the service has changed significantly within the last few years due to external pressures and changes in police authorities.

- The role of the chief constable is being forced, in many respects, by nature of legislation and financial pressures, to assume that of a chief executive rather than one solely concerned with operational policing matters.

- Are we reaching the stage when financial constraints determine policing issues instead the opposite being true?
  Should the cost of policing a large and sustained demonstration or riot early in the financial year substantially effect the policing levels for the rest of the year?
  Recent case law would appear to bear this out.

- The role that accountability has to play may well turn out to be central government control in another guise.

- Many would argue, the authors included, that whilst many facets of the police service can be tailored to a structured managerial framework, many elements are specified by public demand and by other agencies within the criminal justice system.

- Perceived, and real, threats to the police structure have meant that the staff associations have become more vocal and militant on their members' behalf. Any notions of strike action, currently prohibited by legislation, may become more of a spectre if financial restraints start to outweigh justice.

Chapter 3

Strategic Management and Planning

Introduction

> *'When we try to pick out anything by itself, we*
> *find it hitched to everything else in the universe.'*
>
> John Muir

Strategic management is a science in its own right, the subject of numerous courses of up to two or three years duration and innumerable textbooks. We cannot hope to deal with all the subtle nuances of the subject, and the range of management techniques which the global term strategic management encompasses, in one brief chapter.

We can however, attempt to demystify the concept of strategic management, introduce some of the ideas which it addresses and show how these concepts and ideas have been embraced by the police service in recent years. In that respect, this chapter merely whets the appetite. Those wishing to delve deeper into strategic management will find references to several authoritative text books on the subject at the end of the book.

Strategic management has an ever shifting definition. The explanation of what strategic management is depends very much on which text book you happen to be reading. One of the more succinct definitions is provided by the American management theorists, Rowe, Mason, Dickel and Snyder in their treatise on strategic management in 1989.

> *'Strategic management is the process of aligning*
> *the internal capability of an organisation with the*
> *external demands of its environment. The strategic*
> *management process forms the basis to formulate*
> *and implement strategies that achieve an organisation's goals*
> *and objectives.'*

Strategic management is therefore very much concerned with deciding where the organisation should be going and how it should get there. Johnson and Scholes (1989) saw strategic management as being composed of three main elements, namely; strategic analysis, strategic choice and strategic implementation. Put in simple terms, strategic management is about addressing the following questions with respect to the organisation:

- Where are we now?
- Where do we want to be?
- How do we get there?

In addition, it then relates to the implementation of strategies to ensure that the organisation gets where it wants to be as effectively and efficiently as possible. The process of monitoring and evaluation is therefore a crucial element of strategic management.

Unless an organisation is clear about what its purpose is, what it would like to achieve, how it is currently performing and what it needs to do to achieve its aims, then it is clearly not going to be operating effectively. Like a boat without a rudder it will merely drift without direction and it is likely that eventually it will be washed onto rocks and sink. Strategic management and strategic planning might be thought of as fulfilling the same purpose as the rudder on a boat. However, the rudder in itself is worthless. Those controlling the rudder need to know how to use it. In other words, those being asked to fulfil a strategic management role should be equipped with the skills to enable them to do so.

In many respects strategic management in the police service (and for that matter any public sector organisation) is similar to that in the private sector. There are, however, subtle differences, the major one being that strategic management in the private sector is driven by the need to exploit competitive advantage and maximise profits or market share. The police service in the UK has no competitors (yet) and hence is in a monopolistic situation as the sole provider of core policing services (though the situation with respect to more ancillary tasks is less clear). It is also in the non-profit making sector and, as sole provider, already has a 100 per cent market share.

Despite this, the police service should still be clear on what the market, (the public at large), requires of it; where it wants to be as an organisation, that is what its corporate objectives and aims should be; and how it should try to achieve those aims. This chapter will look at basic strategic management concepts applied to the police service. It will also consider how the service has attempted to embrace these concepts and how legislation has helped to encourage the service to do so.

Where are we now?

There are two elements to this question which strategic management should address. Firstly, where are we now in relation to the needs of the external environment in which we operate and, secondly, where are we now in terms of our own effectiveness and efficiency and to what extent do we meet external needs?

In technical terms, this phase of strategic management and planning requires the carrying out of environmental scanning and corporate appraisal.

Environmental Scanning

If they are only used as management jargon, terms like 'environmental scanning' rightly deserve to have a bad name among practical managers. In reality, however, environmental scanning is only a label for a systematic understanding of the current and future conditions under which an organisation operates. It is a part of the 'where are we now' analysis, with an eye to how the real world will develop in the future.

Broadly speaking, environmental scanning is a process designed to assess, from several perspectives, the future conditions under which an organisation will be offering its products or services. Full use of forecasting tools needs to be made, to address both the wider and more focused environments in which the organisation operates. This includes the underlying philosophies and values within the environment as this will fundamentally affect the nature of the organisation.

For example, the police service in the UK is built upon the fundamental philosophy that law and order should be upheld at all times and that a specific organisation should be established and maintained to support that philosophy on behalf of the population. Any shift in this philosophy would have significant effects on the nature and shape of the police service.

The sheer range and diversity of environmental influences on the operation of police organisations is staggering. Some of these are more influential than others but what is clear is that some systematic attempt should be made to assess future trends in such influencing factors. The ability to forecast changes in the environment is crucial as such changes may require a change in strategy. For example, indications might be that some aspects of traffic policing would be seen as less and less of a core policing activity in the coming years, being replaced by more involvement of local government in enforcement and traffic management. If this were the case then there would be little sense in pursuing a broadly based strategy of developing specialist traffic units with their own custom built facilities. The identification of such a trend should lead to a change in strategy, perhaps to retraining traffic officers, a limited tenure in traffic posts and more involvement in partnership activity. It should be noted that this is purely an example and in no way suggests that this will in fact happen. A properly designed environmental scanning system, however, will indicate the pressures and probabilities.

A systematic approach to environmental scanning is necessary because all organisations work in complex environments. It is particularly important to police organisations because of the wide range of external influences which may affect them. Failure to take account of the short, medium and long-term trends in the environment will mean that a police organisation can only react to developments, rather than being able to influence decisions.

Technically, therefore, environmental scanning can best be defined as the identification of future trends in the external environment that could affect the performance of an organisation. It does not normally include analysis of the internal (organisational) environment. The term is usually taken to mean the analysis of the external environment within which the organisation operates.

In strategic planning, environmental scanning enables opportunities and threats to be identified as part of a strengths, weakness, opportunities and threats (SWOT) analysis. This focus upon the external environment is not always understood by those who are interested in policing futures. However important they may be, organisational strengths and weaknesses (and policing systems developments more generally), are best located within the remit of internal (corporate) appraisal (see Stoffels, 1994 and Wright, 1996).

A considerable amount of environmental scanning has already been carried out in the police service. For example, during 1995 the Association of Chief Police Officers (ACPO) produced an extensive analysis of environmental influences and their implications for the police service at the national level. Their *Through the Millennium* paper was circulated to every police force in England and Wales (ACPO, 1996). During 1995/6 Staffordshire University facilitated workshops to identify trends affecting the police service and to discuss appropriate methodologies. Many police forces (and other police organisations such as National Police Training) have carried out environmental scanning for their own purposes.

It is almost impossible to list all external environmental influences on the organisation. However, it is possible to identify those factors which have been important in the past and which should be considered in any environmental scanning exercise. An analytical framework is required to enable all organisations to assess the complexities which confront them in the short, medium and long-term. This is particularly important for public sector organisations where market analysis of the kind employed in business and commerce is not generally viable. The most frequently used approach for environmental scanning is to analyse a range of factors across the political, economic, social, technological, legal and ecological domains. The acronym PESTLE (and its variants) provides a useful guide and is widely discussed in the literature:

- Political: Will a change in government and/or philosophies at a national, local (and even the global) level affect the organisation?

- Economic: Are there likely to be changes in the economy and/or funding which will affect the organisation?

- Social: Are there likely to be changes in the fabric, demographics and views of society which will affect the organisation?

- Technical: Will technological developments affect how the organisation operates or present new challenges in the delivery of its services?

- Legal: Are there likely to be changes in the legal framework within which the organisation operates which affect the basic operations of the organisation?

- Ecological: Is there likely to be any change in the nature of the physical environment in which the organisation operates?

The information generated under each heading should be used to assess the effects of possible changes including the development of new technologies and processes, innovations in institutional relationships, changing demographics and so on. In practice, a computer database is a useful tool to manage the information. This is by no means an exhaustive list but goes some way to illustrating the complexity of environmental scanning. Unless these environmental influences are considered then an effective strategy for the organisation cannot be developed.

Looking at the list above in a police context also gives some indication of the turbulent environment in which police managers have had to plan and develop strategies in the last few years. Changes, or the possibility of changes, in each of those areas have had a significant effect on the strategies of police forces and the service in general. Managers deserve sympathy for having to develop a strategic approach to police management whilst so much change has been happening in the environment. Trying to forecast the nature and direction of change and build strategy upon those forecasts has often been a thankless task.

The success of environmental scanning (and ultimately, the quality of strategic decision) depends on the quality of the data which is gathered and the accuracy

Figure 3.1: Multiple scenarios for strategic planning
Process to create scenarios for each domain of the PESTLE model and to apply to strategic planning

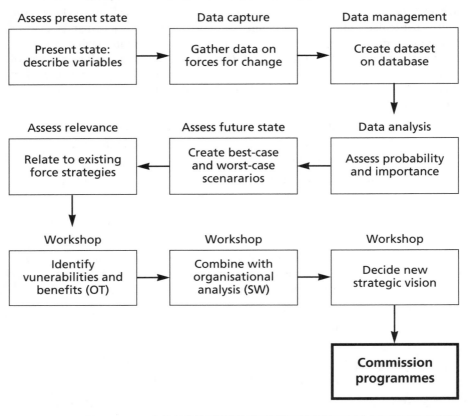

with which the probability and importance to the police of each item are assessed. This is a matter of judgement and is not an exact science. The subjectivity of each item of data needs constantly to be borne in mind. However, the generation of a limited number of scenarios provides a useful tool to focus the large amount of information which is gathered during a futures assessment. The process of developing such multiple scenarios is shown above.

Scenarios concentrate on qualitative argument and focus upon the key issues which are generated during the environmental scanning process. Preferably, they will describe two possibilities for a given set of conditions, depicting alternative best and worst-case futures. This indicates the extremes within which strategic decisions may be affected. Recognising the errors of previous scenario writers in industry, where multiple-scenario planning and selection of the 'most likely' case resulted in costly investment errors, scenarios are best presented in these starkly contrasting pairs. This encourages managers to question their strategic assumptions. Using this approach, the scenarios can be regularly reconsidered as part of the normal planning cycle. Higher levels of predictability will be observed as the system progresses and planning horizons of 5-10 years should eventually be practicable.

Vulnerability analysis is a useful way of taking this process forward. All too often, environmental scanning documents, however well researched, just sit on the shelf and provide no practical benefit. Looking at the vulnerability or benefit presented by each scenario helps strategic managers to determine whether their organisation is in a potentially endangered situation or is well-prepared to cope with possible change. In planning seminars, the most conservative assessment of the consequences, or 'down-side risk', can be established, should the potential threat or opportunity materialise. In this way, the potential impact of a particular threat or opportunity can be mapped against the organisation's ability to respond. In the final phase of the process, instructions are given by the top team to incorporate their thinking into draft strategic plans and practical programmes.

Corporate Appraisal

Concurrently with an assessment of external influences there needs to be a consideration of the effectiveness of the organisation in taking account of external influences and meeting its objectives.

The subject of objectives is one which has received considerable attention in recent years with respect to the police. We will return to it later in the chapter, but it is clear that all organisations should have some broad idea of what they are there to do. This often goes under several names; strategic vision, corporate vision, mission statement are but a few. What is required in very broad terms, is the philosophy underpinning the organisation. In 1990, ACPO published its *"Statement of Common Purpose and Values"*, reproduced below, which effectively fulfils this requirement:

> 'The purpose of the police service is to uphold the
> law fairly and firmly: to prevent crime; to pursue and
> bring to justice those who break the law; to keep the Queen's
> peace; to protect, help and reassure the
> community: and to be seen to do all this with integrity,
> common sense and sound judgement.

> 'We must be compassionate, courteous and patient,
> acting without fear or favour or prejudice to the rights
> of others. We need to be professional, calm and restrained
> in the face of violence and apply only that force which is nec-
> essary to accomplish our lawful duty.

> 'We must strive to reduce the fears of the public and,
> so far as we can, to reflect their priorities in the action
> we take. We must respond to well-founded criticism
> with a willingness to change.'

The clear identification of such a corporate vision is the starting point for any corporate appraisal process. When the organisation knows and agrees what it should be doing then it can assess how well it is currently doing it through a series of techniques. Not surprisingly, during the corporate appraisal process, organisations often realise that either they do not have a clearly stated corporate vision or they have one but that it is poorly defined. This may be equally true of the police service as of many private sector organisations. Carrying out some form of corporate appraisal, however, can act as a catalyst to organisations to develop such a vision where none exists, or to look critically at existing ones. If this is done properly it can, and should, be a lengthy and complex process incorporating much consultation.

A corporate vision or statement of common purpose should not be seen as just a few platitudes which can be put together easily. It should embrace the philosophy of the organisation and as such be the driving force behind everything which that organisation and its staff does. Everyone in the organisation should be aware of it and fully committed to it. How many people reading this book knew what the ACPO Statement of Common Purpose was before they read it earlier in the chapter? How many have thought about it and how it affects them in carrying out their job?

Armed with a view of environmental influences and the corporate vision, managers have at their disposal a wide range of corporate appraisal techniques. Many of these relate purely to profit driven organisations operating in a competitive environment. The American management scientist, Michael Porter, has been prolific in this area. His analysis of competitive forces, analyses of market structures, market power and product portfolios cannot easily be utilised in the non profit making environment of the police service and other public sector organisations. They are, however, becoming increasingly relevant and should not be discounted.

One simple technique has already been mentioned which can give some indication of the current performance of the organisation. That is, the so-called SWOT analysis. Quite simply this requires a fundamental review and structured analysis of the Strengths and Weaknesses of the organisation and the Opportunities open to, and the Threats faced by, the organisation. This should involve some real analysis and not be merely a listing of a collection of perceptions of managers in an organisation.

The aim of SWOT analysis is to identify how far current organisational strategy is relevant to, and hence able to respond to, the needs of, and changes taking place in, the external environment. If done properly, it should help to identify the direction of future strategy and as such is a crucial process in strategic planning. Environmental scanning should have identified some of the opportunities and threats facing the organisation. When considering the internal strengths and weaknesses there are several themes which can give structure to the analysis. Therefore, strengths and weaknesses of the organisation need to be considered in relation to a number of factors, including:

- Resource capabilities, personnel, financial and technical
- Organisation and management structures
- Resource utilisation

- Corporate vision
- Corporate performance
- Systems

The issues can be identified, often through brainstorming, and it is not uncommon for scores to be attributed to strengths and weaknesses (and also opportunities and threats) to give some degree of prioritisation. Although a relatively crude technique, SWOT can give a clear picture of the corporate position of an organisation. It can facilitate the systematic analysis of the extent to which an organisation can cope with its environment. It is therefore an invaluable aid to the strategic planning process. However, due to its inherent simplicity, SWOT analysis is not without its critics.

One of the more widely accepted techniques which has been developed to supplement SWOT is Value Chain Analysis, developed by Michael Porter in the early 1980s (Porter, 1982). VCA concentrates upon the resource capabilities and utilisation in organisations and helps to identify how these can contribute to the strategic performance of the organisation. Porter identified five main groupings of primary activities of an organisation:

- Inbound logistics: *the intake of materials, people, ideas etc.*
- Operations: *the transformation of raw materials into products and services*
- Outbound logistics: *the delivery of the services or products*
- Marketing and sales: *the promotion of the products or services*
- Service: *follow up support facilities available to the consumer*

Cutting across each of these groupings are four groups of support activities, which are:

- Procurement
- Technology development
- Human resource management
- Management systems

VCA is very much directed at profit making organisations. From a private sector point of view value chain analysis looks at those strategically important value activities and linkages between them as a basis for identifying strengths and weaknesses and potential for competitive advantage. In a non competitive environment this is not necessarily applicable. However, VCA can supplement SWOT analysis with respect to non profit making organisations. It not only forces such organisations to assess which activities are strategically important to them and their customers, "value activities", but also provides a framework in which to consider resource utilisation with respect to those activities and support activities.

In a police context then, operations is quite clearly a value activity; that is, the delivery of policing services to the public. Marketing and sales may be less so but their value is likely to greatly increase in importance in the near future as the push towards privatisation and outsourcing of policing functions continues. Unless the public is aware of the range of policing services available then it may not be making full use of the service and perhaps have a false perception of the service as a result.

From a VCA point of view, police strategic managers need to ensure that resources are available and utilised in the appropriate proportion across the primary activities. They also need to ensure that the relevant over arching support activities are appropriately resourced. For example, are the relevant financial procedures and personnel policies (management systems) in place to facilitate the effective completion of primary activities? It is worth considering whether local financial management and limited post tenure in the police service are actually contributing to the effective delivery of policing services.

Value chain analysis can prove an effective addition to SWOT analysis as it requires reasons to be identified why particular activities or resources should be viewed as strengths or weaknesses. In so doing it recognises that organisational capability is strongly related to the way in which resources are deployed and controlled. Appropriate resources, effectively deployed and well managed, can be a major contributor to organisational success. Inadequate resources, poorly utilised and badly managed, can either individually or collectively be a prime cause of organisational failure. Those interested in considering VCA in more detail are recommended to look at Michael Porter's book for a full treatise on the concepts and application of the technique.

There are numerous other techniques for appraising the performance and capabilities of an organisation. Whichever technique is adopted corporate appraisal is often the most painful and difficult stage in the strategic planning process. If done properly it will question established practices and procedures and may mean facing unpleasant facts. As such, the process may be seen as threatening to managers in the organisation and be resented as a result. Those tasked with corporate appraisal must be aware of this and handle the process with a high degree of tact and sensitivity.

Corporate appraisal must be sold to the organisation and individual mangers as a constructive process which will facilitate the continued development of the organisation and its staff. Managers should be encouraged to make a positive contribution to the process and not view it as a threat. Clear terms of reference for the appraisal must be established and the involvement of as many managers as possible should be encouraged. This fostering of ownership of the appraisal should lead to an acceptance of the process and elicit an honest response from managers in the organisation.

Where do we want to be?

Once there is a clear view of the performance and capabilities of the organisation and the environmental influences, a clear view of where the organisation wants to be needs to be developed.

The stages in strategic management and planning are in no way mutually exclusive. As noted above, a clear identification of corporate vision needs to be established at the corporate appraisal stage. However, in the light of the appraisal process and environmental influences, changes may be required to the corporate vision or mission.

It is clear that at this stage there must now be clear agreement on:

- The corporate vision or mission of the organisation
- The objectives of the organisation
- The goals or milestone events which must be met if objectives are to be achieved.

This sounds a very simple process. It is imperative that much time and thought is given to this stage, however, as it will influence the future direction of the organisation and hence its prospects for survival. There is often much confusion regarding what is a mission, an objective, a goal and a strategy and it may be useful now to consider some simple definitions.

Corporate Vision or Mission Statement

As noted earlier in the chapter, the corporate vision should embrace the philosophy of the organisation and be the driving force behind everything which that organisation and its staff do. Richards (1978) sees this as:

'...a visionary projection of the central and overriding concepts on which the organisation is based.'

It logically follows, then, that any significant disagreement regarding the corporate vision of the organisation is a serious impediment to the strategic planning process. Any differences of opinion need to be addressed at this stage or there will be confusion regarding the strategic direction of the organisation.

The ACPO Statement of Common Purpose was referred to earlier in the chapter. In the light of the above definition, you may wish to consider if that provides an appropriate vision for the service as a whole. Where forces and individual departments have adopted their own mission statements you may also wish to consider them in the light of the definition.

Objectives

The concept of objectives is an emotive one which has often been the source of considerable confusion, especially between what constitutes an objective and what constitutes a goal. A succinct definition of objectives is provided by Ansoff (1965) in his seminal text on corporate strategy. Ansoff considers objectives to be,

'...decision rules which enable management to guide and measure the firms performance towards its purpose.'

This definition has been supplemented by numerous writers since it was first produced. Some have seen objectives as being established within the planning process, others see objectives driving the planning process. There is a broad agreement that there are different levels of objectives with different characteristics throughout an organisation.

The simple definition provided by Ansoff, however, clearly identifies the characteristics of objectives. They support and guide the decision making process and they should be the basis of any evaluation or assessment of the firms performance. In effect, they state desired outcomes but not how those outcomes should be achieved.

Our work on the management of crime prevention initiatives has revealed very real confusion regarding the nature of objectives. To illustrate, we have seen several forces set an objective of establishing a vehicle watch scheme. We would argue that the force could merely establish such a scheme without any regard to what the scheme would be seek to achieve and logically argue that it had met its objective. On making this point to police managers, it was often agreed that the objective (or desired outcome) was actually to reduce the level of vehicle crime and that the establishment of a vehicle watch scheme was merely one of a number of activities designed to achieve the objective. Viewing objectives as desired outcomes is a clear and simple way of distinguishing them from activities or tactics.

The concept of objectives is so simple and yet all organisations, including the police service, seem to have real problems in embracing the process of objective development and implementation.

During the early and mid 1980s the concept of rational management and policing by objectives (PBO) began to emerge in the UK. Developed in the USA by Lubans and Edgar (1979), PBO is based on a four stage planning cycle. The stages relate to the development of a mission statement, a goal statement, objectives and action plans, with each of these stages being more specific than its predecessor. For a variety of reasons this failed to fire the imagination of the service as a whole.

There was confusion with the terminology and, in some cases, PBO was seen as an end in itself rather than a means of making operational policing more effective. There was also a degree of cultural rejection of the process. PBO was seen to be steeped very much in the private sector. Many of those tasked with implementing PBO were firmly of the belief that the police service was different and that private sector management techniques could not and would not work in such an organisation as the police.

Since the late 1980s, there has been a subtle change in the attitudes of many of the senior and executive officers in the service. Many now accept that, in managerial terms, the police service is not really very different from any other organisation and hence there is no reason why management techniques adopted in other organisations should not work in the police service. There is a growing acceptance therefore of PBO type approaches to the strategic management of forces.

The government has sought to promote this trend further by setting "key objectives" and requiring forces to set corporate and divisional objectives through policing plans. In this way the government is forcing the service to adopt the concept of objective setting and planning. It is also accepting the premise that objectives can be defined at different levels of the organisation.

Corporate objectives are likely to be formulated by senior managers and give direction to the activities of the disparate parts of the organisation. They are clearly aligned very closely with the corporate vision and are in effect a way of 'operationalising' the vision.

Objectives can also be set at divisional or departmental level. The corporate objectives are handed down to lower levels of the organisation and translated into divisional or departmental objectives. Such objectives relate only to the operations of the particular division or department but should embody the requirements of the corporate objectives. It is more likely that there will be multiple objectives at the divisional/departmental level and the corporate objectives should ensure that such objectives do not conflict in any way.

In policing terms, the key objectives, set by the Home Secretary, determine the corporate focus of the service as a whole. Within that framework each force is required to take due note of its own particular problems and the needs of the communities which it serves, to develop objectives for the force and each division and department.

The pain which forces have gone through in developing such objectives has been considerable, due in part to the confusion regarding what constitutes an objective and its purpose. Objectives have been seen as a threat rather than an aid to effective management, which is their real purpose.

In many cases, the objectives set as part of this process, have been poorly defined. When one refers to Ansoff's definition above many do not meet the criteria. However, the process has been a valuable learning exercise and it is hoped that, in subsequent years, setting effective and well defined objectives will become easier.

In their work on the evaluation of crime prevention initiatives, Berry and Carter (1991) identified that, if objectives were to be of value to an organisation and its staff, they should meet some simple criteria.

- The objectives should be meaningful to those being asked to work towards them. For example, patrol officers should not be asked to achieve objectives couched in financial terms.

- The objectives must be realistic and achievable. There is no greater de-motivating influence than being expected to meet an objective which is totally unrealistic and plainly unachievable. Faced with having to achieve 50 per cent reduction in all crime across the force over a 12 month period officers will either forget to submit crime reports for recording purposes (not advisable) or not even try to achieve the objective. An objective so clearly unrealistic will either result in the adoption of shady practices or the demotivation and disillusionment of those required to meet it. Great care therefore must be taken in setting realistic objectives.

- Where possible, objectives should be measurable. This is consistent with Ansoff's definition which indicates that objectives should facilitate the measurement of performance. Therefore, rather than state that an objective of the force is to reduce crime, it may be better to quantify this in order to make it measurable. A more appropriate objective might be to reduce overall recorded crime in the force by 2 per cent over a 12 month period.

The concept of measurable objectives is one which has been embraced by the government. The authors recognise, however, that it is possible to have both quantitative and qualitative objectives, the latter of which are often very difficult to measure. The well quoted example is the objective of reducing the fear of crime. It is relatively easy to set such an objective but far more difficult to measure progress towards achieving the objective. It is not impossible, however, and the reader is referred to Berry and Carter (1991), which explores the concept of proxy measures.

One of the prime tasks of any strategic planning process is to bring a degree of clarification to the confusion which, even in the private sector, often surrounds the subject of objectives. It is not uncommon to find different departments of an organisation working to opposing objectives, each unaware of the others and each certain that they are acting in the best interests of the organisation. A clear set of corporate objectives which shape divisional/departmental objectives should ensure that the opportunity for such a situation to occur is minimised and enhance the co-ordination of effort towards achieving a shared vision.

Goals

There is often considerable confusion between what constitutes an objective and what constitutes a goal. The distinction is quite simple and well presented by Ackoff (1970), who suggests that:

> *'Desired states or outcomes are objectives. Goals are objectives that are scheduled for attainment during the period planned for.'*

Goals are in effect the milestone events which must be achieved by agreed dates if the objectives are to be met. Strategies are the activities to be undertaken in order to meet the goals. A simple example will help to make the distinction. An objective might be to go on holiday to Florida during April. The goals to achieve this objective include:

- Booking the holiday by the end of February
- Paying for the holiday by mid March
- Being at the airport two hours before the flight time

Strategies to achieve the second goal may include; checking the bank balance, arranging a loan or overdraft and saving hard during January and February. Though this is a simple example it does illustrate the distinction between objectives and goals. Managers, including police managers, often find great difficulty in coming to terms with the concepts of objectives, goals and strategies. In reality, they are adopting these concepts in their everyday lives as this simple example shows.

In a police context, then, an objective might be to establish full multi-agency co-operation in the community safety arena of a force within three years. A goal might be to establish a strategic community safety planning group by the end of the first year. The strategies devised to achieve such goals and objectives would include, identifying all of the agencies which should be included, identifying the policy and decision makers in those organisations and assessing the level of commitment.

Put simply, objectives are 'what we want to achieve', goals are 'what we must achieve by set times in order to achieve the objectives' and strategies are 'what we will do in order to achieve the goals and hence objectives'. Each supports the other in a hierarchy as illustrated in Figure 3.2.

The establishment of clear goals can therefore enable an organisation to check that it is still on course to achieve its objectives and examine any reasons for

Fig 3.2: The strategic management pyramid

deviation. Failure to achieve a goal might indicate the need to look again at strategies or even objectives. Brought together, vision, objectives and goals help to give direction to the organisation. That is, they help to identify where it wants to be.

We have already begun to look at the next stage in the strategic planning process – the strategies themselves. At a local level, the identification of strategies is a simple process. At a strategic level, in a disparate organisation such as the police service, this process is, not surprisingly, far more complex.

How do we get to where we want to be?

At this stage in the strategic management process there should be a clear view of the corporate capabilities of the organisation, the factors influencing the environment in which the organisation operates and the desired outcomes which the organisation wishes to achieve. This stage of the process is therefore very much about the identification of strategic options and strategic choice. It is about considering the alternative courses of action open to the organisation and choosing the most effective one(s). This will also incorporate the identification of the appropriate resourcing strategies and organisational structures. When considering strategic options, Johnson and Scholes (1989) have identified three issues which need to be addressed.

- Generic strategies
- Alternative directions in which strategies might be developed
- Alternative methods by which strategies might be developed

Generic Strategies

Generic strategies are those strategies which the organisation (in the public sector) will chose to maintain and improve its quality of service, within the financial and resource constraints under which it operates. In a police context, generic strategies would include those related to patrol activities. In terms of the Posen review of a few years ago, they are core activities. From a strategic choice point of view, there is little disagreement that such activities must form the backbone of the activities of the organisation. The issues which must be addressed are those which relate to the resourcing and funding of such activities, a consideration of the appropriate focus for such activities and, increasingly a review of alternative methods of delivery.

Alternative Strategic Direction

For public sector organisations such as the police, the identification of alternative directions in which strategies might be developed is often a very difficult process. The ongoing debate regarding preventative or proactive policing as opposed to detective or reactive policing is evidence of this. Forces are facing the choice of whether to adopt the more integrated crime management strategies or retain the crime detection and crime prevention functions as separate departments. This is a clear example of strategic choice between alternatives which the service faces.

Alternative Methods of Strategy Development

The previous two issues are concerned with the directions in which organisations might develop in order to sustain and even improve performance. However, there needs to be some consideration of the method or means by which each alternative strategy is to be developed. These methods might include internal development, joint development or even external development or 'outsourcing'. For example, if it was decided to service all force vehicles every week as a means of improving patrol capabilities then quite clearly there are alternative methods of adopting this strategy. It could take place internally through the establishment or expansion of in house maintenance facilities or jointly with a local garage. This strategy could even be progressed externally by 'outsourcing' the vehicle maintenance functions and requiring local garages to tender for and provide all vehicle maintenance services.

If followed logically what should emerge from this process is a range of options regarding the strategies to be adopted and the method of delivery in the pursuance of the goals, objectives and ultimately the vision of the organisation. The diagram in Figure 3.2 shows how the various components of the strategic management process are integrated.

The next stage is to evaluate the various options and chose the mix which will enable the organisation to pursue its objectives effectively and efficiently.

Strategy Evaluation

Some means of evaluating the relative merits of alternative strategies and methods of delivery needs to be identified and adopted. The process of strategy evaluation requires two issues to be addressed.

1. The Choice of Criteria for Evaluation

Evaluation criteria can be into split three broad categories:

- Suitability: *Criteria need to be identified which assess the degree to which the options address the issues identified at the corporate appraisal and objective setting stages. In other words, to what extent do the strategies build on the strengths of the organisation or seek to address the weaknesses? In addition, do they fit with the identified objectives and goals and the underlying vision of the organisation?*

- Feasibility: *Criteria should assess the extent to which options are practical. They should identify whether or not the options can be implemented and consider the resource implications, such as funding, staffing, technical support of each of the options.*

- Acceptability: *Criteria also need to assess whether or not the consequences of adopting an option are acceptable both internal to the organisation and externally with respect to the client group of the organisation.*

For example, in pursuing an objective of faster response times, one strategic option might be to issue every officer in the force with a patrol car. This option might be a suitable means of achieving the objective but it is unlikely to be feasible and certainly not acceptable to many of the officers of the force and members of the public.

The criteria used to evaluate strategic options is critical to the choice of the best mix of options. If options are evaluated against inappropriate criteria then it is possible that the wrong strategies might be adopted with potentially serious consequences for the organisation.

In addition, criteria may conflict with each other and the process of strategic evaluation often involves the resolution of these conflicts to bring consistency to the criteria.

This in turn may require a number of 'trade-offs'. For example, feasibility criteria for a range of multi agency strategies might require options to make no financial burden on the police. Other criteria might state that only strategies which require all agencies to make some financial contribution to their implementation will be acceptable. Here, the criteria are clearly in conflict and this must be resolved before the evaluation process can proceed.

2. The Choice of Evaluation Technique

Once the evaluation criteria have been identified there are a range of techniques which can be used to assess the various strategic options. Some of these attempt to assess the level of risk and/or predicted return associated with each option. A large number of text books consider these techniques in far more detail.

There does, however, need to be some mechanism for screening the options to identify the most suitable, feasible and acceptable with a low risk factor. There are a number of different approaches to the evaluation process. Three of the more common methods used are :

- Ranking: *Each option is scored against a predetermined set of factors related to the evaluation criteria and a ranking of options is constructed. Whilst this is a relatively simple process, the assignment of scores is by definition a subjective process. In addition, the implementation of the options with the highest scores does not necessarily ensure that the best mix of options emerges.*

- Decision trees: *Each option is again scored against a predetermined set of factors but a ranking emerges as the lesser options are eliminated. A few key criteria are identified and options are progressively scored against those key elements, such that at the end of the process only the few (or even one) meeting the key criteria are left. Again this is a relatively simplistic technique and as such is of limited value when attempting to evaluate a complex mix of strategic options. However, decision trees can provide a useful first cut of options.*

- Scenario modelling: *Under simulated conditions each option is evaluated against a range of possible future scenarios. This method will clearly identify and eliminate those strategies which do not fit into the scenarios and will help to identify the most effective mix of strategic options. For example, strategies for increasing the proactive patrol function of the police might be evaluated against a combination of scenarios including:*
    - *increased/decreased government spending on the police*
    - *a change of government*
    - *increased/decreased public concern regarding crime*
    - *decentralised/centralised control of operational policing*
    - *increased/decreased privatisation of policing functions*
    - *increases/decreases in force establishments.*

Scenario modeling is of great value where the organisation is operating against an uncertain background and where it needs to be able to respond quickly to a variety of possible future events. In this respect it is very well suited to the police service in the UK at present. It is, however, a relatively complex process which is often time consuming and resource intensive but it is undoubtedly thorough and will usually result in the selection of the most appropriate strategic options.

The adopted mix of strategies is then considered in terms of the financial, organisational and staffing required to implement them and plans prepared for their provision. Strategic management is thus about reviewing the processes outlined in this chapter and ensuring that the organisation continues to know where it is, where it is going and how it is going to get there. It is, therefore, an ongoing process. This chapter has attempted to present strategic management as a series of simple and logical steps designed to give direction to the organisation and its component parts. In essence, that is all that strategic management is. Why then have many organisations struggled to embrace the concepts and manage them?

The Failure of Strategic Management

A number of factors will affect the success of strategic management in any organisation.

Senior Management Commitment

Unless there is commitment to the processes of strategic management and planning at the very highest levels of the organisation, then the whole concept is doomed to failure. The most senior managers are required to establish corporate vision and objectives and are often best placed to carry out much of the corporate appraisal work. Without their commitment true strategic management and planning cannot take place.

Acceptance

Not only must senior managers be fully committed to the process of strategic management but also middle and junior managers in the organisation must accept the process if it is to be adopted effectively. It is the middle and junior managers who are likely to be responsible for implementing the strategies identified as part of the strategic management process. As such they must have some sense of ownership and acceptance of the process. Without this the process is also unlikely to be effectively implemented.

Lack of Consultation

There is a danger that those tasked with strategic management lose touch with the realities of the every day operations of an organisation. This can give rise to 'ivory tower' management whereby objectives and strategies are handed down by those "who know best" with minimal or even a total lack of consultation. All parts of the organisation should have the opportunity to comment on the setting of objectives and the adoption of strategies. A lack of such consultation will inhibit the commitment of staff to the strategic planning approach.

Confusion

Throughout this chapter there have been several references to the fact that people often become very confused when faced with the jargon of strategic management. This confusion and misunderstanding can, and often does, lead to the failure of strategic planning and management. To counter this the introduction of strategic management and planning processes must be accompanied by clear definitions of terminology and appropriate training. There must also be refresher training for those joining organisations operating such managerial and planning philosophies.

Lip Service Strategic Management

The confusion often surrounding the strategic management process sometimes leads organisations to believe that they are operating true strategic management and planning processes. In reality, they are often using a few 'buzz' words and producing a brief document which represents something of a wish list rather than a strategic plan.

This in turn may lead to unrealistic expectations of the process and when the 'plan' fails to deliver results then there is a stage of disillusionment. Ultimately the strategic management processes fall into disuse as a result, discredited and abandoned.

All members of the organisation must be made fully aware of what strategic management and planning is and how they should embrace its processes if it is to stand any chance of success. Hussey (1976) summarises this point most succinctly:

> 'Although few people would throw away a car that
> will not start, it is unfortunately true that many
> companies will discard their investment in corporate
> planning when this fails to fire. And it is doubly
> unfortunate when the cause of failure is preventable
> and often as trivial as a lack of an ignition key.'

The potential benefits of strategic management and planning are huge but individuals need to be able to see them and know how to access them. They need to know how to start the strategic management car and how to drive it in order that they can reach their intended corporate destination.

Chapter Summary

- Strategic management is concerned with the identification of where the organisation is now, where it wants to be and how it can get there.

- The organisation needs to identify the environmental influences which affect its operation and the behaviour of its 'customers'.

- The organisation should carry out an in depth appraisal of its performance and capabilities, using a variety of techniques. One such commonly used approach is SWOT analysis, a review of the Strengths and Weaknesses of the organisation and the Opportunities and Threats facing it.

- The organisation must have a clear vision, objectives and goals which define its strategic direction.

- These should trigger the development of a range of strategic options designed to meet the vision, objectives and goals.

- The strategic options should take account of generic strategies of the organisation, alternative directions for the strategic development of the organisation and alternative methods of delivery of the strategies.

- Each strategic option should be evaluated against agreed criteria, using accepted techniques such as ranking and scenario modelling.

- Strategic management and planning can fail to deliver results for a variety of reasons including the lack of senior management commitment, a lack of acceptance by all in the organisation and a misunderstanding of its purpose and terminology.

Chapter 4

Managing Finance

Introduction

If there is one issue surrounding the modern police service which is always likely to stir up debate, it is the financing of the police and their management of that finance. The philosophy of the UK Government since the early 1980s has been one of reduced public spending and the effective and efficient use of publicly financed resources. The police service has therefore come increasingly under the spotlight and its level, method and use of financing has been heavily scrutinised over the last 10 years.

The Audit Commission has been actively reviewing police financing and this has manifested itself in at least four papers which addressed the subject of police financing in the last four years.

The question might be posed, why should police managers concern themselves with finance? Surely that is the province of the police authority and specialist managers within the force. While this is undoubtedly true, increasingly the management of finance at an operational level is an issue which police managers are having to address. The provisions of recent legislation have merely furthered this trend.

Through the provisions of the 1994 Police and Magistrates' Courts Act (PMC Act) there is added pressure on forces to devolve budgets down to operational units as far as is practicable. This in turn means that police managers at BCU level will increasingly have to manage finances as well as staff and other resources. Police managers have primarily been trained to become police officers. They are increasingly required to be not only managers, but to a certain extent, accountants. This chapter is designed to give an understanding of basic financial management concepts as they apply to managers in the police service. It is not intended to be a detailed treatise on the intricacies of accountancy. There are innumerable excellent text books on the market which fulfil that purpose.

In the ten years from 1979/80 to 1989/90 expenditure on the police rose by nearly 50 per cent in real terms and stood in excess of £3 billion at the end of the nineteen eighties. During the early years of the 1990s this trend has continued upwards, and in 1997/98 the figure is almost £7 billion. For this reason alone, the management of finances in the police service deserves to be considered.

Historical Perspectives on Police Financing

Prior to April 1995, funding of the police service in England and Wales was provided by both central and local government. Some 51 per cent of the net revenue expenditure and approved capital expenditure (for example, for new police stations, headquarters, etc.), was met by the Home Office. Further central funds were provided through revenue support grants made by the Department of the Environment and the Welsh Office to fund local authority services in general.

The balance of funding (estimated to be 30% by the National Audit Office in 1991, though clearly this figure varies from force area to force area) was met by local authorities. The council tax and non-domestic or business rate was the source for such funding.

This double source of funding was rooted in the desire to make the police both locally and nationally accountable and in many respects underpinned the tripartite agreement referred to in an earlier chapter.

The police authority and their force invariably drew upon the financial management services of their county council and adopted their financial regulations. For forces covering more than one county, such as West Mercia or Thames Valley, one of the county councils would act as lead authority for financial management purposes.

The extent of financial delegation and budget flexibility varied greatly between forces dependent upon both the financial regulations of the host authority and the management styles of the police authority and the executive officers in the force.

The same was also true on the subject of 'virement', the process whereby sums can be transferred from one budget head to another. For example, if the force fuel budget is underspent by say £10,000 but the overtime budget is at its limit and a major incident requires the spending of an additional £5000 on overtime, it may be possible to transfer or 'vire' funds from the one budget heading to the other. A study by the Audit Commission in 1991 found however that the extent of virement also varied greatly between forces. A series of case studies showed that in one force there could be no virement without prior approval of the police authority, while in another up to £50,000 could be vired by the chief constable without any requirement for further approval.

During 1994 however, a piece of legislation was enacted to change fundamentally how forces were funded and how those funds should be managed.

Police Financing Under the Police and Magistrates' Courts Act

From April 1995 all provincial police authorities have become precepting bodies and their expenditure has been limited by a capping level related to a standard spending assessment, or SSA, calculated for each authority. Authorities can therefore spend on police forces up to a limit prescribed by central government. In addition, the police specific grant from the Home Office is paid as a cash limited sum to police authorities; the sum paid being determined by a formula devised by the Home Office.

These changes have effectively taken control of police finances out of local government hands. The police authorities can decide how to spend the sums allocated but have no control over the level of finances allocated.

A major reason behind this centralisation of police financing is to prevent political interference at a local level in the running of the police force. The most well documented example is that of Derbyshire Constabulary in the late 1980s and early 1990s.

While central government provided their 51 per cent of funding, the local authority consistently failed or refused to make up the difference in funding. As a result, for a number of years, the force was heavily underfunded resulting in deteriorating resources (police cars that would not start, police stations using portakabins).

In turn the force failed three times to achieve a certificate of efficiency from Her Majesty's Inspector of Constabulary, which further adversely affected the level of central funds provided. Throughout all of this the officers of Derbyshire continued to operate with considerable effectiveness and the authors found them some of the most able and competent officers encountered across the country.

The local authority refused to provide the funding as they felt that central government should be providing more. Central government grew increasingly frustrated that the effective operation of a police force was being hampered by political manoeuvring of a local authority.

The provisions of the 1994 PMC Act mean that the situation in Derbyshire cannot happen again. By controlling centrally the level of funding allocated to each force the government has removed the opportunity for local politicians to interfere with the level of funds allocated to policing.

A more subtle point is that by centralising the control of police finances, the government is clearly isolating itself. The blame for inadequate levels of funding cannot now be ascribed to local politicians. Any controversy surrounding the level of police funding will be laid at the door of central government as the sole allocator of such funding.

There has already been considerable argument regarding the formula used to allocate funds to police authorities. Early attempts at using the formula resulted in many authorities facing up to 20 per cent reductions in budgets, while a few others faced considerable increases. Concerted opposition from ACPO resulted in a review of the formula but it is clear that many forces must look critically at the use of the finances allocated to them.

Two other provisions of the 1994 PMC Act have major implications for the management of finances in the police. Under the Act, police authorities have to provide a local policing plan to the Home Secretary which takes into account his key performance objectives and the needs of the local community. In addition to setting out objectives for policing, the plan must also state the proposed allocation of financial resources.

The police will thus have to show how resources available to them are to be used. This in turn will require forces to further devolve their budgets and move even closer to more locally based financial management.

A further financial implication of the Act is that it enables forces to accept 'gifts and contributions' towards the discharge of its functions. In other words, a force may accept and even actively pursue sponsorship as a means of supporting its funding. This concept, relatively new to the police, will be explored in greater detail later in the chapter.

Local Financial Management

Audit Commission Paper 10 *Pounds and Coppers: Financial delegation in provincial police forces*, published in 1991, laid out clear guidelines to forces seeking to devolve financial management to a local level. It also encouraged forces to do so, outlining the many benefits which could accrue from such a course of action. Despite this, a further study in 1994 by the Audit Commission revealed that only approximately 10 per cent of the revenue budgets in forces had been delegated in any way.

This report, *Cheques and Balances*, reinforced the pressures building on forces to devolve financial management to a local level and offered further guidance. It stated that financial responsibility should be aligned with management control but devolution of such responsibility should not take place just for the sake of it. Budgets should be delegated down the chain of command to the appropriate level and the report suggested that overtime should be authorised by an inspector, although the budget holder is often a senior officer one or two ranks higher in the hierarchy.

The report goes on to suggest that there are three stages in achieving full financial delegation in the police service.

The first phase is the delegation of selected revenue budget heads, such as police overtime, heating and minor repairs. During this phase, headquarters retains a strong influence over the management of finance. There is limited virement and authorisation is required prior to any such spending.

The second phase enables other more substantial budgets such as civilian pay, transport and training to be devolved. Headquarters is effectively easing its control role with a shift towards more of a resource management philosophy rather than financial management. The rules regarding virement ease, though limited prior authorisation might still be required for certain items.

The third phase is that which reveals maximum feasible devolution of finances, with the delegation of funding to cover such core activities as police staffing but excluding pensions. In this situation, the BCU commander becomes the key resource manager using costed local policing plans as a vehicle for financial control and expenditure. Headquarters then fulfils essentially a strategic role ensuring that the organisation as a whole meets its corporate aims and objectives.

Many forces are still coming to terms with phase one and beginning to progress towards phase two. Few are yet prepared for phase three in terms of both philosophy and organisation but the provisions of the 1994 PMC Act will ensure that forces will be required to move that way in the coming years. Police managers will increasingly have to move towards the concept of being resource managers, one of those resources being finance.

In their 1991 report, the Audit Commission suggested that there were several stages which forces need to address regarding their infrastructure before local financial management could be implemented:

- Financial specialism needs to be established at headquarters.

- The forces' financial systems need to be reviewed to identify whether they can support the major informational requirements of local financial management.

- Cost centre structures need to be introduced into forces if they are not in place already.

- Financial regulations need to be reviewed to assess if they are appropriate for local financial management and provide the desired level of authority. This includes virement regulations.

- A policy and plan needs to be developed which govern those budgets to be delegated, when they are to be delegated, and to whom.

- Clear lines of reporting responsibility need to established between budget holders and force managers.

- A policy needs to be established which details what happens to any savings achieved through effective financial management.

- The management information needs of budget holders need to be identified.

Financial Budgeting

Financial planning relates to the translation of activities and their resource implications into financial terms through preparation and use of financial documents. The most commonly used document is a budget, which has many uses and can fulfil several roles throughout the organisation. In a police management context the primary concern is with using budgets as a means of planning and control. This section outlines the different types of budgets, how they can be developed and how they can be used by police managers.

A budget expresses the resource requirements of an organisation in financial terms, usually on a monthly and annual basis and often split into departments and/or divisions. Therefore either at organisational or departmental/divisional level, a budget is an effective plan for resource usage.

There are several types of budgets which might be encountered in a police environment. Examples are outlined below.

Revenue Budgets

The most common type of budget found at operational levels, these outline proposed expenditure on items which require continual funding. Examples might include overtime, vehicle mileage and staffing costs. Elements of these budgets are now being devolved to divisions/departments for them to control and the pressures are growing for most, if not all, revenue budgets to be so devolved. Therefore, we may not be too far from the day when the BCU commander has sole control of all of his staffing budgets. He or she may be allocated a sum of, say, £1 million to cover staffing costs in the division for the year, including overtime. It is then up to the commander to manage that sum effectively as, once it is used up, requests for top up funding will either be frowned upon or rejected. This places additional responsibility upon the already sagging shoulders of BCU commanders and its impact should not be taken lightly.

Capital Budgets

These relate to the flow of funds pertaining to a particular project or specific decision. Invariably capital budgets are related to the acquisition of fixed assets for the organisation and invariably they are developed and controlled at force headquarters.

Capital budgets are developed to plan for resources such as new computer and communications equipment, vehicles and buildings. They relate to one-off projects and as such they cover a finite time period, although this may be a few years.

If a force decides to buy a new command and control computer system it is likely to carry out a capital budgeting exercise. This will seek to identify:

- What fund outflows and inflows are associated with the procurement of the system.

- The implications of different means of financing the procurement, for example, outright purchase, lease or loan.

- How worthwhile the project is likely to be, through some form of justification exercise *(see chapter 9)*.

Utilising a range of 'what-if' processes the appropriate financial flows will be identified and the capital budget formalised. This can then be built into the planning process of the force to ensure that suitable financial arrangements are in place to enable the capital project to take place.

Departmental Budgets

These outline the resource requirements and plans in financial terms at a departmental or divisional level. They are clearly important documents to departmental or divisional managers and it is important that they are prepared carefully. They will underpin much of the planning process at divisional/departmental level and decisions based upon an inaccurate document can be potentially damaging.

Consolidated Budgets

These statements relate to the resource requirements in financial terms for the force as a whole. As such they are more of a strategic planning tool than departmental budgets in that they identify revenue and capital requirements for the whole organisation. This is clearly the province of the executive officers, force finance officers and the police authority. They are tasked with developing and managing such budgets though the relationship with departmental budgets is clear. The nature of that relationship, however, is governed by the method used to develop budgets in the force. This will be explored later in the chapter.

Thus, in the post 1994 PMC Act world it is likely that BCU commanders and departmental managers will be increasingly responsible for the development and management of departmental revenue budgets. Consolidated budgets and capital budgets will however remain the province of force central managers at headquarters.

Developing Budgets

There are several approaches to developing budgets, each placing different requirements upon those tasked with their development.

Incremental Budgets

The quickest and easiest way of producing a budget, this method requires taking the previous year's budget and adding a factor for inflation across the board. Due account is taken of any wide variances to the previous year's budget and provisions made for similar future variations. For example, the previous year's force vehicle fuel budget might be inflated by 3 per cent in the following year across the force as a whole. However, the force overtime budget might have been overspent by 10 per cent. Decisions have to be made regarding whether the following year's budget should take account of this variation, that is apply a larger inflationary factor, or not. The benefits of incremental budgeting are that it is quick and relatively easy to produce a budget in this way, particularly the revenue budgets. However, there are a number of disadvantages:

- As they are historically based, they do not take full account of likely monthly variations in financial trends. This devalues them as a planning and control tool, particuarly at divisional or departmental level.

- They require no detailed analysis of the operations of the organisation. They merely reflect previous trends. If, therefore, there are problems within the organisation of a financial nature, this form of budgeting may not identify them. An incrementally produced budget may therefore actually promote the continuation of methods of working which are less than effective or even harmful to the organisation. For example, an incremental budget will look at the amount allocated in the previous year for petrol for patrol vehicles and add an inflationary factor. This will facilitate the continuation of petrol powered vehicles when, perhaps the force should be looking at diesel powered vehicles as a cheaper, more effective alternative.

- They will retain the political and organisational status quo. As such, they are a poor catalyst for change even where there is agreement within the organisation to changing strategies.

For these reasons, alternatives to the incremental method of budgeting have emerged in the last 20 to 30 years in the private sector. These have been mainly in response to change within organisations and the wish to use budgets as one of the vehicles for change.

Zero Based Budgeting (ZBB)

This arose initially in the private sector in the USA and was developed primarily by the Kodak Corporation. It requires managers to propose and justify their departmental/divisional budgets in relation to the alternative uses of those financial resources. Through using ZBB, the historical size of the various budgets is given no weight in identifying the sizes of future budgets. The manager starts with a blank piece of paper (zero base) and has to assess and justify how many resources, in financial terms, he or she needs, to provide the services for which he or she is responsible. The existence of a budget in a previous year is therefore not an acceptable argument in this case. Taking our previous example then, instead of adding 3 per cent to last year's divisional fuel budget the BCU commander under ZBB is required to state how much he or she needs to provide fuel for vehicles in the division to meet the required service levels. Quite clearly, this supports the concept of 'value for money' as all future spending under this approach has to be justified and is open to scrutiny. It has several advantages:

- It forces managers to look at alternative ways of providing a service, as in our example of petrol and diesel vehicles.

- It forces the organisation to take a critical look at itself and in so doing minimises the risk of continuing poor practices.

- It takes more account of outputs than the traditional methods of budgeting. That is, the manager has to look at what services he or she provides and then decide the inputs required to provide those services. The incremental style budget merely requires the manager to look at the level of inputs used previously and add a little more, with scant regard for the outputs which they produce.

There are however a number of potential disadvantages to the adoption of a ZBB approach:

- The development of ZBB is a relatively technical process and often requires a full understanding of business processes throughout an organisation in order to clearly identify the costs and resources needed to operate effectively. For example, when the head of the community relations department at headquarters has to develop a zero based budget, to what extent should he or she be considering divisionally based crime prevention officers who are almost exclusively used by the BCU Commander? These ZBB skills are not often readily available in force which will either require the costly 'buying in' of specialist advice or a budgeting process which is less than effective.

- For the reasons outlined above, the zero based budgeting process is relatively time consuming and resource intensive. Managers in the police service are often short of both.

- By going through the process of zero based budgeting, the resources required to operate, in financial terms, often exceed the finance and funding actually available. This may lead to a review of the budgetary process and even negotiation to arrive at financial requirements which match the available funding.

In the UK both the Audit Commission, with a brief to consider local government, and the National Audit Office, with a similar brief in central government, have adopted a strategy of value for money audits to support their work. It is clear that ZBB can in turn support the push for better value for money as it requires all resource requirements to be justified.

In recent years however, a third form of budgeting has emerged in the public sector in the UK in response to this push for greater effective and efficient use of public funding. The police service, as part of the public sector, has also directly experienced this newer approach.

Cash Limited Budgeting

In this situation a limit is put on the amount of finances available to an organisation, which then has to decide how to allocate those resources to best effect. In response organisations will either adopt an incremental or zero based approach and adjust until the limit targets have been achieved. In many respects, then, cash limited budgeting is in fact a form of financial environment in which the budgeting process takes place.

To differentiate between the methods of budgeting, in simple terms, zero based budgeting is a 'bottom up' analysis of the resource requirements of an organisation; cash limited budgeting is a 'top down' imposition of the finances available to be allocated to resources and incremental budgeting is a 'halfway house' which crudely maintains the status quo of resource allocation between functions.

Managing Budgets

Once a clear policy has been identified and implemented regarding the responsibility for budgets and virements, those tasked with such responsibilities need to be given the tools which enable them to manage.

Crucial to the process of managing budgets is the provision of accurate and relevant financial information. *The subject of managing information and management information is dealt with in considerable detail in chapter 8.*

To manage budgets effectively, however, it is suggested that the manager will require the following financial information on a regular basis for each cost centre under his or her control.

- Total budget for the year
- Budget for the year to date
- Expenditure, actual and committed, for the current year to date
- Actual spend to budget variance for the current year to date
- The balance of the budget left to spend in the current year.

The provision of this information on a regular basis, perhaps monthly, will enable managers to review the level of their current expenditure actual and committed; identify the extent of any over or underspends against budget and consider the level of finance still available to them.

The over and underspend position is particularly important as it will help the manager to identify if any virement might be required in the future.

A process of ongoing assessment of the financial position through perhaps monthly review meetings will enable any major budget variances to be explored. In this way problems can be identified and corrective action or contingency plans be put in place. For example, a series of serious public order incidents in a division may have led to an overspend against the overtime budget. An early identification of this overspend can trigger the implementation of virement procedures or the use of contingency reserves held centrally.

It is therefore strongly recommended that regular budgetary review meetings take place at the appropriate levels and that the process be underpinned by accurate and timely financial reports to the budget holders.

Paying for Capital Projects

The payment of revenue items is a relatively simple allocation of funds, often through the issuing of cheques. For example, a force knows that it must meet its wages bill every month and pay the full amount at the required time.

Capital projects can, however, be paid for in a variety of ways and the method chosen can have widely differing impacts upon the amount of funding to be provided by central government to support the force. Indeed, being creative and inventive in the methods of paying for capital projects can actually help forces facing tight financial limits.

Outright Purchase

Assets can be bought outright by the force and hence become its property immediately. Capital items such as a small number of personal computers or motor vehicles can be purchased in this way. They represent a one off charge against the force and there is often a contingency budget for small capital purchases. This method of payment becomes less attractive when major capital projects are considered. For example, it is highly unlikely that a force will pay outright for the building of a new police station or the purchase of a force wide crime reporting computer system. The strain on the limited police budget would be unbearable and would be likely to bankrupt a force at a stroke.

Forces need new police stations however and updated vehicle fleets and therefore other methods of payment for such capital items must be found.

Lease

Capital items, such as vehicles, can be leased to forces. Rather than pay outright a force may lease its vehicles from a specialist leasing company. For a leasing charge the force can use vehicles and the leasing arrangements often include some form of agreement regarding the maintenance of the vehicles. They often also include the automatic replacement of old vehicles with new vehicles on a regular basis, such as after two years of the vehicle's life.

The advantage of this is that the leasing charge is considerably lower than the cost of outright purchase. In addition, the leasing market is so competitive that some excellent deals can be struck with organisations who see the police service as a flagship market in which to establish a presence. The payment of the lease therefore becomes a revenue item, catered for every year in the annual budget.

The disadvantage of this method of payment is that, effectively, the capital items are never owned by the force. In theory, if the force defaulted in its payments, the vehicles could be recalled by the lease company leaving the force potentially without any transport facilities. In addition, if the leasing company ran into difficulty the force could find the assets frozen (that is, they would be unable to use the vehicles) or recalled by a receiver, or left without a maintenance and replacement programme.

Sale and Lease Back

This method of payment is a way of converting capital items into revenue items and generating cash. Although not common in the public sector, it is relatively widespread in the private sector. As forces come under increasing financial pressure this method of payment may begin to be attractive.

An asset owned by the force is effectively sold to a leasing company, thus releasing cash, and then leased back to the force for the payment of a leasing charge.

For example, a force which currently owns its vehicle fleet may sell all of the vehicles to a lease company for, say, £1 million. These are then leased back to the force for perhaps £300,000 per year. The net effect operationally is nil. The force still has the vehicles and has generated funds and spread the payments for the vehicles.

The disadvantage of this method is that effectively the force is paying twice for its assets; once to buy and once to lease. In addition, the lease payments are often more expensive in the long term than outright purchase. The disadvantages relating to pure leasing outlined above also apply. However, as a means of generating funds and easing financial pressures somewhat, this method is quite attractive.

Loan

Capital items such as buildings can be paid for through loans,. A force can receive a loan to pay for a new police station, rather like a mortgage, which it must repay in regular instalments over an agreed period of time.

The advantage of this method of payment over leasing is that eventually the asset becomes the property of the force. It also allows the payment to be spread in more manageable amounts which become a revenue charge on the budget.

However, if the payments are not made, the asset can be repossessed. In addition, loan payments are expensive because interest has to be paid and over the years the force may pay two or three times the value of the asset.

Extended Hire

A relatively new method of payment has emerged during the 1980s usually relating to the procurement of computing and information technology. A form of lease arrangement, these schemes require forces to make a regular hire or lease payment for the use of IT. For an additional sum they are entitled to have their hardware and software upgraded with the latest editions or versions as soon as they become available.

In the fast developing world of information technology this might appear attractive. Forces can ensure that they have the very latest equipment and software at their disposal at relatively minor extra cost.

The problems of leasing are present but more subtle operational problems can occur with this method of payment, especially in relation to IT. Information technology systems are difficult to implement, though when established can provide significant benefits to the force. The process of regular upgrades, sometimes twice or three times a year, can actually be counter-productive as it disturbs the established and settled system. The process of upgrading may require systems to be shut down for a period, which obviously hampers operations and the new hardware and software might need a certain length of time to bed in. Small but irritating problems may be encountered with the upgrades which in themselves are not significant but added together become counter productive.

Forces should therefore think carefully about whether they can accommodate the disruption which is almost bound to follow the upgrading process, if they adopt this method of payment.

As with all of the methods outlined above, care must be taken to ensure that the appropriate method of payment is selected; that which provides the required goods, under the relevant conditions within the funding limits under which the force operates.

Sponsorship

As noted above, the 1994 PMC Act made provision for the police to accept sponsorship and other grants which could be used to support the delivery of police services. Previous experience of sponsorship in the police has been almost totally in the crime prevention arena.

Crime prevention officers in recent years have become adept at seeking out funds from a variety of sources. Many force-wide and even divisionally based crime prevention initiatives are now sponsored by a range of organisations. In an increasingly multi agency environment the number of initiatives so funded is set to increase.

Examples of such sponsorship include the part funding of vehicle watch programmes by insurance companies and the financial support of vehicle crime campaigns by the major motor manufacturers. In March 1997, Gwent and South Wales forces accepted seven vehicles from Vauxhall in a three year sponsorship deal to help them promote crime prevention. A multi-national burger chain has also offered considerable support to anti- truancy and juvenile crime reduction programmes.

Organisations may wish to sponsor police for several reasons but clearly any such support is likely to be a significant boost to the public relations efforts of sponsoring organisations. It should also be remembered that private sector organisations are there to make a profit and any decisions to sponsor the police are likely to be of a commercial nature; the pay off being increased sales and ultimately profits.

Who Will Sponsor?

The police can approach a range of organisations for sponsorship but the first port of call is often the private sector. There seems to be a perception that the private sector in its various forms (for example manufacturing, retail, service) is awash with spare cash. Forces just need to think of a number and ask for it and the various organisations will hand over the money gladly. The reality is often far removed from this scenario.

The economy is still emerging from a long and protracted recession which has seen many organisations either go out of business or struggle greatly in order to survive. There just is not a surfeit of cash in many organisations. Even the larger national and multi-national companies have to think very carefully before committing even modest sums to police based activities which appear to have little tangible reward. Initial approaches to private sector organisations for any significant sums are therefore either likely to be met by outright rejection or be subject to detailed scrutiny. Officers approaching such organisations for funding must therefore be prepared for this.

Other organisations which may be prepared to sponsor and support the police include public sector organisations such as local authorities and health authorities. In this time of increasing multi-agency working there is now a willingness between organisations to work together to address commonly perceived problems in an integrated way. The resulting growth in community safety programmes at a district local authority level has presented opportunities for funding and support for the police. It is important at this stage to note that sponsorship does not have to be of a purely financial nature. The donation of resources to support the work of the police is equally effective and welcome.

In a multi-agency environment, agencies have offered if not finance then resources such as staff, to support the work of the police.

A well publicised example is the Staffordshire truancy project which, although originally developed by the police, is sponsored and supported by organisations such as local retailers and the county education authority. Though minimal funds were provided to support this project, it could not have taken place without the resources donated to the project.

Financial support for police work may be available from other sources. The single regeneration budget (SRB) programme launched by central government in 1995 brought together a number of funding programmes such as Safer Cities and City Challenge. The SRB can be used to support police work again in a multi agency environment, for example in funding projects designed to address drugs and prostitution problems.

Funding for similar work may also be available from sources such as the National Lottery fund and the Millennium fund. In addition, there are a wide range of funding sources which could be approached to support the research and development work in forces, though some of these may require the force to work in conjunction with higher educational institutions. Examples of these funding sources include the Rowntree foundation and the Leverhulme trust.

Obtaining Sponsorship

Once potential sponsors have been identified officers need to approach them with a clear plan. This plan should include the following as a minimum.

- A clear outline of the problem which is being addressed, for example car crime in an area.

- A summary of the strategic aims and objectives of the proposed activity to address the problem, for example to eliminate the car crime problem.

- A brief description of the activities being planned, for example new lighting in a car park, increased numbers of patrols and CCTV.

- A clear description of what the funding is required for, for example to part fund the CCTV system.

- An estimate of the amount of funding or support required, for example £5000 towards the cost of new lighting or provision of car park attendants perhaps by a local authority.

- The monitoring procedures which will ensure that the funds or resources are used effectively.

- The benefits of sponsorship to both the force and the potential sponsor.

At all times the WIIFM factor needs to be addressed. Any potential sponsor will look at such applications for funding and ask 'What's In It For Me?'. The benefits to the potential sponsor need to be stressed, especially when dealing with private sector organisations. While some organisations are more public spirited than others, at the end of the day, they cannot continue to throw money at such projects indefinitely. Unless they can see that by supporting police work there will be some long term benefit, then they are unlikely to offer sponsorship.

In the example above, it may be that a supermarket chain can be persuaded to part fund a CCTV system on an adjoining car park. The provision of the CCTV may in turn attract more people to the car park as they feel it to be safer. This may in turn attract more people to the supermarket and hence increase the sales, market share and profit of the store. Faced with this argument, the donation of a modest sum to support CCTV suddenly becomes an attractive commercial proposition. When dealing with the private sector in particular, if the 'What's In It For Me' can be stated in financial terms, it is far more likely to receive serious attention.

In addition, an outline plan which addresses the issues highlighted above, provides evidence that the proposed use of resources has been clearly thought through and is not just a speculative approach with the begging bowl. Indeed if sponsorship is sought from funding bodies or programmes such as SRB, a detailed plan is required before any application for funding will be considered. The detail required by SRB in particular is especially daunting and will clearly dissuade any less than serious applications for funding.

The development of the opportunities provided by sponsorship mean that police officers have to develop yet more financial management skills. In the world of local financial management officers are having to develop skills in managing costs. In the world of sponsorship these skills will need to be supplemented by others which will enable income to be sought and managed.

Chapter Summary

- The Police and Magistrates' Courts Act 1994 centralised the control of the level of police funding in the Home Office.

- The Act encourages the delegation of financial management to a local level through the requirement for costed local policing plans.

- The Audit Commission have laid down guidelines to support forces in their efforts to move towards local financial management.

- Budgets can vary in type (revenue, capital) and be prepared and managed at different levels in the organisation (force wide, divisional).

- Budgets can be developed using a variety of methods including incremental, zero based and cash limited.

- The effective management of budgets rests on the provision of accurate and timely financial information to the budget holder and regular reviews.

- A variety of methods can be used to pay for capital items and the method adopted will have significant implications for the force budget.

- Sponsorship can now be sought by police from a variety of sources and take the form of financial or other resource support, for example staff.

- In seeking sponsorship forces must develop a clear plan for the use of the resources requested.

- When seeking sponsorship, the benefits to the force and the sponsor must be clearly identified.

Chapter 5

Managing People

Current Practice and Procedures

'Man is the measure of all things.'

Protagoras

Management has been called 'the art of getting things done through people'. This definition by Mary Parker Follett, calls attention to the fact that managers achieve organisational goals by arranging for others to perform whatever tasks may be necessary and not necessarily by performing the tasks themselves. A more complex definition might be:

> *'Management is the process of planning, organising, leading and controlling the efforts of the organisation's people and also of using the resources of other organisations to achieve stated goals.'*

The type of organisation we work for, conditions what we do as managers and what we see, or come to see as the *normal* type of management style, that is, the way we relate to others in the organisation and to those external to the organisation with whom we have contact, the effectiveness of the systems and controls which govern the way our employees work and the way the organisation clearly sets out (or not as the case might be) its goals and objectives. It operates with a hierarchical line of control which tends to be accepted by its employees as the 'best' way for that particular organisation to achieve its objectives, though in most cases, this is certainly not an accurate assessment of the situation.

External perception, or perhaps misconception, of the structure of an organisation is of an integrated whole with all its constituent parts (management and employees) working with a precisely defined unanimity of purpose to satisfy its customers, precision in action! This is far from the truth, the human factor intervenes to dispel this myth.

People are not uniform in their abilities, their experience or their approach to any particular task. They cannot be rigidly categorised and put into little boxes, people only achieve their full potential if they are given some degree of latitude in which they can apply their experience, initiative and common sense to the particular task to which they are assigned. Over prescriptive use of job descriptions can be stultifying and demotivating. This is perhaps where the over bureaucratic rigidly disciplined type of organisation fails to achieve the full potential of its employees and where those organisations which have a better understanding of how to exploit the full potential of their employees have achieved real leadership in their field.

It is important, before looking at the current management style operating generally in the majority of police forces throughout the U.K., that the part played by the influence exerted by society and the environment in the development of that style and of the resultant structure during the twentieth century should also be looked at. It is because of those very influences that current practices and procedures have evolved and we have the structures and controls that currently exist.

What degree of change, (or lack of change in some cases), has been brought about by these influences? The type of policing we have today has changed

Fig 5.1: The management process

dramatically from what it was during the initial formation of local police forces throughout the country. This was perhaps the only time in its history that the public at large, truly had community policing. Today this perception of community policing is being hailed as a possible solution which will provide an effective strategy to reduce the incidence of crime in the community. The wheel turns full circle!

What we have today in many local police forces is, in light of current management practice and thinking , an over bureaucratic and rather autocratic organisation which, in the main, continues to perpetuate the management policies of yesterday. One of the main reasons for this may be the fact that many in the organisation consider that management within the police environment is 'different' and that normal management principles do not apply. This is far from the truth, management is a generic term and its application applies to any type of organisation; it applies to managers at **all** levels within the organisation and is concerned with effectiveness and efficiency.

The basic principles apply across the board and the outcomes (effectiveness and efficiency) are a requirement for any organisation which wishes to succeed and achieve their objectives.

If we accept the fact that change has been slow to come in the police service, we can perhaps research the reasons for this and gain a better insight into why things are done in the way in which they are. There always has been, and indeed there is, a need for an organisation such as the police to be a well disciplined body of men and women. Trained to react to the most extreme situations in a structured and logical way, a strict set of rules had to be observed without questioning the reasons for these rules or the correctness of the approach in any particular situation. This has, without doubt led to an autocratic style of management which requires an unquestioning response which still exist in many forces today, that is, management by edict.

The fact is that modern thinking on management has changed and in practice has proved that discipline, improved reaction to situations, more productive solutions to everyday problems can be achieved without the need for the autocratic approach which looks for unquestioning obedience to slavishly following the edicts of senior management.

The current role of the manager is to plan and organise the tasks of his/her subordinates in the most effective way in order to achieve the required result or results. Does it have to be carried out with unquestioning obedience as is often the case or are there better ways of ensuring the end result? This will be discussed in some length later in the chapter when we look at some of the basic management skills.

The 'Lean' Organisation

'Every dogma has its day.'
Abraham Rotstein

Since the publication of the first edition of this book, some of the emphasis on individual aspects of management has changed. Management in the generic sense is alive, is fluid, reacts to the current needs of society and as such is undergoing constant change. Some of these changes make for better management, others are retrogressive.

Unfortunately management principles are not written in tablets of stone and cannot be, due to its need for flexibility. Only by trial and error can the right management style be found to suit current requirements. There are however, certain basic concepts that do not change and these form the basis on which all good management actions are based. Nevertheless it is in the way these are mixed and the relative emphasis that is given to them which determine the success or failure of that particular management style.

It is a fact, that in the way the world economic situation is developing, there is a prime need to be more effective than our neighbours. This means fine tuning our organisation to be ever more capable, to be consistently good at what we do and to strive constantly to be the best in our own field of operations.

One answer to the new needs of any organisation is the concept of the 'lean machine'. The term 'lean production' was first stated in the 1990s with the publication of *The Machine That Changed the World* by J. Womack, D. Jones and D. Roos. This model was based on largely on the car industry but has been expanded beyond this narrow field to embrace all types of organisations. The first or transitional phase is to help the organisation become leaner by restructuring, delayering and downsizing. The trick is knowing where to stop. When has the organisation reached its optimum size for continued effective operation? The watchwords must be *proceed with caution* otherwise employees will become demoralised and any potential gains will be lost.

Few would dispute the fact that the most valuable and important asset that any organisation can have is its people, and the effective management of people is one of the most important basic tenets of any well run organisation. Unfortunately people are also the most expensive and variable items in an organisation's budget and with the ever increasing fiscal restraints being imposed due to world competition, they are usually the first to be looked at by senior management when setting out to impose savings. Provided that this is not carried to extremes, there is nothing wrong with this policy, but as with many new policies, the pendulum can swing too far and the move will have disastrous results.

It is once again unfortunate that this policy can be imposed without any real idea as to how the remaining personnel can continue to perform their increased duties in a manner which is at least as good as before or more often the demand is for better performance. As with many 'flavour of the day' concepts, it was adopted by organisations who were looking for the panacea, had no real concept of how it should work, and as a result was wrongly applied sometimes with appalling consequences.

Re-allocation of work and areas of responsibility are almost always a consequence of this type of change. It is therefore of vital importance that proper assessing and developing of people is carried out as this is the key to maximising the potential of any organisation. This is best achieved by using the appropriate structure and systems which can and do enable this to happen. An example of this can be seen in the increasing move towards the civilianisation of many posts where it has been seen that these could be more effectively carried out by staff with different skills to those required by the police themselves.

It is abundantly clear to those who have been in management for any length of time that the most difficult part of the move towards a leaner organisation is the management of people. They are a constant variable, have to be trained, motivated, led, directed and encouraged, each at different time frequencies and with differing intensity and priority. The lean machine type of organisation cannot operate successfully unless these aspects are carefully addressed. Managers can no longer be sure of being able to operate in a restricted field, but are required to be multi-skilled, be more flexible and be able to confidently manage the wide diversity of needs that the modern organisation has.

The awareness of this need for a flexible and highly skilled approach within the police service is exemplified in the increasing stature given to the position of personnel officers whose responsibility it is for the development and training of all those within the organisation. The West Yorkshire Force has recently appointed a civilian human resource manager who reports directly to the Chief Constable, effectively giving the position the equivalent of the rank of Assistant Chief Constable. The Metropolitan Force have also raised the profile of HR policy in an initiative involving consultation with community leaders.

The Transparent Organisation

We live in a world that is more demanding not only of the goods and services it requires but also of the way these are provided and how they react with the environment. 'Green' issues, human rights and sex discrimination are very much to the fore in the public domain. There is an increasing demand for greater transparency in the operation of organisations. The police service is perhaps particularly vulnerable on this aspect as to much of the populace, its management, structure and day to day operation is pretty much of a closed book. It is only recently that a number of incidents has raised public awareness and called into question just how our guardians of law and order do operate. It is very much a case of not only that justice must be done, but that justice must be **seen** to be done. This has been highlighted recently in a number of forces throughout the country where there has been a demand for re-examination of police actions. The Hillsborough disaster inquiry is a particular case in point; others involve the questionable conviction of IRA suspects and their subsequent release. Questions have been asked and the need for more transparency made obvious.

The pressures being exerted on organisations throughout the country to become fitter, leaner and more effective are exemplified in the introduction of new procedures for the evaluation and assessment of police officers. Under new rules which come into force in 1998, they will then be treated in the same way as under performing employees in other sectors. The new police procedures will be linked to appraisals with line managers and will include a series of warnings leading to a formal hearing, after which an officer could be required to resign. The introduction of these new procedures will also bring about changes in the way officers who have been involved in corrupt practices will be dealt with. This is part of a growing trend for efficiency and must not be taken out of context. Peter Moorhouse, chairman of the PCA has said that there is no reason to believe that there are a large number of officers who are performing below standard, that they are no different from any other organisation. The question only involves a small minority of officers who must improve or be given some sort of administrative discharge.

Organisations operating in every field are becoming aware of the need for transparency in the way their organisations are conducted. The lead has been taken by many of the largest commercial and public service organisations in the country (e.g. Bedfordshire County Council, Royal Mail and Scottish Hydro-Electric) and parliament is now very aware of this need and is taking action to ensure that this will apply to our system of government. The following is a quote from Rolls Royce Aero Engines Ltd., which illustrates their appreciation of this fact.

> *'It is becoming apparent that customers, in addition to demanding quality products and services from their suppliers, are taking an increasing interest in the way that suppliers manage their business. In the field of equal opportunities, customers are starting to want assurances that the appropriate policies are in place and operate effectively. This gives them confidence that suppliers are managed professionally in all aspects of business and not just those directly associated with the production of a quality product or service.'*

This interest that is being shown in how organisations manage and react to their environment is as a result of a population that is becoming better informed and is eager to show that it has a stake in what is happening and what is done and wants to be confident that the structure of civilisation is improving. They want to be assured that fair and equable policies are being pursued by every organisation, that race and sex discriminatory practices are no longer tolerated and that the quality of service being provided is up to the current standards required by them. The police service is particularly exposed in this respect, they are constantly under the spotlight from the media and as such have to be seen to be scrupulously fair at all times, no matter what the provocation may be. This can make the manager's job in the police environment particularly difficult and the need for adequate training all the more necessary.

Pyramid Management

The organisation of forces is in the traditional hierarchical style, with a pyramid of management starting with the chief constable, (chief executive in commercial organisations) followed by the assistant chief constables (the board of directors in industry). The rest of the structure again follows traditional lines with the senior management (superintendent), middle management (chief inspector, inspector ranks), and first line management (sergeants). This traditional structure has largely been abandoned by industry in favour of a flatter, more compact format which has been found to be more effective and less expensive. So far this style of management has made little impact on police management. The Sheehy report made some attempt to modernise the police management structure and adopt a style which would have fewer layers of management. This met with such severe opposition that it was dropped at an early stage in the progress of the Bill to implement the recommendations of the report. It was resisted on the basis that what applied in industry and commerce could not be compared with the requirements of management in police forces.

Decision making in a police management context, takes place almost uniquely at the top. In many cases, little in the way of consultation takes place further down the management scale. Information is usually gathered from a sufficiency of relevant sources, regardless of level, but it is often only a data gathering exercise and little or nothing is sought as to opinions at the lower levels in the management scale. The analysis and decision making tends to be for higher levels of management only.

Effective and efficient use of resources, both human and financial, is nowadays an essential prerequisite for managers in industrial and commercial organisations. This is an aspect of management in the police environment which has not as yet preoccupied managers to anything like the same extent that it has in industry. Different pressures exist in the different areas. There is a demand for profitability in the industrial sector which does not exist in the police service. As against that, there is great pressure on the police to provide successful outcomes in the combating of crime, and in many cases, this far outweighs the careful husbanding of financial resources.

It is only very recently that managers within forces have had to look more carefully at how they could deploy their resources to best effect. The Police and Magistrates' Courts Act, which became law in late 1994, makes it incumbent on chief police officers to submit what is in essence a business plan laying out the strategy, the objectives and the projected costs for the coming year to the revised composition of the Police Authority. Each Basic Command Unit (BCU) has to submit their own individual forecast of cost, resource requirement and operational activities to force headquarters. This is then embodied into the force business plan for approval by the Police Authority and funding by central government. This aspect and its implications is discussed in more detail in chapter 3.

Performance appraisal has now been adopted as part of management in the police. It is a matter of opinion as to how effective this is in an organisation which is usually considered to be autocratic. Certainly it has been effective in industry but there it operates in a more open style of management where the interchange of ideas and opinions takes place on a two-way basis, each party to some extent appraising the other. The criteria on which the appraisal is based have to be on a mutually agreed basis, otherwise targets and other performance criteria are being imposed on the subordinate which he/she may not be able to meet and indeed they may be almost impossible to achieve.

Many of the accepted techniques of modern management styles have been adopted in part and grafted on to the existing police management style. Some have been successful but more have failed to live up to the expectations which were based on the results in industry. It is questionable as to how many of these new management techniques can live happily in partnership beside the old style management concepts and how effective they are in this type of environment.

McGregor's Theory X and Theory Y

Douglas McGregor's (1960) theory X and theory Y are assumptions about human behaviour in the workplace by managers. He sees two radically different sets of assumptions made by managers about their employees. The first sees employees as being inherently lazy, requiring coercion and control, avoiding responsibility and only seeking security. This is theory X.

The second set of assumptions (theory Y) sees the employee in a much more favourable light. In this case employees are seen as liking work, which is as natural as rest or play; they do not have to be controlled and coerced if they are committed to the objectives and goals of the organisation. Under proper conditions they will not only accept but also seek out opportunities for responsibility; the majority of people are able to exercise imagination and ingenuity at work.

Theory X and Y have made a major impact on management thinking in organisations and have led to the development of many of the current styles of management in favour today.

These are obviously very black and white classifications of management styles; many organisations operate with a mixture of the two, though how far this contributes to effective and efficient management is a moot point. It would be interesting to develop on the success or failure of the current mix operating in a *force which you know.*

Motivation

> 'We know nothing about motivation.
> All we can do is write books about it.'
> > Peter Drucker

The definition of motivation is variable dependent on the position and status of the definer. The Oxford English dictionary defines it as 'concerned with or having the quality of initiating action'. From the point of view of the manager, it is a management process. It is something managers do to induce others to act in a way which will produce the results which both they and the organisation desire.

The individual has a different concept. He/she sees motivation as purely self encouragement towards their own particular goals. Landy and Becker (1987) described it as a psychological concept which relates to the initiation, direction, persistence, intensity and termination of behaviour. Both aspects of motivation are relevant in the management process as both contribute to the development of the individual within the organisation and the contribution that they can make in the furtherance of the corporate goals.

Maslow's Hierarchy of Needs

What can managers do to motivate their subordinates? Abraham Maslow (1943) propounded a hierarchy of needs theory, which was composed of five basic need categories (fig. 5.2). These are physiological, safety, belonging, esteem and self actualisation.

Physiological needs are the basic requirements for survival. Humans must have food in order to live, and shelter too survive. Physical well-being must be satisfied before anything else can assume importance.

Safety needs reflect a desire for protection against loss of shelter, food and any other basic requirements for survival. Security needs also involve the desire to live and operate in a stable and predictable environment.

Belonging needs reflect the person's desire for love, affection and belonging. The need to interact with others and have some social acceptance and approval is generally required by most people.

Esteem needs are those human desires to be respected by others and to have a positive self image. People strive to enhance their status in the eyes of others, to obtain a good reputation or superior ranking in a group. When these needs are thwarted, feelings of inferiority and/or weakness can occur.

Fig 5.2: Maslow's hierarchy of needs

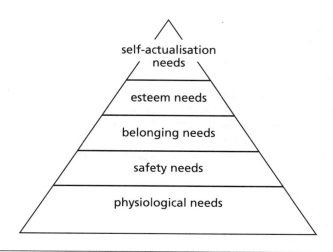

Self-actualisation needs are the individual's desire to do what he/she has the potential to do. This is the highest order need.

Maslow claims that the higher order needs (belonging, esteem, and self-actualisation) are not considered important until the lower order needs have been satisfied or at least partially satisfied. Maslow states that a person is not motivated by a need that is satisfied. Once a need is satisfied, the person is concerned with the next need in the hierarchy.

Herzberg's Hygiene and Motivating Factors

The application of the needs theory poses problems for managers as to how they can translate the 'needs' into management strategy. Research by Herzberg, Mausner and Snyderman (1959) provides some guidance for managers in solving motivational problems. There had been a long held assumption that if a person was dissatisfied with one aspect of the job, (for example, pay) all that had to be done was to increase the remuneration. This would lead to greater satisfaction, better motivation and better performance. It is generally recognised that the police service is nowadays one of the better paid organisations in the U.K., however, it is questionable if this has done anything to improve motivation. Indeed one only needs to read some of the articles in magazines aimed at the police service to appreciate the despair and lack of motivation that appears in the light of the current crime situation. Herzberg and his fellow workers concluded that there were two factors which influenced people in the workplace, each working in a different way. He called these hygiene factors and motivating factors.

Hygiene factors do nothing to increase satisfaction, but satisfaction decreases if they are not present. These are associated with the context of a job. They include working environment, status and organisation policy. The most important hygiene factors, or dissatisfiers, were as follows:

- Company or organisation policy and administration
- Supervision – the technical aspects
- Salary
- Interpersonal relations – supervision
- Working conditions

Herzberg noted that these factors were more related to the *context* or environment of work than to the job content.

Motivating factors are related to high job satisfaction and willingness to work more effectively. When present these factors may induce more effort but if absent will not normally produce dissatisfaction. Motivating factors are associated with the content of the job and include such factors as responsibility, achievement and advancement or promotion. The most important motivators to emerge were the following:

- Achievement
- Recognition
- Work itself
- Responsibility
- Advancement

Herzberg pointed out that these factors were intimately related to the *content* of work.

Horses for Courses

An individual's striving for a particular goal results from:

- The strength of the particular motive or need
- The expectations of success
- The incentive value attached to the goal

There are other factors which enter into the equation, principle among which is the variability of human nature. This requires the manager to be aware of the different approaches to motivation dependent on the particular employee. Employees with a high need for achievement tend to be motivated by challenging and competitive work situations. Those with low achievement needs would tend to perform poorly in similar situations. This highlights the need for the manager to be able to match the individual to the job. Employees who have high achievement needs will perform better in situations which are challenging, complex, satisfying and stimulating.

Employees with low achievement needs prefer situations of stability, security and predictability. This type of employee tends to respond better to a considerate, understanding approach rather than a high pressure stress inducing management style. David C. McLelland (1961) in his research on motivation suggests that managers can to some extent raise the achievement-need level of employees by creating the proper work environment – permitting subordinates a measure of independence, increasing responsibility and autonomy, gradually making tasks more challenging, and praising and rewarding high performance.

There is great variation in the way in which managers in different organisations practice the art of motivating employees. Many may prefer the tried and tested theories of motivation such as Herzberg's because they are perhaps easier to apply. Although the basic concepts of these theories still hold good, there is a constant progression of ideas on the subject and current thinking requires a more knowledgeable manager who has the ability to understand subordinates, carefully plans what he/she will do, and is consistent and patient in the carrying out of these plans.

Richard M. Steers and Lyman W. Porter (1983) suggest some implications of current theories of work motivation for managers:

- Managers must actively and intentionally motivate their subordinates
- Managers should understand their own strengths and weaknesses before attempting to modify that of others
- Managers must recognise that employees have different motives and abilities
- Rewards should be related to performance, not to seniority or other non-merit based considerations
- Jobs should be designed to offer challenge and variety. Subordinates must clearly understand what is expected of them
- Management should foster an organisational culture oriented to performance

- Managers should stay close to employees and remedy problems as they arise
- The active cooperation of employees should be sought in improving the organisation's output; employees are, after all, also stakeholders in the organisation

The good manager who can understand and motivate his staff will have mastered one of the key areas for successful management.

Leadership

'Leadership is action – not position.'
Donald H. McGannon

Leader rather than manager? The answer is neither. Leadership is an integral part of a manager's skills and is used to maximise the potential of people in the organisation. It is frequently confused with motivation. Motivation is the internal desire to act in order to meet actual or perceived needs. Leadership, while often dependent on someone who is motivated to lead, is focused on the individual who provides a motivating climate for the teams or groups within an organisation by task design and attention to outcomes. Leadership is essentially externally focused, whereas motivation is primarily internally directed. It can only really operate in a team environment where the effective leader gets things done by a concerted effort involving some or all members of the team. Leadership plays a key role in human resource management and depends largely on the ability of the leader to communicate his/her enthusiasm, vision and sense of purpose to the team. Effective leadership depends on three variables: the leader, the led, and the situation.

The leader's aim should be to accomplish successfully the allocated task with the help of the team and this has three main objectives:

- To gain the commitment and active cooperation of the team
- To set agreed objectives which are realistic and achievable
- To make the best uses of the available skills and energies of the team

What makes a successful leader? The old cliché states that leaders are born, not made. This, in line with most of these ancient sayings, is not true. What is true is that it comes more naturally to some managers than to others, but it is a management skill that can be acquired by almost anyone.

Henry Mintzberg (1973) carried out extensive research in which he studied managers who had formal authority and defined 10 managerial roles that leaders must play:

- Figurehead
- Leader
- Liaison
- Monitor
- Disseminator
- Spokesperson

- Entrepreneur
- Disturbance handler
- Resource allocator
- Negotiator

Mintzberg highlighted the leader role, saying:

'The influence of the manager is most clearly seen in the leader role. Formal authority vests the manager with great potential power; leadership determines in large part how much of it he/she will in fact use.'

Why do subordinates accept directions from a manager? Is it, as in the case of the police that the direction is accepted as an order, or are there perhaps better reasons why this happens? What are the real sources of a leader's power and influence? There are five recognised bases of a manager's power (J. Stoner and C. Wankel, 1986):

- Reward power: *where the manager has the ability to reward the person for carrying out orders or other requirements*
- Coercive power: *where the manager has the power to punish the employee (rightly or wrongly) for not meeting his/her requirements*
- Legitimate power: *or authority where the manager is lawfully entitled to exert influence (e.g. establishing reasonable work schedules)*
- Expert power: *where the perception is that that the manager has relevant expertise or special knowledge and can apply this in specific areas*
- Referent power: *where the example of the manager motivates subordinates to emulate his/her work habits*

The effective leader starts with varying amounts of basic talent and builds on this throughout his/her working career. They carefully observe on how things are done to achieve the best results, or not done resulting in failure. They build up their expertise by learning and analysing both successes and failures and using that experience to achieve a surer way forward to realising future success.

What is a Leader?

What is a leader? Many attempts have been made to provide a competent definition and most have failed. There are so many aspects to which combination of skills and abilities are required by the successful leader, such as personality traits, the factors influencing success and the qualities required. John Adair, considered to be the British expert on leadership ranked the following attributes considered by senior management as the most valuable in enabling them to perform their tasks:

- Decisiveness
- Leadership
- Integrity
- Enthusiasm
- Imagination

- Willingness to work hard
- Analytical ability
- Understanding of others
- Ability to spot opportunities
- Ability to meet unpleasant situations
- Ability to adapt quickly to change
- Willingness to take risks

Managers can condition themselves to recognise the importance of these factors, learn them, practise them and improve their ability to use them in their everyday work. The aptitude for leadership can be developed, and although a number of the abilities may be inherent, others can be developed and strengthened in order to achieve an effective overall leadership style.

Types of Leader

There are a number of different types of leader and these can be broadly classified as:

- Autocratic: *The leader who imposes his/her will on subordinates and requires those subordinates to be at all times compliant to those wishes and to do as they are told*
- Democratic: *Those who achieve their objectives by encouraging the active participation of both peers and subordinates in the decision making process. This type of leader will rely more on persuasion and well founded reasoning rather than the use of his/her superior position of power*
- The visionary/enabler: *This type of leader has been identified by Dr. John Nicholls as the true leader, inspiring people with his vision of the future, their participation in it and commitment to it*
- The Manipulator: *Those who are concerned with operating/manipulating the internal system(s) with little regard for the individual, their feelings or their abilities*
- Charismatic: *The leader who has the natural characteristics of personality projection and motivational qualities, and will have developed these to his/her best advantage*
- Non-charismatic/pragmatic: *This type of leader has developed a quiet confidence based on experience and knowledge. Has a cool analytical approach to dealing with problems*

None of these types portrayed is wholly illustrative of any particular type of leader, most leaders will have a mix of these qualities in varying degrees and will alter their style to meet particular situations. Nevertheless, there is a predominance of approach which is conditioned by the dominant characteristics of the leader.

Leadership Approaches

How then does the effective leader decide on the best type of approach to any given situation?

Figure 5.3: Fiedler's model

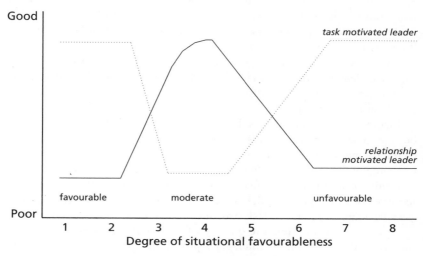

Leader/member relations	good	good	good	good	poor	poor	poor	poor
Task structure	high	high	low	low	high	high	low	low
Leader position power	strong	weak	strong	weak	strong	weak	strong	weak

One of the best known theories on leadership was developed by Fred E. Fiedler (1967). While a number of criticisms have been leveled at his theory from researchers who have questioned the measures used in assessing the dimensions involved in his model, his conceptual development of the factors involved in leadership is straightforward and basically sound.

Fiedler's model shows the effect of leadership styles on leader performance according to situational conditions.

Fiedler's model (fig. 5.3) shows the effect of leadership styles on leader performance according to situational conditions. The vertical axis on the model shows the range of organisational performance achieved by the leader. The dotted V and the inverted V trace the effects of the task motivated leader and the relationship motivated leader on the performance level, depending on the degree of situational favourableness (high to low). Situational favourableness is directly related to leader-member relations, task structure, and the leader position power, which can be clarified by asking the following questions:

- Leader-member relations: *How well does the leader get along with his/her subordinates?*
- Task structure: *How well defined are the steps to perform the task?*
- Leader position power: *How much power does the organisation give to the leader in his/her position, e.g. the ability to reward or punish?*

The model predicts that the best leadership style to obtain good performance within an environment having high situational favourableness is the task-motivated leadership style (good leader-member relations, high task structure and strong leadership position power). As the degree of situational favourableness decreases to the moderate level, the relationship-oriented leader is most likely to obtain good results from his subordinates. Note that either the task-motivated or relationship-motivated leader may get along well (or not so well) with subordinates. The former type of leader focuses on getting the job done, while the latter focuses on getting people or groups motivated.

Fiedler's basic contention is that given technical qualifications, most people will be able to be successful leaders. He summarises his position by saying '...the secret of improving leadership effectiveness lies in matching the leader and the situation or changing the leadership situation so that it fits the leader's personality.'

Further research done by Feidler and Chemers identified three elements (fig. 5.4) in the work situation which help determine which leadership style will be effective – leader-member relations, task structure and the leader's power position.

According to Fiedler, the quality of *leader-member relations* is the most important influence on the manager's power and effectiveness. If a sergeant for example, gets on well with the rest of the group, if group members respect him for reasons of personality, character, and/or ability, then he may not have to rely on formal rank or authority. On the other hand, a manager who is disliked or distrusted (the autocratic sergeant) may be less able to lead informally and may have to rely on firm directives and orders to achieve the required results. This is exemplified within the normal working environment where a sergeant in charge of a squad can, without resorting to 'pulling rank' and ordering some action to be taken, achieve better results and a greater degree of co-operation from the group (by the power of his/her personality acquired through experience and the ability to understand human nature) by merely asking that something be done.

Task structure is the second most important variable in the work situation. A highly structured task is one where the step by step procedures or instructions for the task are available; group members therefore have a very clear idea of what is required. Managers in these situations automatically have a great deal of authority. There are clear guidelines by which to measure the performance of the person, and the manager can back up his/her instructions by referring to the rule book or

Fig 5.4: Feidler and Chemers effective leadership styles

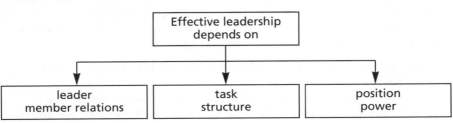

manual. Illustrative of this is the good management of a crime prevention initiative where the planning has been well done, the problem defined, the objectives clearly outlined, the strategy and actions determined, effective performance indicators outlined, and everyone made aware of the reasons for the initiative. Members of the group who will carry out the initiative have well defined tasks and the group leader can easily determine the effectiveness of each individual. The Centre for Public Services Management and Research at Staffordshire University (Berry and Izat, 1995) have constructed for the Home Office a framework which would be the source for reference.

When tasks are unstructured, e.g. committee meetings, group member roles are more ambiguous because there are no clear guidelines on how to proceed. The manager's power is diminished, as group members can more easily disagree with, or question, the manager's decisions or instructions.

The leader's *position power* is the final variable identified by Fiedler. Some positions such as chief constable carry a great deal of power and authority. The chair of a voluntary organisation on the other hand has little power over the people in the organisation. High position power makes a leader's task much easier and enables him/her to influence subordinates, low position power on the other hand makes the leader's task more difficult and he/she will have to resort to other means of influencing the people involved.

In the police environment there is certainly a high degree of position or rank power which should theoretically make the job of the manager much easier. However, if the manager is not sufficiently team oriented (the leader/member relations are poor), the most important influence on his/her leadership is lacking and the manager will have to resort to issuing orders which are prescriptive, are likely to be resented by his/her subordinates, will result in a poorer input from them and a less than desired outcome to the task. This power structure is traditional in the police service and its abuse will probably be self evident to many of the readers of this book.

Is it therefore wrong to have such a strong rank power position? Successful management requires position power as one of the three factors which Fiedler identified as being crucial to effective completion of the task or project. If it is applied properly and used to guide the team members in their approach to the particular task, allowing the members to feel that they have a high degree of participation will result in better input from the team, a high degree of motivation and a more effective use of the resources to achieve the desired outcome.

The Current State of Play

There is little doubt that at least some forces within the U.K. are moving towards this management style where the priorities are as outlined by Fiedler, i.e. firstly, leader/member relations, secondly, task structure and thirdly, position power. This is replacing the more traditional approach where the priorities were position power, task structure and leader/member relations in that order. Was this structure successful? Many arguments can be made on the subject, both for and against, but it is a fact that both the environment and management styles are in a constant state of evolution. Management must change to meet the new needs which are constantly being thrown up by the changes in the environment; what was effective then will not necessarily be effective in the current situation. How will the police service of tomorrow evolve, how can it become more effective, what style of management will evolve?

The change in the understanding of how human resource management works has brought about changes in the way we utilise the human resource part of the equation in the effective achievement of the task outcomes. Current thinking places good leader/member relations as a prime requirement for the successful and effective completion of the team task.

Vroom and Yetton (1973) identified three major concerns that a leader has to face when making decisions on problem solving and task orientation. These are:

- The quality of the decision
- The degree of acceptance of the decision by subordinates
- The time frame within which the decision must be made and the action initiated. They made four assumptions relative to this. These are:
  - autocratic decisions are faster
  - subordinate participation creates acceptance
  - group decisions are most effective when applied to unstructured shared issues
  - involvement develops subordinates' abilities

This latter assumption will be developed further in the next section.

The old style management approach which placed position or rank power as the absolute priority could and did often achieve task completion, but at what cost? Until fairly recently there was low accountability within the police service on the aspects of use of human resources and of their costs. Autocratic decisions were made by middle or higher management to devote a given number of resources to a problem and to stay there until there was an acceptable result; the decision was not questioned, the costs were not considered, the only important factor was achievement of the objective. Value for money was not a consideration.

The higher degree of accountability which is now being required of the police service means that ineffective use of resources and an extended time scale is no longer acceptable. Managers have to look for better and more effective ways to achieve improved performance and results. A rapidly changing environment imposes the requirement for a more informed management style which can optimise the resources available, particularly the most expensive and the most variable – the human resource.

Basic People Management Skills

'Nothing is more terrible than activity without insight.'

Thomas Carlyle

In the authors' opinion, managers, in the main, practice one of two types of management – passive (reactive) and active (proactive). By far the most popular is the passive style of management. This involves the manager in feeling more needed as he/she is constantly reacting to situations, directing and participating in stemming the 'fire' and when the situation has been resolved, (no matter how temporarily) feels that they have justified their existence and provided value for money to their organisation.

This type of manager is largely motivated by interest in satisfying their own ego and is often indicative of a person who is not really in charge of the situation and feels vulnerable. This feeling of vulnerability convinces the manager that the only way he/she can justify their position is by making themselves (in their opinion) indispensable. They will relate to their superiors the 'successes' in tackling and overcoming the perceived problems of the day and will try to convince them of the effectiveness of the actions which they have directed. Within the police service there are many officers to whom one can relate as practising this type of management. Passive style managers can convince themselves that they are following all the normal principles of good management, involving employees, discussing the effectiveness of the particular actions taken and creating team spirit. Sadly they have missed one of the most important aspects of good management in that they have little idea of the actions they and their team should be taking in the field of prevention. They are almost totally reactive and have little or no experience of the value of proactivity in the prevention of problems in the workplace.

The truly proactive manager on the other hand practices all of the above concepts but is constantly seeking to anticipate what is going to happen, predicting future problems and generating actions which will either minimise or eliminate those problems. He/she utilises all the expertise available in the 'team' to define the problem(s) and to generate appropriate action(s) to achieve the objective of reduction or elimination.

If this does not happen, the manager will never be truly effective and the team under his/her control will spend a large part of their time in tackling and trying to find solutions to the numerous small 'fires' which are generated daily in most organisations – the firefighting solution. The proactive manager on the other hand will, with his/her team have considerably reduced the incidence of this type of problem and will be able to devote more of their efforts to achieving the aims and objectives of the organisation and less to the myriad of small recurring problems which plague many such organisations.

A common belief in the police environment is that they are of necessity reactive and there is very little scope to be proactive. How can we predict when and where crimes will take place is a commonly voiced statement made to back up the reactive approach. If policing were purely reactive, there would be little point in branches of the organisation, such as the CID, gathering intelligence, if not to actually prevent a particular crime, to have the resources on the spot to apprehend the perpetrators, and hopefully to prevent future crimes by these particular criminals. Crime prevention is steadily gaining a higher profile and increasing importance in the fight against crime. It is the manager who can plan an initiative which is both resource and cost effective and achieves its objectives who is demonstrating their skills and competency as a manager.

Team Management

The competent management, motivation and involvement of teams is another basic skill without which the good manager cannot function. The interest which we have in teams relates to those circumstances in which groups are more effective than individuals acting alone. Groups can:

- Accomplish complex problems and interdependent tasks that would be beyond the ability of an individual working alone
- Solve complex problems that require inputs from a number of different sources and expertise
- Provide a means of coordinating activities
- Facilitate implementation through generating participation and commitment
- Generate new ideas and creative solutions within the model
- Provide an opportunity for social intercourse which improves morale and motivation

Group dynamics play a large part in the effect that a manager has in achieving success in his/her job and much research has been done in this field to determine optimum group size, composition and effectiveness in differing types and sizes of organisations, under differing circumstances and with differing aims. In most situations there is clear indication that teams or groups with greater than ten members are less effective than smaller groups and that where a larger human resource input is required it is better to increase the number of teams rather than increase the group size providing that there are clearly defined tasks for each group and that all tasks are integrated and geared towards achievement of the overall

---

Fig 5.5: Some key factors in group behaviour

objective. Some of the more important factors in the behaviour of groups is shown in fig. 5.5.

Communication, (another of the basic management skills) is a critical factor in the effectiveness of the group performance, in the inter-relationship within the group, and is easier and is more effective in compact groups. Larger groups can become more process oriented and less task oriented due perhaps to the more complex processes required to effectively control, integrate and coordinate the activities of the group and to ensure a level of internal communication sufficient to achieve the group objective.

The makeup of the group is also important and the good manager will ensure to the best of his/her ability that there is a sufficient range of skills and width of experience to guarantee a reasonable chance of the group succeeding in their allotted tasks.

Belbin *et al* carried out a systematic study of management teams and concluded that that six roles were needed in an effective management team apart from specialist and functional roles. These six were expanded to eight (Belbin 1981) which are:

- Company worker
- Chairman
- Shaper
- Ideas man
- Resource investigator
- Monitor/evaluator
- Team worker
- Completer/finisher

These categories emphasise both the importance of task orientation and the social/emotional area (team maintenance). The Belbin approach to team composition is widely used during residential management training courses where an essential factor for the success of the programme is that the members of the teams formed for the duration of the residential are compatible with each other and can each supply a different area of expertise. It is used during the residential part of the Certificate and Diploma in Management courses which are run for police managers.

Managers must always be aware of the frictions that can be generated within a group, but the mode of team working is distinct from the accommodation of conflict as a management approach to action and decision taking. Nevertheless, within the general mode of team working there can always emerge a degree of interpersonal conflict and this can be both constructive and destructive. In the constructive mode it can stimulate different solutions to problems, encourage creativity and participation in brainstorming, and can bring into the open interpersonal and/or interdepartmental conflicts of long standing. In the destructive mode it can produce polarisation and subsequent dislocation of the entire group, lead participants to use blocking and defensive attitudes, subvert the group objectives and stimulate win/lose conflicts. The manager must always be aware of both the advantages and the dangers inherent in groups and be ready to exert his influence to minimise anything which might reduce its effectiveness, including its structure and composition at the outset.

Customer Awareness

One of the more important of the basic management skills is the awareness of the importance of the customer in everything that is done. In the industrial and commercial fields, it is not difficult to determine who is the customer, or it would so appear at first sight. It is however slightly more complex than merely identifying the *external* customer, this is the less difficult aspect of awareness of customer importance.

It is when we begin to develop the concept of *internal* customers that problems arise. In the industrial and commercial fields, identification of the external customer is fairly straightforward, it is almost always the persons or organisations who buy their goods or services. It is less easy in the police environment where there are a number of different groups who could be considered as external customers.

Whom do we serve? Is it the Home Office, the legal system, the police authority, the local community or perhaps all four? Do we try to satisfy all of them at the same time – many of them with conflicting views on what the police should be doing to be most effective in the fight against crime and in the provision of services to the community at large? These are questions that have to be addressed by managers if they are to construct an effective strategy and set relevant objectives which satisfy the priorities, on which they have decided.

If we accept that the external customer plays a vital role in everything we do within the organisation, then we can see that awareness of this need to identify who is or are the external customer(s), is of prime importance. There has been a recent shift of emphasis within the police environment from an organisation which tended to try and achieve their objectives in splendid isolation, to one which realises that regular and frequent contact with other agencies and statutory bodies within the community is essential. It has been realised that only by finding out what is seen to be important to the 'customer' (the community at large) and by seeking their involvement, can that customer be satisfied.

The significance of the vital role played by the customer is one of the basic skills of management, but it is only in recent years that it has come to be appreciated as the *raison d'etre* for the existence of the organisation. In other words – no customers, no need for the organisation!

The concept of the *internal* customer is arguably equally important and has been highlighted by the increasing move to develop the idea of **total quality** within organisations. The aim of total quality is to introduce minimum standards of quality into every operational and management level of the organisation and into every action or process that is carried out. It seeks to instill the idea of constantly striving to improve on these standards and introduces the idea of 'what we do today is not good enough for tomorrow.'

The concept of the internal customer is inextricably linked with the concepts of total quality. In essence, what it says is that every individual action we undertake contributes to the overall effectiveness or lack of effectiveness of the organisation as a whole and that the next person in the chain for whom we are carrying out that action is **our customer**. The quality of each and every action that we undertake becomes important, in that the quality of what we have done will reflect on the subsequent operations that may have to be carried out and will influence the final outcome. It is also interesting to note that we in our turn will become the *customer* in the chain of actions and events carried out by any organisation and our effectiveness will be conditioned by the work carried out by our *supplier* and passed on to us for our input to the process. It stresses the chain reaction and domino effect of everything we do in our workplace and places the responsibility on each employee to set standards for the outcomes which he/she would want to receive were they the customer.

The quest for quality in order to satisfy (no not just satisfy, but delight) our customer is never ending if we adopt the attitude that tomorrow we will continue to strive to improve on what we did today. Quality of service is becoming a prime concern within most police forces, but if it is to be successful then quality of management must also become a prime concern. Without emphasis on *quality in management*, it becomes impossible to implement good practice in the planning and implementation of the actions which are required to achieve both the day to day and the longer term objectives. The new accountability being imposed on the police service by the Police and Magistrates' Courts Act makes it all the more necessary that we look to the quality and standards that are required of those who are required to manage the organisation.

Chapter Summary

- The need for achieving the potential of employees is discussed.

- Many police forces are said to be over bureaucratic and autocratic in their style of management. The question is asked about the necessity for this and the alternatives which can provide a better and more effective management style.

- The current role of the manager is primarily to plan and organise the tasks of subordinates.

- Police forces have adopted a traditional management style with an extended pyramidal structure. The newer concept of a flatter structure with fewer ranks is considered better.

- The 'lean' organisation is now a fact of life and managers have to adapt to operate within its demands.

- Performance appraisal is now an integral part of management. It can and does help in the move toward better performance by both subordinate and manager.

- Employees need to be motivated to achieve their own personal goals and those of the organisation. The key motivating factors are – achievement; recognition; work; responsibility; advancement.

- Managers think that they can *manage* the achievement of objectives. Leaders focus on achieving commitment and co-operation to achieve agreed objectives. Leaders operate on three bases: leadership/member relations, task structure and position power.

- Managing people effectively needs a proactive approach by the manager.

- There are innumerable instances of where teams provide a better means of operating effectively within an organisation. It is considered essential in the police environment. The manager needs to be aware of the strengths and weaknesses of the individuals within the team.

- The importance of the customer, (both internal and external) and the advantages of recognition of this fact to the organisation, are outlined.

Chapter 6

Managing Professional Conduct

Introduction: The Professional Context

> *'The difference between the amateur and
> the professional is that the professional does
> the right thing in the right way, whether they
> feel like it or not.'*
>
> Anon

In this chapter the management of the professional conduct of police officers is considered from several viewpoints, focusing on the practical implications for supervision, audit and training.

Modern policing is complex. As John Kleinig (a notable American commentator on world-wide issues in police ethics) has claimed, it is the whole context of policing which makes thinking about law enforcement ethics necessary. As he rightly says, this is:

> *'Not because there is a morality peculiar to law
> enforcement, but because the police role and
> the circumstances under which police must make
> their decisions are often novel, complex and
> time-constrained.'*
>
> Kleinig (1995)

The term 'policing ethics' has not generally been popular with working police officers. Many police officers regard themselves as the guardians of public behaviour but often find it difficult to accept that there needs to be an examination of their own conduct beyond their legal responsibilities. It is not only the idea of 'ethics' which causes misgivings. The very term 'professional' itself can also have negative connotations. For example, the so-called 'professional foul' in soccer is one committed by a player with a cynical intention to gain an unfair advantage over the opposing team.

In this chapter, we use the term 'professional conduct' in a positive sense, meaning an acceptance of agreed standards that are shared by all practitioners. This chapter will suggest that whether we call it 'ethics' or not, professional conduct needs to be managed exactly like any other aspect of policing.

In Britain, the development of the so called 'new police' brought about the professionalisation of the police in the early part of the 19th Century. Before that it was the prevailing morality of the communities within which local policing took place that influenced conduct. Although the Royal Commission on Police Powers and Procedures in 1929 argued that the police had never been recognised as a force distinct from the general body of citizens, the professionalisation of the police certainly made a difference to their ethical status.

As we remark elsewhere in this book, public scrutiny and criticism of the British police have continued to develop in recent years. Miscarriages of justice leading to formal enquiries into police practice or to civil litigation have fuelled much of this criticism. Amongst many others, cases such as the Guildford four, the Birmingham six, the investigations into the West Midlands Serious Crime Squad, the Carl

Bridgewater murder and the conviction of John Donald (a Regional Crime Squad officer) for corruption, have all affected the public perception of police.

Historically, one of the strengths of British policing is the closeness between the police and the public. The reality, however, is that the professional police are subject to pressures that the public do not share. This does not explain misconduct of the kind revealed in some of the notorious cases mentioned above. It does, however, lead us to ask additional questions about how and why such things can happen in a well-managed profession dedicated to good order and proper conduct in the public-at-large.

At least part of the answer can be found in the fact that although the police may still regard themselves as ordinary citizens, in reality they have additional power, problems and responsibilities. They have to operate within constraints and to satisfy demands that other citizens do not experience. Alongside this they are often subject to cultural and organisational pressures that can affect attitudes unless good management and training help them to resist the temptations. This chapter sets out some of the arguments and suggests how good management and training can help to promote high standards of professional conduct.

Policing and Human Rights

The relationship between policing and human rights makes a suitable starting point. British police officers, as officials of the Crown, have a responsibility to pay particular attention to human rights. Human rights are important to policing for two main reasons. They are important because they are the key principles that underpin the legal and moral accountability of police in a democratic state. They are also practically important because they act as a check upon the conduct of police within the real-world context in which they operate.

The aftermath of World War II saw new developments in universal human rights in the realisation that widespread violations required international measures to counter them. The adoption in 1948 of the United Nations (UN) Universal Declaration on Human Rights was the most important global development. In adopting the Declaration, the UN General Assembly proclaimed it as 'a common standard of achievement for all peoples and all nations'. The covenants associated with the declaration are legally binding for those states that have ratified them.

The European Convention on Human Rights came into being in 1950 following the UN Declaration. It reaffirms the fundamental freedoms that underpin democratic systems of government operating under the rule of law. The range of articles was subsequently amended by the protocols of 1970, 1971 and 1990. It also provides a series of procedures for adjudication and compensation. Its supra-national nature recognises the limitations of individual governments to protect human rights. Although the Convention is not directly incorporated into European law, it is acknowledged in the preamble to the Single European Act (1987) and the Maastrict Treaty. The European Court of Human Rights takes it into account in assessing the actions of member states. Although the Convention on Human Rights is in the process of being incorporated into English law. It provides a source of principles upon which the courts can draw. It also provides a framework for human rights that is particularly relevant to policing.

Rights can only be realised if the individuals to which they apply are part of a community that is subject to the rule of law. Although in this country we do not yet have a written constitution or a formal Bill of Rights, the existing human rights conventions provide a moral support for law. It is their universal status which puts the obligation upon citizens and governments alike to respect their application. As one eminent commentator has noted (Nino, 1996) at the most fundamental level, human rights;

> '...constitute an indispensable tool for avoiding the kind of catastrophe that often threatens human life... misfortunes occur not only because of the scarcity of resources, but also because many use their fellow humans as just another resource, either for their own benefit or to realise peculiar visions of the absolute good. This practice of using men and women as instruments is even more disastrous if, as often happens, it is carried out by the powerful, by those who have access to weapons or other means of subjecting other people to their will on a large scale.'

The antidote to this kind of disaster is the recognition of human rights, including their recognition by powerful organisations such as the police. At the highest level, the various declarations provide the means through which the arbitrary use of power can be controlled. In democratic states this is underpinned by the doctrine of the rule of law. Although there may be controversies as to how the law is to be interpreted, the rule of law represents a higher-order expectation that the law will be applied fairly to all citizens.

The relationship between the police and the people and between the domestic law and human rights principles is mediated by pillars of specific legislation, the application of which is subject to oversight by parliament and the judiciary. The model in fig 6.1 shows an idealised framework for these relationships. The model also shows the linkages between the need for public order (at the societal level) and the need for safety and security (at the level of individual citizens). There is likely to be tension between these two levels unless the relative role and importance of each is understood by government and its officials in public administration, especially by the police.

Although, at the time of writing, the linkage has not finally been formalised by incorporation into our domestic law, the various human rights conventions provide a bridge between these ethical and legal worlds. They are ethical in that they suggest that being human is alone a sufficient ground for attaining a dignified life free from arbitrary power. They have legal status because they are acknowledged by parliament and the judiciary in the formulation and application of our domestic law. For this reason, if for no other, police have a responsibility to adhere to them in the exercise of their power.

Because its primary purpose is not the protection of the state but the independent and impartial administration of justice, the judicial system itself provides a series of safeguards for individual rights. In Britain, the courts have been bold in the application of judicial review to ensure that the authorities only exercise power within the limitation of the law.

Fig 6.1: Model of relationship between people and police – law and rights

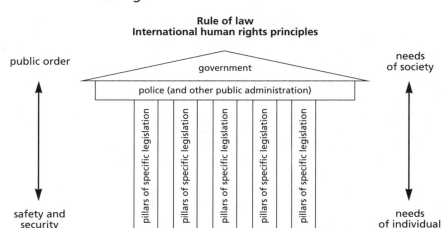

The following human rights measures affect policing both directly and indirectly:

- UN Universal Declaration on Human Rights (1948)
- European Convention on Human Rights (1950)
- Council of Europe Declaration on the Police (1979)
- UN Code of Conduct for Law Enforcement Officers (1979)
- Basic Principles on Use of Force and Firearms by Law Enforcement Officers (1990)

The first four of these are extensively discussed in the Council of Europe publication *Human Rights and the Police* (Alderson, 1984). For European police forces, the European Convention on Human Rights provides a framework of categories against which police actions and policies can be assessed. These include the right to life (Article 2); freedom from torture or other inhuman or degrading treatment or punishment (Article 3); the right to liberty and freedom from arbitrary arrest (Article 5); and the right to a fair trial (Article 6). All police officers and managers should be aware of the main articles of this Convention.

The Council of Europe Declaration on the Police (1979) and the UN Code of Conduct for Law Enforcement Officers (1979) also provide a series of rules, standards and guidelines with which an effective and legitimate police is expected to comply. The UN Code of Conduct is supplemented and extended by the Basic Principles on the use of Force and Firearms by Law Enforcement Officers, adopted by the Eighth UN Conference on the Prevention of Crime and the Treatment of Offenders (held in Havana in 1990). This limits the circumstances under which coercive force should be used. The use of force is discussed in more detail below.

The Police Discipline Code

In addition to the authority of human rights conventions and the requirement to adhere to the rule of law, police conduct is subject to other rules and sanctions. From the beginning of modern policing, written orders have been given a primary role in countering police misconduct. In the early days, although many of the orders dealt with minor incivility or drunkenness on duty, others dealt with more serious matters such as the excessive use of force and corruption. It is often said that the large volumes of force general orders and instructions, which have continued to expand until recent times, are simply catalogues of past mistakes. It is certainly true that the rules and sanctions that exist in legislation, in the police discipline code and in standing orders, have been predominant in the management of professional conduct, although some foraes now emphasise guidance rather than instruction in their official documentation.

The Statutory Instruments which have been issued by the Secretary of State under the Police Act, 1964 and subsequent legislation, have in themselves provided a series of sanctions on police conduct (Police Regulations, 1995: Police (Discipline) Regulations, 1985 and other associated Statutory Instruments) The Police (Discipline) Regulations provide the mechanism for disciplinary proceedings and set out the discipline code itself in a schedule. The list of offences for which an officer may be subject to disciplinary proceedings is extensive. They include:

- Discreditable conduct
- Misconduct towards a member of a police force
- Disobedience to orders
- Neglect of duty
- Falsehood or prevarication
- Improper disclosure of information
- Corrupt or improper practice
- Abuse of authority
- Racially discriminatory behaviour
- Neglect of health
- Improper dress or untidiness
- Damage to police property
- Drunkenness
- Drinking on duty or soliciting drink
- Entering licensed premises without good cause
- Criminal conduct
- Being an accessory to a disciplinary offence

Invoking the discipline code is often the last resort in the day-to-day management of police conduct. Most discipline charges are derived from complaints investigations rather than from action which is initiated by supervisors. In this sense, the discipline code does not provide a flexible tool for management. At best it is a deterrent. At worst it is a blunt instrument leading to punishment. In recent years, because of this limitation, consideration has been given to developing an advisory code of police ethics which might be both symbolic and practically useful to managers in encouraging high professional standards.

Developing a Code of Professional Conduct for Police

In Britain since 1979, successive governments have demanded greater value for money and accountability from all the professions, including the police. The creation of an ACPO Quality of Service committee in 1991 emphasised the rise in the strategic importance of quality control in policing and it is within this committee that the initiative to produce a code of conduct has been pursued. However, progress towards defining a code of police conduct has been halting. A draft was circulated within the Service in 1993 but did not reach the status of an endorsed statement. No public sign has yet been seen of the results of the consultation procedure which followed the publication of this draft.

Local policing is very often concerned with managing local disputes using pragmatic and conciliatory strategies which depend upon gaining the trust and co-operation of the public for their success. This is far removed from the issues which face a regional crime squad unit or the anti-terrorist squad, for example, in deciding how far it is justified to go to save life or to defeat professional criminals. The fact that discretionary authority exists right down to the basic working level in British policing (the constable) makes the construction of a code to cover all eventualities a difficult task.

A detailed ethical code to cover all policing is virtually impossible to complete. However, a code of general principles may be beneficial, in the way that a written constitution or human rights convention is beneficial, as a statement of requirements for police conduct. Arguably, statements of this kind already exist in the Police Discipline Code and the Statement of Common Purpose and Values agreed between ACPO and the Staff Associations. The strategic role of this statement is discussed in Chapter 3.

The danger is that a code which contains principles at a very high level of generality is difficult to relate to the wide variety of policing activity. Such a code requires continual interpretation and may have little real effect upon working practices. As will be suggested below, a more rewarding approach might be to conceptualise ethical problems in policing as conflicts between value systems, one of which is the very system of legal rules and procedures within which policing is meant to operate.

Management as 'Enforcing the Rules'

Apart from the introduction of policing skills into probationer training and new programmes for interviewing training, most attempts to improve police conduct have focused upon the prevention of malpractice by a progressive tightening of the rules. The Royal Commission on Criminal Procedure (1981), for example, which led to the Police and Criminal Evidence Act, 1984, effectively tightened the rules governing the detention of prisoners in order to reduce malpractice. This act was important because it put into place new accountability procedures which were intended to make police practice more transparent to the public through the courts. This has provided a strong influence upon police investigation. Similarly, the Royal Commission on Criminal Justice (1992) was important in setting new ground rules for investigative interviewing.

If it is true that such tightening of law and procedure can be effective in regulating some aspects of police behaviour, why not counter all potential police misconduct by enforcing the rules? Some commentators have argued that that is precisely what must happen because the consequences are so serious both for individual prosecutions and for the criminal justice system as a whole (Zander, 1994). In court cases where the procedural rules are breached, the doctrine of the so-called 'fruit of the poisoned tree' will apply, resulting in all the evidence being excluded. This emphasis upon compliance with the rules rather than the search for truth has been the case in the US courts for some years. Against this background, it is not surprising that efforts to ensure compliance with the rules have become the predominant tool in trying to influence police conduct.

However, some of the recent cases in Britain that have received extensive scrutiny are not simply about failure to comply with the rules. In terms of managing police conduct, what is instructive about these cases is not only the breaking of the rules but the reasons for breaking them. Even in cases which appear to be straightforward malpractice, it is necessary to explore the motivation of individual officers to learn the right lessons. And where officers *do* follow the rules, they may still feel a tension between their desire to see justice done and the requirements to conform to due process, particularly where they empathise with victims. This tension can have serious stress-related side effects leading to a generalised reduction in performance, matters of extreme importance to management.

The problem of the inadequacy of rules as the primary tool for influencing behaviour also has to be seen against the implications of decades of business management research. Formal rules are often seen as a barrier to effectiveness or as a symptom of organisational conflict. To be effective, rules and regulations have to be translated into 'rules-in-use' through which the often contradictory demands of legal formality and organisational work are kept in some kind of rough and ready balance.

Despite these criticisms, it must be conceded that a code of general principles can provide a statement of expectations for police conduct. It should be strongly emphasised, however, that this does not mean that the rules of themselves guarantee that their requirements are always followed. Research indicates that, although they may be *necessary* conditions for regulating police behaviour, prescriptive rules alone are not *sufficient* to do so. More needs to be done by means of active management to provide the sufficient conditions for regulating the police and to ensure that the organisation as a whole promotes high standards of professional conduct.

Dilemmas of Policing: Managing Value Conflicts

Research carried out in England by Wright and Irving (1996) showed that police attitudes were strongly affected by a range of dilemmas and value conflicts which they experienced in their work. The research revealed a range of problems covering the whole range of police work, including patrol, criminal investigation, dealing with death and trauma, conflicts between the formal requirements of the criminal justice system and the need to ensure justice for victims, especially those of child abuse. Conflicts of loyalty to the police organisation ('the job') colleagues, friends and family were also common. Some of the value conflicts were close to true ethical dilemmas where two equally repugnant real-world options confronted police. Others were difficult choices between conflicting values.

Given that much police work involves the sorting of other peoples conflicts and the control of a wide variety of deviant behaviour (such as the application of social norms or values on behalf of society) the occupation faces new recruits with a moral minefield. The operational culture tends to offer the more experienced officer ways of coping with this minefield by simplifying the issues and constraining the scope of what they are expected to consider in making decisions. Pressure on individuals to adopt these coping tactics can be intense. Yet where the exigencies of a situation or the pressure of alternative value systems intrude, the individual is bound to feel conflict.

The value systems involved in policing decisions are often personal to the officers themselves or derive from the operational culture in which they operate. The informal rule system which controls many aspects of police behaviour is, as many commentators have pointed out, often not compatible with the legal structures within which policing is meant to operate. Personal value systems derive from membership of family, religious and other groups in the world outside policing. Values derived from the operating culture of policing emphasise the need to look after one's colleagues, the need to get the job done and to achieve justice in spite of, rather than through, the application of due process.

The research identified examples of actual value conflicts that police officers had encountered in their work. The specific objective of the project was to identify and refine a series of anonymous but realistic case studies based upon officers' operational or managerial experience. Graef had used a similar approach in his work *Talking Blues*, illustrating the pervasive influence of the culture on police officers' attitudes (Graef, 1989). Although it has not yet been adopted, this research could support a professional development programme, enabling newly appointed officers to pre-play a range of options in preparation for meeting them in real circumstances and to manage a situation before it gets beyond their control. Express commitment to high standards of conduct should be encouraged in workgroups. In this way, a new officer's ethical approach to his or her work would rapidly become known.

A Model of Police Value Conflicts

The dilemmas and value conflicts revealed during research showed that 72% of the cases concerned problems over the occupational culture or the job itself. 56% concerned relations with colleagues, 40% were concerned with conflicts between the formal requirements of law and informal pressure to ensure justice. 24% were concerned with conflicts with the public world outside the police and 16% related to issues concerning friends and family. Clearly, some scenarios will include conflicts of more than one category. Figure 6.2 *(on next page)* shows the interaction between the self and the various categories of problem.

Fig 6.2: A simplified model of the interaction between internal and external values

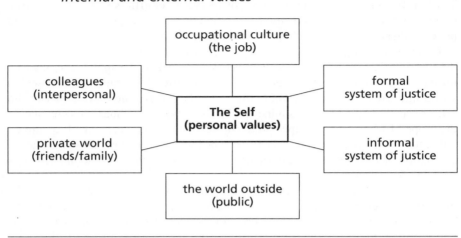

Conflicting Loyalties and the Organisational Culture

Managing the behaviour of individual police officers is an important factor in achieving high standards of professional conduct because compliance with the rules can be so strongly affected by the organisational culture. The pressures upon police to solve highly publicised murder cases, to identify and prosecute terrorists, to arrest the perpetrators of organised crime or to maintain public order can be pervasive influences upon conduct. These organisational pressures are transmitted to individual police officers and may affect their professionalism unless officers have learned through training or experience to be impartial.

Research into organisational behaviour in Britain and the US has shown that the effect of formal sanctions may not overcome these powerful and immediate organisational pressures. The norms of the workgroup may be more powerful than regulations or court decisions in shaping police behaviour. Police interpret the law, operating with strong informal, discretionary concepts of justice which they believe they share with the public at large. In cases where the official rules seem to operate against these informal concepts of justice, police will interpret them to preserve what they perceive as just ends.

The problem of conflicting loyalties signifies very deeply held commitments which, when they come into conflict, are primary causes of police stress The key point is the moral ambiguity which they appear to entail, particularly when an officers thinks that the rule of law or the requirements of procedure cannot be accorded professional predominance over the need for loyalty. Any system which seeks to change police attitudes needs to take these loyalties into account and to provide mechanisms which enable police to avoid them.

In a sense, it is already too late to remedy the problem after the conflict of loyalty has arisen. This is particularly the case in dealing with loyalty to a colleague who may have used excessive force or in conflicts between the formal requirements of the law and a perceived need to ensure a just outcome. These cases are impossible to remedy after the event because the attempt to ensure justice may involve assaults, system-bending or the creative re-construction of events. It is very unlikely that police officers will be willing to discuss these problems because to do so could end a police career or even result in prosecution. Rather than to rely upon the ultimate sanctions of the discipline code or the criminal law, it is better not to rely upon the blaming culture. Managers and supervisors need to be aware to the dangers, to pre-empt the situation and to guide inexperienced officers away from these pitfalls.

Conflicts of Loyalty Relating to Colleagues

Conflicts of loyalty to colleagues are a major issue. The following scenario provides an example of how a conflict of loyalty can arise in everyday policing:

> In this case, two uniformed officers on patrol in a police van were called to deal with a fight in the street. On their arrival at the location they found two young men confronting a youth who was shouting and screaming at them. They quickly separated the protagonists. Both of the young men were the worse for drink. One of the young men, who had been wearing spectacles, had a small cut on his nose. One of the uniformed officers officer dealt with the youth and the other officer dealt with the two young men.

> The two young men were recognised by the uniformed officers as members of the police force who were employed on plain-clothes duty. The uniformed officers felt that this situation confronted them with a conflict of values. They knew that the right procedure would be to deal with the assault and to report the matter. However, the circumstances of the case made this course of action difficult. Apparently, the youth who had remained at the location had been one of a group who had been stopped by the two intoxicated 'on-duty' plain-clothes officers. The youths had resented the situation and one of them had hit the plain clothes officer.

> Because the uniformed officers knew the plain-clothes officers well and because of the loyalty they felt to them as colleagues and to the force as a whole, the uniformed officers decided to take no further action. They sent the youth on his way and persuaded the plain-clothes officers that this was the best course of action. The plain-clothes officers agreed that they had been wrong to intervene because of their intoxication and asked the uniformed officers not to report the matter to their superiors.

The uniformed officers felt that this placed them in a dilemma. They were aware that the control room would require an explanation to cover their deployment. On the other hand they felt that a full explanation would initiate a formal enquiry and compromise the loyalty which they felt to their police force and to their colleagues. For this reason, they decided to give a brief but inaccurate account to the control room. To provide some extra cover for this questionable action, one of the officers later gave an informal (true) account of the incident to his supervising Sergeant. This provided the Sergeant with a consequential dilemma, thus extending the problem.

This incident is a typical example of the conflicts of loyalty which can arise for street-level operational police officers in the exercise of their discretion. In this case, supposed loyalty to colleagues conflicted with loyalty to their organisation and to procedural requirements. Similar problems can arise over conflicts of loyalty to friends and family or to other members of organisations to which police officers may belong in their private capacity.

Conflicts Between Formal and Informal Justice

Many cases raise more serious difficulties especially where officers are put into a difficult position where colleagues have failed to follow the rule of law in dealing with offenders. In some cases an officer is placed in a dilemma between considerations of loyalty and what the law requires. In other cases, officers feel obliged to take action to secure justice for victims or the general public where they believe that it is unlikely that the criminal justice system or rules of procedure would enable them to do so.

The support of commentators for the appeal to moral ambiguity in some cases of this type is limited. For example, in a case where an officer received considerable public support for a minor but unlawful assault upon a youth who was causing a disturbance, McKenzie has rightly argued that the application of ethical and legal principles and the notion of fairness should be predominant (McKenzie, 1995).

More serious cases of this kind entail what has become known as 'noble-cause corruption'. Frustration at being unable to achieve what is viewed as a just outcome in a criminal case is a major problem. The resort to 'dirty' methods is undoubtedly a convincing mode of justification for some police officers who deal with people who they believe to be guilty but who they cannot convict of their crime within the criminal justice system. This resort to 'dirty' means in these cases usually gets labelled as 'noble cause corruption' and there is little difficulty in understanding this as malpractice.

However, where there are serious dilemmas about ends and means, which may include the need to save life, the problem is more complex. The so-called 'Dirty Harry Problem' (from the films portraying Harry Callahan, a fictional American detective) is probably the most extreme example of this kind, where the ends to be achieved are urgent and unquestionably good but only some 'dirty' means will work to achieve them.

Fig 6.3: The 'Dirty Harry' problem

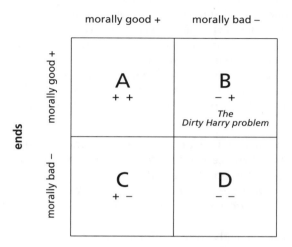

In Harry's case, the problem is the difficulty of reconciling ends and means, as shown in Figure 6.3. This case has been extensively discussed by Klockars (1980). Where the ends and means are both morally good, no problems arise. Similarly, we have no difficulty in understanding that morally bad ends are corrupt, whether good or bad means are used to achieve them. The difficulty arises for some police officers when the ends are undoubtedly good but where questionable means must be used to achieve them.

Problems of this kind can work against compliance with rules, including the human rights conventions. Responsibility to rise above these ordeals rests with the individual police officer but the police organisation also has a role. Although it is right to say that it is important for individual police officers to develop the strength of character to deal with such situations, it is also necessary to recognise that this is not only a matter for the individual. Good training and supervision also play an important role.

Conflicts Relating to the Performance Culture

Developments in police management have required officers to operate to local or national canons of effectiveness. Effectiveness is related to the concept of utility, measured in terms of outputs and outcomes. It is primarily concerned with ends rather than means. In its most crass form, it is totally uninformed in relation to ethical content.

For policing, as elsewhere in the public sector, the last two decades of this century have been characterised by the adoption of systems of accountability where primary emphasis has been placed upon the quantification of performance. From Home Office circular 114/83, which required police forces to adopt measures for objective-setting and the rational management of resources, through to the papers of the Audit Commission, there has been considerable pressure upon police managers and operational staff to achieve quantifiable results. Since the early 1990s, this pressure has been compounded by the requirements from government for police to focus their performance upon objectives which are centrally determined and which reflect the policies of the executive.

Most commentators agree that such performance indicators are an important way through which to direct and monitor police activity. The Cassells enquiry, for example, agreed that they serve a useful purpose and that they need to be expressed in terms:

> *'...which fully recognise both the national leadership*
> *task of the centre and the role and responsibilities*
> *which the police are called upon to discharge*
> *through the way they operate in practice.'*
>
> Police Foundation/Policy Studies Institute (1996)

Whilst this is undoubtedly correct, this claim leaves many unanswered questions about the effect which the performance culture is having upon operational and managerial practice and behaviour. It also leaves unanswered questions about the ethical and human resource aspects of policing practice which need to be taken into account if leadership from central government and from those who are responsible for managing the police is to be credible.

At the level of the viability of central and local performance indicators, the chain of cost – input – output – outcome which is advocated by the Audit Commission does little to encourage an integrated methodology for achieving excellence. In a technical sense, it does not account for the ethics of processes which act as intervening variables and radically affect the outputs and outcomes which might be achieved. In the worst-case scenario, the separation of performance from ethical considerations produces examples of malpractice which can be increasingly expensive. The real costs of failing to include professional conduct within the performance concept include the reputational damage which can be done to police organisations resulting from criminal prosecutions of individual police officers and the high levels of financial damages resulting from civil litigation or out-of-court settlements.

In research studies, officers have described the problems of the requirement to obtain results which they believed work against their deeper duty and responsibility to help the public. Problems of allocating sufficient time to victims were mentioned in this context, amongst other factors (Irving *et al*, 1996). Research on value conflicts has also shown that for some officers, compared to duty to provide practical advice and support for the public, the requirement to concentrate on the 'figures' was dysfunctional and stressful (Wright and Irving, 1996). These difficulties can only be corrected by management adopting measures which formally recognise the ethical side of performance.

These problems mean that the quantitative concepts which have hitherto been virtually the sole method for judgement of performance can no longer be sustained in the face of increasing ethical pressures upon police organisations. Some forces have already started to recognise that management needs to go further than meeting the requirements of systems which are primarily driven by output per unit cost. The strategy of the Metropolitan Police, for example, now emphasises that for overall excellence in performance it is necessary to '...have the right people doing the right things in the right way.' Whilst recognising that policing needs to work within an agreed envelope of expenditure and to set objectives accordingly, initiatives of this kind bring human rights, fairness and other ethical considerations into play in contextualising the notion of performance.

Problems of the Use of Force

The use of force always requires justification whether it is used by police or by individual citizens. In a democracy, police authority to use force represents a very serious ceding of power which needs to be carefully regulated and monitored. Coercive force is not only permitted but is actually unavoidable under some circumstances. This, in itself, can lead to moral conflicts.

As a first principle, the amount of force used needs to be proportional to the ends to be achieved. In essence, this means that it should be minimised. For example, if police can arrest a killer without the use of deadly force then they should do so. The doctrine of minimum force has long been accepted as the crucial principle in judging the extent to which police are justified in applying force as part of their coercive power. This has been codified in the UN Code of conduct for Enforcement Officers (1979) and the Council of Europe Declaration on the Police (1979).

In some circumstances the police are empowered to use lethal force. The use of firearms is the usual (but not the only) way in which this authority is implemented. The UN code (in common with regulations in many police forces) regards the use of firearms as an extreme measure. They should only be used when a suspected person offers armed resistance or jeopardises the life of others and less-than-lethal methods are not available.

Many police forces have adopted containment and prolonged negotiation to resolve armed incidents. Disabling techniques, including TASAR high voltage guns and CS gas have also been provided. But even in police forces (such as in Britain) where the police are not routinely armed, reserve armed facilities are made available at very short notice. It should be noted however, that the same principles about the use of force apply to all methods whether potentially lethal or non-lethal, namely minimalism and proportionality. Because they are considered in legal judgements and in other forms of accountability, these concepts need to be recognised by squad and local managers making the ground-rules clear to their officers. Similar ground rules need to be established and firm action taken by management over the use of informants and in other cases where dis-information may be contemplated as a tactic to combat organised crime.

Training and Professional Development

It is against this complex sociological, psychological and organisational background that the key problems of professional police conduct should be understood and managed. As should be evident from the above discussion, the suggestion that police malpractice is simply a failure to comply with the rules does not accord with the real-world complexities and ambiguities of policing. More exhortation to comply is not what is required. Several distinct responses are required from the organisation and from individual managers, covering training, audit, monitoring and active supervision.

Firstly, police officers should be encouraged, as part of their professional training, to develop a *repertoire* of professional strategies to deal with their conflicts. Because peer-group pressure can be so powerful, only an appropriate programme of professional development will enable police officers to handle the extraordinary ethical difficulties of the job. Training in knowledge, skills and attitudes for police recruits has been developed to a high standard. However evaluation of this training has always emphasised that when newly trained probationers come into contact with the "real world" of policing, they immediately acquire a set of behaviours to enable them to cope with the job. Many of these coping behaviours are idiosyncratic to a point but they are also handed on from one generation of officers to another and constitute an important part of the operational policing culture.

Career-long development programmes are needed to complement the rule systems and provide an effective framework through which individual and corporate professionalism can be achieved. Practical programmes of professional development should be provided from the recruit stage onwards, including effective team training within the workplace itself. This would help to counter any adverse effects of the strong police culture into which new personnel are inducted. Because so much of policing is about conflicts between values, police officers need to learn early in their careers about value conflict and differences in the value systems within which they operate.

Behavioural change is a long-term process, predicated upon a clear understanding of the pervasive culture of policing and the individual and collective need it fulfils. For a professional development programme to be successful it must meet a need that is at least as powerful as that expressed by the culture. It must enhance professional status and support self-regulation. It must be powerful enough to provide officers with strategies upon which they can draw when they meet difficult circumstances in their professional careers. Such an approach must be highly credible to experienced practitioners. To make such a programme effective, moralising language needs to be avoided. The problem of moralising is a real and practical issue for working police officers because it strikes to the very core of their perceptions of their own authority. The sense that police are being provided with sermons about their behaviour is only likely to be exacerbated by "talking shops" that do nothing to address the real difficulties inherent in the job.

Ethical Leadership and Active Supervision

Secondly, a major issue in managing police organisations is ensuring that the declared values enshrined in senior management policy and strategy are carried through middle management down to the lowest operational levels. This is a problem for all large organisations but it is particularly so for police because of the high level of operational discretion available to constables and sergeants.

Because of the way in which they have developed, all police forces are disciplined hierarchies. This means that there is a responsibility upon supervisors and senior police managers to monitor and control the activities and conduct of those for whom they are responsible. In some police organisations, however, the focus has been primarily upon organisational effectiveness and efficiency, rather than upon ensuring legitimacy. This has been brought about by the primacy of output measurement discussed above, which can emphasise producing 'results' and getting the job done at the expense of ensuring that it is done within the due processes of law.

The belief that policing is only about fighting crime, rather than the exercise of due-process under the criminal justice system, is a dangerous a model for police officers to follow. In such cases, if supervision is inadequate, an emphasis upon controlling crime by any means can lead to malpractice and abuse. This needs to be countered by good management and supervision which recognises the potential problems and puts into place local measures which ensure that effectiveness is not achieved at the expense of legitimacy.

In the workplace, the deficiencies of traditional coping strategies, based upon apparently supportive but often idiosyncratic group attitudes, need to be recognised and effective systems of supervision and team management initiated to counter them. This would help to resolve the anomaly between the requirements of formal systems and the informal culture which is the main influence upon professional conduct. By developing the team to cope with complexity and ambiguity in the exercise of their discretion, managers empower their officers to deal with value conflicts before they arise.

Ethical Audit

Thirdly, although the importance of the corporate governance of policing has been recognised through the adoption of the ACPO statement of common purpose and values, this has not necessarily been followed through into actual policing practices at the grass roots. The reason for this is that policing has a complex constitutional structure but no corporate centre which can fully control policy or initiate ethical audits for the police service as a whole.

As will be evident from the discussion above, the audit of police forces usually focuses strongly upon effectiveness as the key measure of performance. In general, this form of audit ignores the ethical dimension. Similarly, in specific cases of malpractice, questions of conduct are invariably subsumed under legal or disciplinary procedures involving a *post hoc* review of culpability, with the focus upon the attribution of individual or collective blame. Rarely is the health of a police organisation systematically audited against an agreed set of ethical and human rights standards.

This has not been the case in some parts of the private business sector which have come to realise the importance of ethical audit to their business. Business conduct starts with specific and identifiable moral dilemmas which emerge in the course of business activity. Because these dilemmas are complex, those who are concerned with them, both as practitioners and observers, should not be concerned to moralise but to offer a framework through which they can be understood and tackled. This implies the use of a logical framework for their analysis.

Because individual and corporate professionalism cannot directly be guaranteed by open scrutiny in cases where operational effectiveness might be jeopardised or lives put at risk, it is necessary to have in place other systems of accountability which act as surrogate controls. In its ethical component, therefore, corporate governance of the police is about who is accountable to whom and at what strategic level. It is about what checks and balances can be put into place to ensure the ethical health of the police organisation.

Despite this acceptance, and whilst most police forces would claim to be ethical organisations, it is far from clear how this claim might be validated. Because police work and the dilemmas it produces are complex, there is great value in the development of a logical framework for ethical analysis and audit. According to Clutterbuck and Snow (1990), ethical audits should attempt to answer the management's need for information on where the organisation is now and where it ought to be, in terms of its values. They should cover policy, systems and standards and the means for monitoring and analysing performance in the areas of ethics and social responsibility. The key questions which need to be asked include:

- What documentation sets out the organisation's policies in this area?
- What knowledge (internally and externally) is available about those policies?
- Do the policies reflect the current state of thinking on the subject (best practice)?
- Are systems and standards in place which measure the 'right' things?
- Are such systems and standards are being implemented effectively?
- Is there year-on-year analysis against well-defined ethical targets?

Unless ethical audits which incorporate these questions are seriously embedded in the regular planning process, commitment to ethical principles and human rights will remain just superficial lip-service commitments. They will not be geared to the real business of running the organisation.

Other Monitoring Measures

In many cases, individuals keep their value conflicts to themselves and are reluctant to discuss these issues with either their supervisors or immediate colleagues. This is because cases can involve criminal or disciplinary offences and to discuss them would spread responsibility. The perceived need for secrecy is an undoubted barrier to the possibility of defusing potentially explosive situations by officially supported counselling within the workgroup. If officers confide in supervisors or colleagues, even under a promise of confidentiality, the admitted malpractice may be so serious that someone within the police institution may feel obliged to resort to 'whistle-blowing'. For the supervisor to keep such an issue confidential raises a secondary value conflict for the supervisor concerned. In this sense, "A problem shared is a problem doubled".

Properly organised 'hot-lines' can provide one way of defusing these situations. Lines of this kind have been used successfully in international aviation, allowing flight-crews to report incidents which may compromise safety without jeopardising their jobs or their loyalty to their companies or colleagues. The Metropolitan Police has instituted a similar facility and only time (and sensitive evaluation) will tell whether it is a successful approach in the policing environment.

Effective managers should continue to develop their own sensors in their work-groups. Awareness of the problems of staff is a day-to-day requirement. Managers need to develop their own tactics and particularly to make clear what are the acceptable limits of conduct. These should not be considered as remedial measures for some kind of sickness. They are simply common-sense ways in which police management can help officers to follow certain patterns of behaviour (such as fairness, honesty and the use of minimum force). Even so, there will still be dilemmas from which they cannot easily escape, given the nature of the work.

Although this managerial approach to police conduct will not totally eradicate the value conflicts which are a major influence on failures to comply with the ideals set out in the law and regulations, officers can avoid the worst consequences. In this sense, well-understood management techniques and effective training can tackle problems which look insurmountable when analysed in the abstract. Only a judicious mixture of these measures (professional development, active team management, ethical audit and monitoring) is likely to be successful in managing police conduct in the long-term.

Chapter Summary

- Professionalisation of the police places heavy responsibility upon individual police officers and upon police organisations to ensure high standards of conduct.

- Respect for human rights principles is the cornerstone of good police conduct. Officers should be aware of, and routinely follow, the principles in the relevant UN and European Declarations and Conventions.

- The Police Discipline Code and other rules and sanctions are necessary but not sufficient conditions for achieving high standards of police conduct. Only self-regulation and good management can provide the sufficient conditions.

- Management is not just a matter of enforcing the rules. Policing is subject to a wide range of value conflicts, including conflicting loyalties relating to the job, colleagues, family, concepts of justice and the use of force.

- Because of the complexity of these conflicts, a four-fold approach to managing police conduct is required. This has individual and organisational components. It includes the provision of effective professional development from the recruit stage onwards; good ethical leadership and active supervision; regular and systematic ethical audit to ensure the health of the organisation; and the development of effective means of monitoring.

Chapter 7

Managing Change and Development

Change and Development

'There is nothing permanent except change.'
Heraclitus

Change has a major effect on people within the organisation and can be another source of stress due to feelings of insecurity that affect those who are involved. The forces for change can come from the environment external to the force or from within (generated by) the organisation or can be brought about by individuals (managers) themselves.

Change in the police forces in the UK, is increasing at an almost logarithmic rate and is due firstly to external pressures being exerted by the community, the media, politicians and the Home Office and secondly to internal pressures by forces such as ACPO, the Superintendents' Association, the Police Federation and generally by managers within the organisation.

A wealth of reports, recommendations and new legislation in the past few years (Sheehy Report, Police and Criminal Evidence Act, Police and Magistrates' Courts Act) is changing forever the way the police service is operated and managed. Change is disruptive no matter how well it is managed and it is resented by people who inherently like things to be the way they were. Change sweeps away many established systems and methods with which the employees had become familiar and imposes new systems, a new structure and the old equilibrium is gone.

Managers can respond to change in ways that are constructive or in ways that are destructive and will eventually destroy the career prospects of the individual. There are two major aspects of change:

- The type of change which is needed almost on a daily basis, where managers react to specific needs and make piecemeal changes to rectify a problem situation and
- The programme of planned change which is put in place to accommodate the externally generated mandatory modifications.

The Need for Planned Change

Do we really need planned change? What are the advantages of this approach? Because organisations such as the police are open systems, dependent on the environment, there needs to be an awareness of the changes that are taking place around them, and the plan must be able to accommodate sufficient modification and structure to this change, which will satisfy these new environmental demands. Only in this way is the currency, the validity and the need for change identified.

There is also a need to address the effect of change at individual level, where, as a result of the overall organisational change, the behaviour of the employees at any or all levels within the organisation are affected. The behaviour of each individual within the organisation (when taken collectively), affects the balance of forces for and against change (fig. 7.1). It is therefore essential that this is taken into account when planning change, and the judicial use of reward and punishment restructured to be compatible with the new planned conditions.

Fig 7.1: Forces for and against change

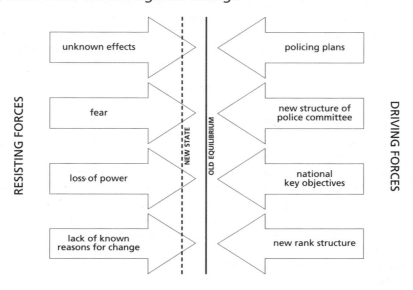

Individual emotions, attitudes and values are not developed rationally or logically but are conditioned by the culture of the organisation and its general perception by its employees. These are unlikely to be altered by appeals to logic or reason, as was evidenced by the opposition to the Sheehy Report and the rejection of many of the logical arguments which were put forward in its support by both politicians and civil servants.

Reshaping of the 'force field' takes place as planned, there is a move forward, a refreeze then takes place which becomes permanent change and in due course the cycle continues to meet the new demands of the environment.

Reshaping (the move forward), can only be achieved successfully if certain vital factors are recognised by the managers of change. Staff must be educated both in the need, and in the reasons, for change. The communication highways within the organisation must be efficient and convey the right information to the right people at the right time. *(Chapter 8 discusses this issue in depth.)*

People (the employees), need to feel that they have a degree of participation in what is taking place; the more participation that is involved, the more comfortable people will be. Change induces anxiety and stress and there needs to be a programme of facilitation and support if this is to be reduced. This in turn reduces the opposition to the changes that are taking place and makes the move forward that much easier.

Getting people to change is no easy task for the manager. There is an inherent opposition to change; people feel comfortable with the situation they know, and are unhappy about the unknown and the effect it may have on them personally. Patterns of belief and values are established over years, and to change these needs an explicit communications strategy aimed at establishing new patterns of belief and values which are compatible with the change. It perhaps involves 'unlearning' of the old values and techniques and the adoption of a new 'comfort' area which embraces the reality of the new changes to the individual's responsibilities and role.

This programme of planned change has been defined by Thomas and Bennis (1972) as:

'The deliberate design and implementation of a
structural innovation, a new policy or goal, or a
change in operating philosophy, climate and style.'

It is arguable that all of these are applicable to the police at the present time. It is however true, that if these changes are to be successful, it needs a greater involvement of management time and resources, and requires both new and different skills and knowledge. If these are not available and managers are asked to cope with these new demands for which they have not been trained and do not have the requisite skills, they enter a phase where the pressures can become intolerable, the manager performs well below his/her norm, and stress can become a debilitating factor.

It is essential that where planned change is undertaken, managers and their staff receive the requisite training to enable them to manage effectively under the new conditions.

The police were in a state of virtual equilibrium, that is, only the normal forces of incremental change were taking place up to perhaps the release of the Sheehy Report (1993) and the release of the White Paper on the Police and Magistrates' Courts Bill (subsequently enacted in 1994). The forces acting for change and the forces resisting were equally balanced and the status quo was maintained. With the introduction of the Act and the repercussions of the Sheehy Report, the position changed, and the driving forces were strong enough to move the centre ground well into that of the restraining forces. It is true that a strengthening of the driving forces almost always results in a similar strengthening of the resistance to change. This was well evidenced, as was stated earlier in the chapter, by the opposition to the Sheehy Report and the subsequent modifications that were imposed on the recommendations.

Why is Change Resisted?

There are a number of reasons why people resist change.

- What is not known causes fear and induces resistance. Restructuring within an organisation can leave people uncertain about their future prospects and even about their current job. People want to feel secure and have some control over the changes that are taking place.
- Not knowing the reasons for the change also causes resistance. It is very often unclear to those involved why the change is necessary at all.
- Change can result in a loss of power and/or a loss of benefits.

All of these are applicable to the changes which are currently taking place in the police environment.

If the police service is to survive the considerable pressures that are upon them, its managers need to be more than good operators at the level of their individual skills. They need to understand the complexities of the processes and nature of change if they are to steer their organisation through the dynamics of the change that is being imposed on them. This means looking again at the analysis of change and perhaps changing the ways in which the academics review the subject as management trainers.

There is no typical narrow approach to the subject of change which works successfully, analysis needs to be extended outside of narrow confines such as those of interpersonal and group analyses. To operate successfully as a manager during changes in the structure, organisation, culture and control of the organisation, the manager must understand and learn from the contextualisation of these changes within the organisation. He/she must take the wider view where the individual's ideas and viewpoints are subservient to the whole and work to make the change effective.

Training and Development

> 'The education of a man is never
> completed until he dies.'
>
> Robert E. Lee

It is perhaps prudent to clarify the distinction between what is training and what can be classified as development. *Training* is directed towards maintaining and improving *current* job performance, while *development* seeks to develop skills for *future* jobs. Both managers and those who are not in a management position may receive benefit from training and development, but the mix of experiences is likely to vary. Those who are not managers are more likely to be trained in the technical skills required for their current position, while managers are more likely to be given help in developing the skills (particularly conceptual and human relations skills) required for future positions. This is not always true in the police service where management skills are often not taught until after the officer has been in a management position for some time, even years. For example a sergeant, (who certainly has a major requirement for management skills) may not have the opportunity to acquire these skills until long after he/she has been in post, other than doing some form of study in their own time and at their own expense.

Figure 7.2 shows a typical composition of an organisation's workforce changes. Managers in organisations do not stay in one position permanently. Those who are successful are usually promoted; those who are not considered suitable for promotion are in most cases subject to tenure and are liable to be moved sideways or even to a less onerous post. The organisation and its managers must acclimatise themselves to a constant change of personnel over time.

Figure 7.2 lays out the process from the feed-in of human resources at the recruitment stage to the feed out of the organisation through retirement, resignation, or discharge. The selection and induction processes follow the normal procedure for the police service, thereafter a lengthy training and development take place

Fig 7.2: The staffing process

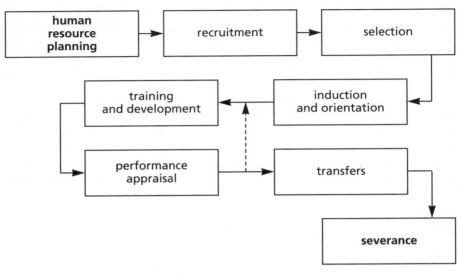

when new recruits are given a thorough grounding in all the aspects of the work which they will be required to carry out. It should be noted here, that the training and development phase also embraces established staff whose specific needs have been (or should have been) ascertained, in the normal chain of events, usually after performance appraisal. The transfers section relates to the movement of personnel between one position and another. Tenure which is a fact of life in the police service, means that there are at any given time, a large number of personnel in the process of transfer who need training.

With new employees, the need for training is self evident as with those newly promoted or about to be promoted. Less evident is the need to train those for whom there is no immediate prospect of promotion and who have been in their current position for a number of years. Training can however build on the foundations already established in their job by enhancing the skills and knowledge required to improve current performance and to develop potential for the future. Once this potential has been ascertained then a development programme can be planned which will develop the individual for a new and more demanding job. If training is to be successful, it must generate change. If it does not succeed in doing this, then it has failed in its objective.

The purpose of training must be to better achieve the objectives of the organisation and to develop professional managers who will manage their staff and resources more effectively. Although moves have been made to make training more relevant, there is still sometimes little correlation between the type of programmes on offer, the aims and objectives of the organisation and the needs of the individual. This is particularly relevant to the police service where much of the training has little bearing on either the actual needs of the organisation or the long term development of the individual. Scatter-gun training methods can produce the clichéd 'jack of all trades, master of none'.

Management Development

Two main routes are open to employees to satisfy their management development and training needs within the police service:

- Internal management courses organised, staffed and compiled by internal trainers; and
- External management training supplied by colleges and universities

Internal courses are designed to fulfil a perceived need with direct relevance to the police service and its operation. External courses run by colleges and universities are geared to fulfilling a need for management skills applicable to all types of organisation. Successful participants will gain a qualification at the end of their course which will be recognised as supplying skills applicable in any industry or organisation. Two main types of qualification are now available at higher level – the traditional Bachelor/Masters degree and the newer National Vocational Qualification (NVQ) to Certificate and Diploma level.

The first step in designing any training and development programme is to identify the needs. There are a number of procedures that managers can use to determine an individual's need:

- Performance appraisal: *the individual's work is measured against the criteria and performance standards required for that job*
- Analysis of job requirements: *reference is made to the skills and knowledge required for that particular position. Those who have been ascertained as having the potential but without the specific skills and knowledge become candidates*
- Organisational analysis: *the structure of the organisation and its effectiveness in achieving its objectives is scrutinised to determine any areas of weakness in performance which may need to be addressed by additional training programmes*
- Survey of human resources: *managers and staff are involved in a survey to determine problems they may be experiencing and the action they consider necessary to solve them*

It is not enough to identify the need for change; individuals who are the targets for a training programme must be motivated to participate in the effort. They need to realise that identified deficiencies in their performance must be eliminated if they are to maintain their current status and position, be promoted, gain relevant pay increases, or achieve other objectives.

Management development is designed to improve the overall effectiveness of managers in their present position and to prepare them for greater responsibility when they are promoted. Because of the increasingly complex demands now being made of managers, management development programmes are becoming more prevalent. It has at last been discovered that it is more cost effective to devote a

127

small proportion of the financial budget to training than to allow experience alone to be responsible for the training . This is unreliable, time consuming and ultimately far more expensive than it would have been to effectively train the manager in the first place. If it is thought that training is expensive, try ignorance as a substitute.

In the police service, there is a tendency for management development courses to be programme centred, that is, a programme is designed and administered to managers regardless of experience, status or ability. Little is done in the way of determining the individual needs which might be required for a particular individual or the skills required for a particular post.

Management development programmes need to become more *manager centred*, that is designed to fit the actual requirements of the personnel attending that particular course. This requires that a needs analysis is done to determine the particular needs and problems that this group of managers may face. The needs analysis must be thorough if the programme is to be properly tailored to the individual or group needs. An example of this is shown in fig.7.3.

Programme centred activities use the scatter-gun technique in the hope that at least some of the content will be useful and contribute to the learning of some of the participants. It is evident that this approach is not cost effective and in the current economic climate is a waste of precious resources. Managers who are expected to participate in the training of their subordinates and in their development require to be trained themselves in the developmental skills. It is doubtful how effectively this is done in the police environment.

Training cannot of itself create potential, it can only help develop it, therefore managers must have the ability to select those whom he/she considers can usefully benefit from attendance at a development training programme. There is a tendency to consider a participant who has successfully completed such a programme as

Fig 7.3: Typical needs analysis

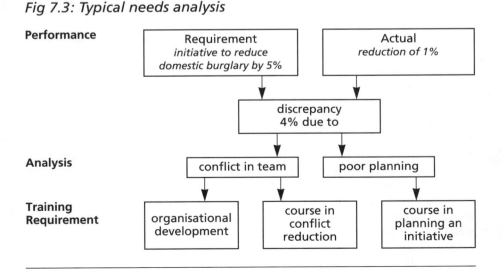

competent to undertake the increased responsibilities, missing the all important fact that he/she will require experience in the work environment in order to supplement the theory acquired in the classroom situation.

It might be useful at this stage to examine what criteria, if any, are used to measure success or failure for participants in a development programme. It is certainly true that in many cases, attendance is in itself the only criterion used to determine success. Performance appraisal for the individual participating in the course is an absolute necessity if the value of the programme and its content is to be ascertained. Competent trainers must design a set of measurement criteria which will give a true evaluation of the performance of each participant during the course. Subsequent appraisal requires to be carried out by the individual's manager on the improved performance on his/her return to normal or revised duties.

Interpersonal Skills

'It takes a great man to make a good listener.'
Sir Arthur Helps

Interpersonal skills are usually defined as relating to communicating and interacting and working with others. It covers subjects such as team leadership, actioning change, negotiating, reciprocal relationships and influencing skills.

There is a growing demand among employers for managers to have highly developed interpersonal skills and the police service is no exception. These skills are crucial to maintaining an effective organisation and to presenting an acceptable image both internally and externally.

In recognition of this, the DfEE commissioned a study on *Changing Roles for Senior Managers*. The report has recently been published by the Institute for Employment Studies (July 1997). Senior managers and personnel professionals from eighteen leading companies were interviewed. Competency frameworks were analysed in half of the companies chosen and in one a forum for participants. Other reports on related subjects published by the same institute cover *Getting the Best out of Your Competencies* and *Skills Competencies and Gender Issues for Pay and Training*.

The eighteen leading employers interviewed in the research for the first report identified interpersonal skills as one of the most important areas where they were lacking in expertise. Greater width of command as a result of flatter, leaner organisations mean managers have to have a wider knowledge of more techniques than ever before. This has been accompanied by a shift in emphasis from management (the autocratic style?) to a leadership style in which the manager is more closely involved with his/her employees. Empowerment of employees means that today's managers have to learn the skills of listening, relating, encouraging and motivating all those in his/her 'team' to make change as non-traumatic as possible but most of all to make it effective.

Managers in the police environment have been indoctrinated into a command and control structure where macho management has been the order of the day. Managers in this type of culture find it all the more difficult to change to utilising some of the 'softer' skills. Today, if organisations want to retain and develop their best performers, their senior managers must be prepared to motivate them, inspire them, assess and recognise their performance and establish meaningful communication on a regular basis, not once a year when annual assessment comes around but on an ongoing regular basis.

Senior managers need to learn to be team players, forge reciprocal relationships with their colleagues and have a close involvement in what the team is doing. The softer aspects of management style and behaviour have now become the focus of considerable attention due to the need for organisations to maximise the performance of their people. Changing managerial behaviour will take time as managers currently believe that their culture has not and perhaps should not be open to interpersonal disclosure. The soft skills are perhaps the most difficult to change as they involve the changing of personal behaviour

Organisations nowadays recognise that if they want to encourage their managers to empower people, they have to invest in personal capability. Many employers however, offer little or no opportunities for training in the areas of team development and group dynamics. One answer adopted by some organisations is to create competency frameworks. These define the important behaviour they want their managers to demonstrate but find hard to articulate. The frameworks could cover such things as self development, leadership, developing others, forging reciprocal relationships, communication skills, and listening and influencing skills; these are becoming an integral part of a managers repertoire.

Performance Appraisal

Performance appraisal is one of the most important tasks that a manager has to carry out, yet it is one which most managers admit to having difficulty in carrying out effectively. Managers find difficulty in judging the performance of a subordinate objectively and relating this to a fixed set of standards. Peter Drucker (1954) is enthusiastic about appraisal:

> *'To appraise a subordinate and his performance is part of a manager's job. Indeed, unless he does the appraising himself he cannot adequately discharge his responsibility for assisting and teaching his subordinates.'*

The nature of an employee's job and the performance expectations attached to it, and the ways in which in which the performance will be measured, should always be made clear at the outset of employment or promotion.

Performance appraisal is an often misused term to describe the *annual* ritual when the subordinate is invited to interview and a list of the successful and unsuccessful activities for the achievement of the imposed objectives is delivered by his/her superior. It becomes almost a castigating session where failures are paraded and little is done to find the real underlying reasons for any lack of success.

This type of appraisal technique is used (or misused) in many forces, where the unfortunate appraisee is only given an idea of how their performance has been viewed at the end of a twelve month period. It has been said to the authors on many occasions that the person being appraised should know within themselves at what level they have been performing. This is wrong on a number of counts; the individual has a much narrower view of their own performance relative to that required when viewed in the division or force context. He/she may not have been clear as to what was really wanted of them and felt that they had indeed performed satisfactorily. It is time we moved beyond this antiquated type of approach, which to be fair many have done so, but many more remain to be convinced otherwise.

Performance appraisal should be related to a process of continuous feedback where during a two-way discussion, subordinates are given information about how well they are doing, problems are elicited and their potential solutions discussed and agreed. Areas of weakness where the appraisee needs to strengthen his/her approach and the progress towards agreed targets and objectives should be discussed.

By all means let us have a formal appraisal system but let it combine the informal day to day intercourse on topical problems and successes with a formal interview on an annual basis when *mutually* agreed targets and objectives are agreed and a constructive review of the past twelve months is carried out. This should be interspersed with quarterly formal interviews when progress towards the targets can be discussed together with any problems not uncovered on the continuous feedback loop.

We now come to what some might consider to be the heretical part; should appraisal be carried out on the superior's performance on the same basis? During the interview, an opportunity is given to the appraisee to discuss any shortcomings in the way he/she has been helped or hindered throughout the period of the appraisal by the actions (or lack of them) by their immediate manager. It is certainly becoming much more common for this now to be part of the appraisal procedure. It is essential that the appraisee feels confident when voicing an opinion, that it will not reflect detrimentally on them personally. This is always a problem in organisations that adopt an autocratic style of management. It can to some extent be overcome by using different approaches to performance appraisal. Two of these are:

- A group of superiors rating subordinates
- Peer group rating of colleagues

Both of these allow the appraisee a greater degree of freedom to speak plainly without fear of reprisal in the form of lack of career advancement.

The approach of subordinates rating superiors is becoming more acceptable in many organisations and is being used as another method of evaluating managers and helping them to improve their performance.

With fixed term appointments appearing for the first time in the police environment, the interplay between appraiser and appraisee becomes even more important. Much discussion has been generated within ACPO as to the merits or otherwise of fixed term appointments. These have been a fact of life for many in other walks of life and their incidence is increasing. There is little doubt that as the trend grows in popularity that there will be increasing pressures on the police service to follow suit.

Development of an individual has two major objectives – to improve their performance within the organisation in their current post, and, if suitable, to enable promotion to take place. The decisions about whom to promote and whom not to promote are among the most important and the most difficult that a manager has to make. Because the possibility of advancement serves as a major incentive for better managerial performance, it is important that it is fair and is seen to be fair – that is, that it is based on merit and untainted by favouritism.

The appraisal of performance should, if it is properly carried out, have identified the strengths and weaknesses of the individual; this identification can be the starting point for a career plan. The personal strategy should be designed to utilise strengths and overcome weaknesses in order to maximise career opportunities.

Career Planning

There are many different approaches to career planning and development but in many respects it is similar to an organisational strategy. An example of this is shown in fig. 7.4.

How clear are managers about the direction they want to take? This is to some extent conditioned by the opportunities that are available within the organisation in which they work. Nevertheless, it is essential that the individual has a clear idea of

Fig 7.4: Career strategy planning

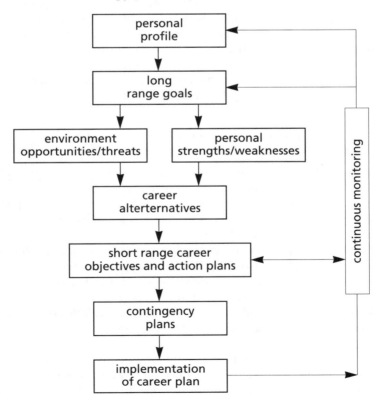

where they want to go. Not everyone is suited to the police environment but they may not find this out until some time after they have joined. If this is the case, then a vitally important decision has to be made. If after discussion with the individual's immediate superior, and also with the personnel function, no clear long term development path is seen, a crucial decision has to be made. This will concern whether or not he/she is suited to this environment and if not, should the decision be taken to work in an environment which is more suited to their skills and personality. Where the individual feels comfortable within the force then managers or potential managers must develop a career strategy if they are to receive satisfaction in their workplace. Managers often resist making a career plan because it can involve taking decisions, in some cases painful decisions.

The choice of one goal limits the opportunities to pursue others. If a career in CID is the objective, and this is pursued, then other options may be limited. People need to be aware of their own strengths and weaknesses, and their attitudes towards work, achievement, material things and change. Managers have a tendency to resist setting firm long and short term goals because of uncertainty in their immediate environment. There is also a fear of failure to achieve these goals because of what it could do to that manager's ego. This is particularly true in the police environment where failure is anathema to the culture and where failure, or perceived failure, by an individual can develop a stress situation. Career planning could, and perhaps should, start during the performance appraisal. At that time, the growth and development of the manager should be discussed. Career goals and personal aims can and should be considered by the person's line manager in selecting and promoting, and in designing subsequent training and development programmes.

Promotion

Promotion is usually seen as a significant way of recognising superior performance. It is however important that recognition is made of the extent of the skills of the individual in question and that they are not promoted to their own 'level of incompetence'. That is that the manager recognises the strengths and weaknesses of the individual and does not promote them to a position where they will not be capable of performing well or where their particular skills are not relevant. This is an important factor in reducing the possibility of stress induced by the inability to adapt to the pressures of the new post.

Promotions can be seen as discriminatory by staff who feel that they have been bypassed and this can have a demotivating effect resulting in a lowering of morale. This is particularly true nowadays with the laws on sex and race discrimination being much more powerful. In these circumstances, it is even more important that the selection process is known and understood by all employees as well the criteria which are used to determine those suitable for promotion. The performance appraisal is a useful time to advise employees of their shortcomings and the fact that perhaps they have reached the extent of their abilities in their present post and that any further potential for advancement may be beyond their capabilities.

Tenure within the police service facilitates the application of transfer between posts without the possibility of promotion. Transfers such as this can be useful in giving employees broader job experience, open new horizons and increase motivation. They can and are in some cases used to facilitate development and give increased opportunity for promotion as an end result. It is also a useful way of creating openings which might not otherwise be available and would create a block to potential promotees.

Management and Motivation of Civilians

> *'There are only two ways of getting on in this world; by one's own industry or by the weakness of others.'*
>
> Jean de La Bruyere

The preceding section has concentrated more on the training and development of serving officers rather than on the growing numbers of civilian staff who are now taking over positions formerly filled by serving officers. Is the style of management required for civilians any different from that required for police officers? The theoretical answer is no, but as we look at the different environments in which they work, perhaps we will come to a different conclusion.

As was mentioned earlier in the chapter, the prevailing management style within the police service tends to be autocratic (not untypical in an organisation where discipline has a high priority), and to demand immediate compliance with the command of a superior officer. This style of management will not work in areas other than those where the employee is part of a uniformed organisation (police, army, prison service etc.) and subject to a high degree of discipline and need for obedience.

Civilian posts are not in this category and police officers cannot obtain the same degree of unquestioning obedience as they can from their uniformed subordinates. *This subject is dealt with in greater detail in Chapter 12.*

Managing your Superior

> *'By working faithfully for eight hours a day, you may eventually get to be a boss and work twelve hours a day.'*
>
> Robert Frost

If there is to be an effective, productive and trusting relationship between the subordinate and his/her immediate manager at whatever level, an understanding of each others needs and a good working relationship needs to be established at an early stage.

The first rule of managing your boss is to really get to know him/her. What does he/she want from:

- Life? *Tangible needs are very often less important than supposed. It is the intangible needs that assume a much greater importance. For example*

Fig. 6.5

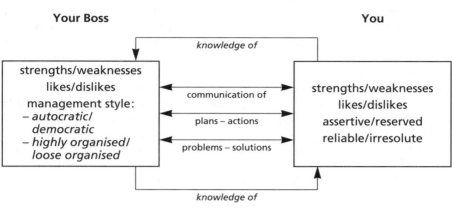

Your Boss

strengths/weaknesses
likes/dislikes
management style:
– *autocratic/*
  democratic
– *highly organised/*
  loose organised

knowledge of

communication of

plans – actions

problems – solutions

knowledge of

You

strengths/weaknesses
likes/dislikes
assertive/reserved
reliable/irresolute

> *they may want a quiet comfortable life, they may seek power and status, they may prefer security to taking a chance or they may have a high need for recognition.*

- Work? *Two aspects are usually evident, the personal objectives and the organisational objectives. The personal objectives can be esteem from colleagues and subordinates, achievement of personal goals, recognition for the work they are doing, survival and self-realisation. The organisational objectives (particularly in light of the new policing plans and the need to work to cash limited budgets) are the provision of acceptable forward planning, the achievement of the goals and targets set at force and divisional levels and the effective use of available resources.*
- Subordinates? *Most bosses want co-operation, to be kept up-to-date with all relevant information, honesty at all times, a high degree of dependability and not to be bothered unless it is a matter of some importance.*

Your immediate superior is also a human being (though this is doubted by many subordinates) and is no different from other managers and employees in that they have their likes and dislikes, their strengths and weaknesses and a style of management which is peculiar to them and is conditioned by their own personality. The strengths of some managers lie in their ability to relate to their subordinates, others in their ability to get things done. Some in their competence and ability to react to uncertainty and risk while in others their strength lies in their aptitude for managing themselves and on their use of time.

Management styles are as different as are managers themselves. Some have an intuitive knack of doing the right things at the right time without really knowing why, others have a highly organised, formal and structured style of managing, maybe autocratic but not necessarily so. This style of managing can also be democratic. Many managers are good at delegation, can stand aside and take an overview of what is being done, other have a need to get involved. Management can be assertive, indeed almost aggressive as practised by some, others can exert their authority by a passive style which can be equally effective.

It is important to recognise the qualities, strengths and weaknesses that are inherent in your immediate superior, to know what you yourself want from life and work, to analyse your own strengths and weaknesses so that you and your boss can work in harmony. For those who want to enjoy work and to progress up the management chain, it is imperative that cognisance is taken of these factors which can and do, influence your career development and promotion prospects.

The relationship between the manager and his immediate superior is particularly important if the team and the organisation as a whole is to be effective. Managers at all levels must work together in symbiosis, where they share their respective strengths, each endeavouring to complement the others known weaknesses and avoiding potential sources of conflict. The working relationship and its effectiveness is as much dependent on the subordinate as it is on the part of the immediate superior. Each must play their part in the development of the relationship and the team spirit, each profiting from the strengths of the other to provide the optimum in benefits for both the managers and their organisation.

Internal and External Consultancy

> *'The one thing more difficult than following
> a regimen is not imposing it on others.'*
> Marcel Proust

With the advent of team operation as a major plank in the management of many organisations, there is a need for more senior managers to acquire the skills necessary to enable valid consultancy advice to be given to managers and team leaders to empower them to deal effectively with problems at a local level.

The internal consultant treads a difficult path in his/her ability to influence the way a particular problem is handled without usurping the power of the manager or team leader to make his/her own decision. If the management style of the organisation is to be more open and responsibility devolved to the appropriate level, then it is important that the manager being advised does not feel that his/her power is being usurped and the ability to make decisions eroded.

Dealing with change can be, and often is, a painful experience. Where the consultant can be of great value is by explaining the need for a certain course of action and perhaps more importantly by listening to what is the manager's evaluation of the situation or problem and his/her proposed course of action before delineating their own ideas as to what should be done. It is a delicate task to persuade a manager that a certain course of action should be taken in preference to the one that he/she is proposing. It is too easy for senior managers to feel that they have more pressing needs and that they cannot spend valuable time explaining the underlying reasons and to resort to demanding that their own particular course of action should be implemented. With the increasing importance of human resource management being recognised in many forces, there is an opportunity for the HRM to act in the capacity of consultant/adviser.

External consultants face similar difficulties to those in the previous paragraph. Forces are more and more coming around to the idea of using the particular expertise that an external consultant may have. It makes sound common sense in any organisation where the expertise may not exist or where it is felt that an opinion formed outside the cloistered confines of the force may be of value, that the opinions and advice of the consultant are sought.

If some degree of expertise already exists within the organisation, the task of the consultant can be all the more difficult. He/she may find it difficult to obtain the relevant information needed due to internal staff feeling that their knowledge and expertise has been devalued. If organisations are to obtain the maximum value from external advice then the way must be prepared beforehand by consulting with the staff concerned and clearly explaining the reasoning behind the decision to seek external advice.

Job Definition – Rigid or Flexible

> *'The art of progress is to preserve order amid*
> *change and to preserve change amid order.'*
> Alfred North Whitehead

The pressures exerted by the need for greater flexibility of the workforce has been brought about by downsizing and has resulted in the fact that there are less people to carry out the same number of tasks.

Job definitions have been thought to focus the employees minds and actions on their areas of responsibility and to make them clearly answerable for any shortcomings. In fact this has worked well for many years when staffing was adequate to allocate employees to specific areas of responsibilities with specific duties. Employees tended to be regarded as components in the management machine, being told what to do and operating within strictly defined limits of responsibility and areas of authority, a situation which lent itself to an easily determined job definition.

The new approach to managing leaner, slimmer organisations where much more flexibility is required makes it increasingly difficult to be as specific on the requirements of the post as was previously the case. If the requirement is for people to be more flexible and to use their own initiative as to what course of action may be required at any given time, then they cannot be restricted to action within specific defined boundaries.

The empowerment of people means just that. They must have the latitude to make their own decisions in the environment in which they are operating, providing it does not conflict with the overall strategy of the organisation. The difficulty arises when they are empowered, and have received little or no training in this area of expertise. In some organisations the empowerment of employees has failed because senior management expected them to be able to shoulder this burden without adequate training. Implementation without training equals almost certain failure.

There is still reluctance on the part of employers to implement a scheme of this nature, fearing that employees do not have the ability to make valid decisions on their own. If only they would realise the potential wealth of knowledge and expertise they are losing because of this. If people are prepared for the task, adequately trained and briefed, the use of people at the point of contact to make timely decisions can and does work with advantage both to the employee, (who gets to use his/her initiative) and to the organisation which gets a faster response to the solution of day to day problems.

Chapter Summary

- The effect of change – its importance, the stress it can induce and the feelings of insecurity it can bring are outlined.

- Two main types of change are outlined – incremental change, the day to day changes that all organisations undergo, and the planned programme of change which reacts to the changing environment. The need for change is explained.

- The 'force field' of forces for and against change is explained and the particular forces operating in the police environment are outlined.

- The implications of the Sheehy Report, the Police and Magistrates' Courts Act and the Police and Criminal Justice Act are illustrative of the forces for change currently operating within police forces.

- The distinction (often blurred) between management training and management development is explained.

- The absolute need for training at all levels within the organisation is outlined as is the advantages of training in areas not always considered as suitable or advantageous to the force.

- Internal and external management training, and the advantages in each area are discussed.

- Determination of an individual's needs as opposed to those of the organisation is discussed and the ways in which the manager can determine these requirements.

- The difference between *programme centred* and *manager centred* courses and the relative advantages or disadvantages is discussed and conclusions drawn.

- Performance appraisal is stated as one of the most important tasks a manager has to perform. Differing ways in which managers approach this task are outlined.

- An important aspect of management – managing your superior is often not given the degree of importance it warrants in career development. Impressing your immediate line manager with your ability to perform well can have a major influence on your career.

- The need is outlined for management to provide the facility for internal consultancy and for the expertise necessary to facilitate external consultancy.

- Job definition – should this be rigid and very explicit or flexible enough to allow the ability to meet change.

Chapter 8

Managing Information

Introduction

> *'Information is expensive.*
> *Lack of it is more so.'*
>
> Lord Rayleigh

Information is something of a Cinderella concept. When someone refers to information, invariably, it is when they are talking about information systems and, in particular, information technology (IT). Too often there is an over concentration on the 'technology' element without the necessary attention to the information element. This has been a significant reason for some of the more spectacular failures of IT systems, both within and outside the police service, in the recent past.

It is easy to forget that IT is merely a tool with which it is possible to process data. Without data it is nothing. Attention needs to be given to information in its own right. It is an immensely powerful resource and yet is so often overlooked or ignored as a concept.

There is an added complication within the police service. Much of the work of the service is underpinned by information in the form of intelligence and 'operational' information. This has clearly led to a concentration of information processing resources in developing the use of such information. This in turn has meant that the effective use of non-operational and management information within the service is still comparatively undeveloped.

With the continuing push for effectiveness and efficiency, forces are increasingly turning to management information as a means of helping them manage. Whilst this is to be welcomed, even in the operational arena, more productive use can be made of intelligence and operational information to support more effective management.

This chapter aims to raise awareness of the importance of information in the police service. It will illustrate the value of viewing information as a strategic resource and recognise the need for an information strategy. In so doing, it will reveal how the value of information within the force can be maximised and will identify the role of police managers in the process.

Data or Information?

Even outside the police service there is often considerable confusion regarding exactly what constitutes data and what constitutes information. The two terms are often used synonymously but without a clear understanding. Although it may only be seen as a semantic point it is worth establishing definitions for the terms data and information. This should facilitate a clearer understanding of the content of this and the next chapter.

Different information and information systems texts will reveal subtly different definitions for data and information.

For the purposes of this text we will view data as a collection of unprocessed facts, associated with a particular activity. Examples might include a vehicle registration number, a crime complaint form number, the location of an incident. Information, on the other hand, can be viewed as data which has been processed into a form meaningful to the recipient.

Using these definitions, then, data becomes information once the facts have been processed. Information places a degree of structure upon the data which should improve the understanding of a particular situation by the recipient of that information.

Therefore using our examples above, a single crime complaint number means very little. A collection of crime complaints, totalled, provides information such as crime statistics. Similarly, a collection and structuring of individual incident location data can help to identify incident patterns.

There are two important principles outlined in the definition of information given above. Information must have some meaning to the person receiving it. Failure to take this into account has contributed to the problem of information overload, referred to later. This also requires officers to identify clearly their own information needs, a subject which will also receive attention later in the chapter.

Types of Information and Levels of Use

Figure 8.1 shows that information in the police service can be classified by both type and level, and gives examples.

- *Strategic information* is, by definition, broad in scope, covering a relatively long time frame (months or even years). It relates to the general direction of the force as a whole and the environment in which it operates.
- *Managerial information* relates to the planning and control processes within the organisation. More detailed than strategic information, it helps managers to manage resources and relates to a shorter time frame (weeks or months). It is also more focused organisationally, usually relating to a functional department or division.
- *Tactical information* is of a short term nature, relating to the day to day operation of the force. It is, by definition, very detailed and likely to relate to a small geographical area, for example, beat area or even street. This information is therefore concerned with short term activities, supporting the carrying out of specific tasks as effectively as possible.

Within the police service there are also two broad types of information, namely operational and non-operational.

- *Operational information* relates directly to the primary operations of the service, that is, the prevention and detection of crime and upholding of the law.
- *Non-operational information* relates to the support processes which enable the force to carry out its primary operations.

Examples of operational and non-operational information at the different levels are shown in figure 8.1. Some would suggest that there is a third type of information, which is management information.

Fig 8.1: Classification of police information by type and level

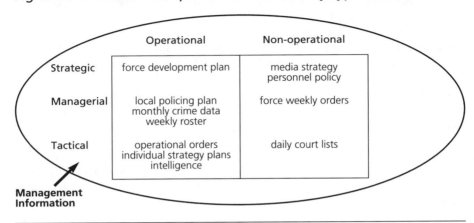

	Operational	Non-operational
Strategic	force development plan	media strategy personnel policy
Managerial	local policing plan monthly crime data weekly roster	force weekly orders
Tactical	operational orders individual strategy plans intelligence	daily court lists

Management Information

Management Information

Before considering management information, it may be prudent to consider the concept of management and managerial roles. Numerous texts have been written about the pure concept of management. One of the most important pieces of work in this area was completed by Mintzberg (1973) who carried out the first major study to identify actual management roles. This considered what managers were actually doing, not what they should be doing. Of the twelve roles identified, some two thirds related to decision making.

A definition for management information might, therefore, be produced simply by adding to the definition of information provided earlier. Management information might be defined as data which have been processed into a form, meaningful to the recipient, and of value in supporting the decision making process.

If this is the case, management information becomes a third type of information within a force which overlays all other types and levels of information. For example, management information can support the decision making process at a strategic, non-operational level. When looking at the development of a media strategy for the force (that is, non-operational, strategic role), decisions can be supported by reviewing the amount of contact over the last year with the different elements of the media. Decisions can then be taken with regard to the required level of contact and the nature and scope of media agencies with whom contact should be maintained.

There is, perhaps, confusion between management information and managerial information. Management information specifically supports the decision making processes across the whole of the organisation. Managerial information is that information which supports the management processes at a functional level only. Figure 8.1 helps to make this distinction.

Too often within the police service, management information is overlooked as an aid to more effective management. There is often the view that looking at information *per se* is of little value; that we should concentrate on information systems and not information.

However, we all operate in an uncertain environment and have to make decisions with less than perfect information. If we had perfect information we could make decisions with 100 per cent certainty and effectiveness. For example, if our friendly neighbourhood villain phoned up to say that he was about to break into the council offices on the high street, the police manager could ensure that resources were in place to catch him – a clear decision and an effective use of resources.

Unfortunately, however, this situation is unlikely to occur. The police manager has to make resource allocation decisions based on incomplete, less than perfect information in an uncertain environment. The more information he or she has, will reduce the level of uncertainty and should lead to better, more effective decision making.

Information technology and systems can only be the tools to process data and provide the information, accurately and quickly, to the user. Decisions themselves can only be made by managers and only on the basis of the information available to them, no matter how provided.

A consideration of the type and level of information within the police service and the managerial role adopted might be thought to be a little too academic. All very interesting, but so what! The next section will show that a clear understanding of such factors is vital if the problem of information overload is to be countered.

Information Overload

Leading management scientist Robert Heller coined one of the neatest definitions of information overload:

> *'Managers are to information as alcoholics are to booze.*
> *They consume enormous amounts, constantly crave more,*
> *but have difficulty in digesting their existing intake.'*

Due to the proliferation of information technology as a data processing medium, it has been stated that 75 per cent of all information available throughout the history of the Earth has been created in the last twenty years. At the current rate of technological development the amount of information will double every ten years.

Historically, many of the early commercial computer systems were 'transaction processing' systems. As the name suggests these systems processed large amounts of data in a standard way. Examples include payroll, invoicing and stock systems. Many of these systems produced a range of management reports almost as a by product, which were often distributed throughout the organisation, whether anyone had asked for them or not.

In the police service, many of the early command and control and crime systems produced just such reports. In most cases, these were, and often still are, distributed without any assessment of the potential users and their needs. A small number of those receiving the information might be interested in it but many will not be, for several reasons:

- Managers receive so much information that eventually much of what they receive remains unread.
- The information is not consistent with their requirements. That is, it is not:
  - produced at the right time
  - in the required format
  - of sufficient detail
- A lack of awareness of what the information is telling them
- A lack of skills to enable the managers to interpret the information
- A lack of skills to enable the managers to decide whether the information is of value or not.

To illustrate this point, Houghton and Willis (1986) carried out some work with Northamptonshire Police which enabled a range of hitherto unavailable information to be provided to force managers. By utilising simple data analysis techniques, better use could be made of information within the force to support management decision making processes. They were thus able to produce such information as manpower deployment, demand patterns for police resources and crime trend analysis. The research found, however, that officers had considerable problems in interpreting the information. In addition, much of the information produced was new to the police managers and this lack of familiarity meant that the information was used less than optimally, if at all. There is a vast amount of information available to police managers; more than can be realistically managed. As long ago as 1984 Youell and Smart, in a study of police management information systems, suggested that:

- Police managers should be educated to ensure that they are aware of what management information is available to them.
- Police managers should receive training to show them how to use such information to best effect.
- Top management within police forces should actively support the development of the use of management information.

Over ten years later, there is considerable evidence that the same holds true.

Resource and Perception Driven Information

Harrington (1991) identified the provision of information in an organisation as resource driven. Information is a resource and as such is available to all. The skill of management is to identify exactly what information is of value, changing the emphasis to perception driven provision of information. The situation in the police service is further compounded by the underlying culture of INTI CIHAHI. This is not an ancient Aztec God or lost Inca city but an acronym for the conventional view of information provision within the police service:

'I Need That Information – 'Cos I Have Always Had It.'

There is an inherent reluctance to challenge the amount, nature and value of information provided to police managers. If a way is to be found through the mass of information bombarding police managers on a daily basis, this challenge has to be mounted.

As an illustration, some years ago, one information manager, new in post in an English force, was horrified to see up to one hundred standard management information reports distributed weekly across the force area. The cost and effort involved in this process was considerable. He therefore prohibited the sending of any of the reports for a two week period and received only two phone calls querying their absence (both from the same officer).

This exercise led to a needs identification programme which established the information requirements of each police manager and attempted to meet them. Where they could not be met, the exercise helped to develop future plans for information provision.

Clearly, then, if best use is to be made of information within the service, there is a need to find a way of assessing its value to the receiver. This will not only help to steer a course through the mass of information received by managers but will also help to make better use of information held within the force and identify any requirements not yet being met. In this way a force information policy and strategy (not information technology yet!) will begin to evolve.

Police managers have a major contribution to make to the process of improving the use of information across the force.

Individual managers must ensure that they have clearly identified their information needs in relation to their various roles and have communicated them clearly to the information providers. Force information managers must ensure that they are providing the relevant information to the right people, in the right format, at the right time and frequency. Force strategic managers must ensure that the resources and infrastructure are in place to enable the force information managers to fulfil those duties. They should, in addition, produce an information strategy and policy which will underpin the development of information as a resource within the force.

The Identification of Information Needs

The identification of information needs is dependent upon a number of criteria. The three main ones are outlined below.

The Managerial Role Being Adopted

Management textbooks are full of theory in relation to managerial roles. Many of the early pieces of work were normative. That is, they outlined the roles that managers should adopt rather than those which they actually adopted. The first major descriptive review of managerial roles was by Mintzberg (1973) and it identified ten separate roles which managers actually fulfilled. These varied from 'figurehead' to 'disseminator' to 'disturbance handler'.

Clearly, the role being adopted will influence the type of information required to help fulfil that role. The information to assist in the role of 'resource allocator' will be markedly different from that required to fulfil the 'spokesperson' role.

Organisational Objectives

Information requirements will be affected by the underlying objectives of the organisation, the department and even specific tasks. This is often when the 'nice to have' versus 'need to know' dichotomy becomes apparent. For example, when attempting to develop a media strategy there is a variety of information which might be available, which could include:

- The current force policy
- The number of people in the press office
- The number of radios in the press office
- The names of local papers
- The names of editors
- The current methods of media liaison
- ACPO guidance
- The standard of decoration in the press office.

However, when one considers the objective of such a strategy, it can be seen that much of the information which it is possible to collate is actually redundant. If the aim of such a strategy is to ensure that relevant information is being presented to the public via the most effective and appropriate channel, then some of the information listed above is not vital. For example, to meet that objective, is it really necessary to know the number of radios and the standard of decoration in the press office?

While this is a simplistic example, it illustrates the point. Referring back to the objectives or aims of a particular task, or even the force as a whole, can help to steer a course through the wealth of information available to police managers.

Individual Factors

The type and range of information required by managers is also influenced by their own personal styles and particularly their cognitive styles. The thought processes which managers use will have a considerable influence on their information needs. This is particularly true when managers are adopting decision making roles.

The analytical manager requires a wealth of information on which to base a decision. The heuristic manager on the other hand is far more interested in broad concepts than specifics and requires more broad based information. The movement of managers up the organisation requires a shift from analytical to heuristic styles.

To illustrate, a police manager might consider a report prepared by staff to support the decision to purchase a new computer. The heuristic manager is likely to require a summary of the main arguments for and against the purchase to support the decision making process. This is unlikely to satisfy the analytical manager who will probably require a full analysis of the arguments including costs, timescales and technical support data.

When assessing information needs, then, police managers need to be aware of those factors. Within that framework, however, they must also be aware of more detailed criteria. In an attempt to ensure sufficiency and currency of information, it is important that police managers consider the following:

- The depth/detail required: *for example, crime data by force or by division or by beat area?*
- The accuracy required: *for example, the divisional overtime budget by thousands of pounds or to the pound?*
- The frequency of reporting: *for example, the breakdown of incidents on a monthly or weekly or daily basis?*
- The speed of reporting: *for example, weekly incident figures by the end of the following week, or end of the following day?*
- The format required: *for example, crime data in a data table or in graphical format?*

It is clear that police managers have a considerable role to play in the effective use of information within the service. By identifying their own needs they can influence the shape of the systems designed to provide such information.

Information requirements, however, can and will change over time as individuals move throughout the organisation, adopt new roles and modify their management styles. The implication for those tasked with providing the systems designed to deliver the information in line with identified requirements, is that they should not develop such systems without continued liaison with the end user.

Provision of Information

It should not be felt that the views of managers regarding their information needs can be clearly gained by merely asking them. A perceptive study by Burgstaller and Forsyth (1973) identified five common responses by managers to the question, 'What information do you need to help you manage?' They classified five types of manager as a result:

- Bottomless Pit Manager: *Requires as much information as possible, 'just in case'.*
- Closed Door Manager: *Requires little or no information, 'just in case'.*
- Accounting Manager: *Only requires information of a financial nature, anything else is not really information.*
- In Basket Manager: *Only requires information which will enable him/her to carry out current tasks i.e. jobs in the in-tray at present.*
- Mississippi Gambler: *Unwilling to divulge information needs for a variety of political reasons.*

While it is unlikely that managers will adopt any of those stances fully, the work has identified some of the problems that information providers need to take account of in assessing information needs.

The role of the information provider is to bring a sense of realism to the identified needs. At the same time the needs have to be elicited in some way from the managers. The role of information professionals, therefore, is to find the most effective way of:

- Identifying information needs
- Collecting the desired information
- Storing the information
- Processing the information, if appropriate
- Disseminating the information

They therefore need to consider not only the systems to gather and process information, but also the means of ensuring that the required information reaches the relevant people at the appropriate time in the desired format. That is, they must consider the communications processes within the force.

Communications Strategies

The word 'communications' has particular connotations in a police environment. It is generally felt that any reference to communications must include radio communication and operational matters.

Fig 8.2: Generic structure for communication of non-operational information

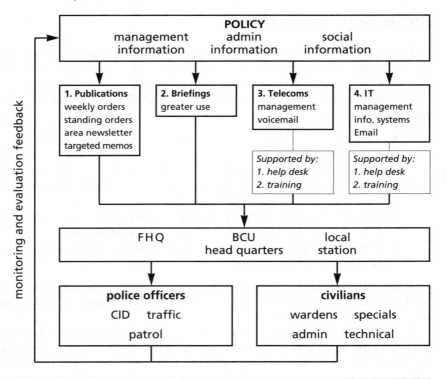

In fact forces must have strategies for the effective communication of both operational and non-operational information. These strategies must specify lines of communication and provide the structures to facilitate the passage of the relevant information to relevant individuals at the relevant time in the relevant formats. Technological aids are merely the vehicles which will enable the required information to be communicated in accordance with the strategies.

Figure 8.2 shows a generic structure for the communication of non-operational information throughout a police force which has been distilled out of a number of studies in recent years. It supports a downward but co-ordinated, structured flow of information with monitoring processes in place to capture feed back.

The structure also promotes bottom up communication of information to management. The proposed information flows are to location rather than individuals and this in turn provides a more streamlined model, consistent with the organisation.

Information Resource Management

Figure 8.3 reveals the cycle which information managers need to consider at all times. Their role is to reconcile managers and information to ensure that the former makes best use of the latter in the most effective way.

What information managers have to consider is a means of integrating information needs, information systems and communications structures within the force. In other words, they should work towards the development, implementation and co-ordination of:

- An information strategy for the force
- An information systems strategy for the force
- A communications strategy for the force.

This approach is known as Information Resource Management (IRM).

Fig 8.3: Information management cycle

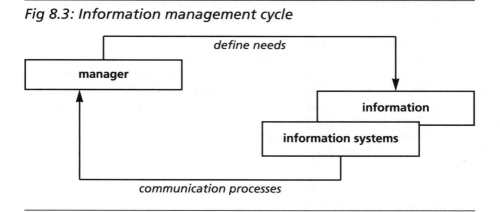

The information strategy defines standards for the utilisation of information across the force area. The information systems strategy specifies the standards for systems devised to gather and process the information. This invariably includes the utilisation of computing facilities within the force. The communications strategy outlines the vehicles for delivering the information to the appropriate manager.

Information Strategy

The prime objective of an information strategy is to maximise the value of information as an integral resource of the organisation. Drucker (1988) recognised that, increasingly, individuals will be responsible for identifying and meeting their own information needs. In this case, the organisation should therefore have a shared or unified vision which lays down corporate ground rules for the use of information. Lack of such ground rules may lead to the fragmentation of information around the organisation and the possibility of extensive data duplication.

This has particularly been the case in the UK police service. Lack of corporate direction with respect to the use of information has lead to multiple information and data sources between and within forces. Crime Pattern Analysis (CPA) is a classic example.

Where forces have been reticent to adopt CPA at a corporate level, 'pockets' of CPA systems have often emerged on some divisions. All are broadly similar, all trying to fulfil the same purpose, yet the presence of multiple systems in different divisions represents excessive duplication which is clearly not an effective use of resources. A clear policy with respect to the use of crime based information as a means of analysing patterns would address that problem. This might include establishing guidelines for such factors as the use of information in a CPA role and the methods of analysis.

An information strategy, therefore, contains the policies and procedures for the identification, management, protection and provision of information and for the sharing of information by authorised users. The establishment of such a strategy is now becoming increasingly accepted in the private sector. The process of establishing and maintaining such a strategy is sometimes referred to as 'data administration'.

Whilst it is not the purpose of this book to offer a treatise on information strategies, it may be valuable to consider some of the tasks required in their establishment:

- Identifying information needs
- Setting data definition standards and procedures for information sharing. This includes ensuring that information is consistent across the organisation, hence addressing problems of incompatibility.
- Identifying and managing corporate data and information flow models.
- Promoting an awareness of the role of information within the organisation, where it is, how it can be accessed and how it relates to other information.
- Establishing controls and procedures for security of information.

American information scientist John Diebold (1980) identified several core stages in the development of an information strategy:

- An awareness needs to be created within senior and executive managers regarding the need for, and value of, adopting an IRM approach. In other words, an IRM culture needs to be established and accepted by executive officers and promoted throughout the force.
- Data and intelligence should be gathered regarding information needs. The infrastructure should also be established to ensure that changing needs can be identified and addressed promptly. There should be regular, perhaps annual, reviews of information needs within forces and whether such needs continue to be met.
- An audit of current information provision should be carried out to identify what information is currently available and to what extent information needs are being met.
- The costs of current information provision should then be estimated. This will include not only a consideration of the cost of technology but also the costs of support staff. For example, when considering electronic mail as a means of providing non-operational information, the cost of staff to support the implementation and running of the system should be considered as well as the costs of hardware and software.
- The gaps between the current levels of information provision and information needs can then clearly be identified.
- From the preceding analysis, an 'ideal' model of information needs and use can be established. This will then form the framework for the development of systems to provide such information. In other words, it is the information policy for the organisation. For example, such an analysis may reveal serious gaps in the current crime reporting systems such that crime data cannot be analysed effectively. An enhanced crime reporting system can then form part of an information systems development strategy.

The establishment of an information strategy should therefore create a stable framework for the effective use of information. In so doing it should ensure that the organisation is better equipped with information and can thus respond more quickly and effectively to particular situations.

In addition, a clear information strategy should facilitate improved cross functional and cross departmental co-operation by making information available across boundaries to a wide group of authorised users. This in turn promotes the development of effective cross functional teams and integration of the organisation horizontally as well as vertically. Increasingly the police service is being required to operate in such a cross functional way.

Traditionally, crime prevention and C.I.D have been mutually exclusive functional areas of police work and never the twain shall meet. In recent times, encouraged by bodies such as the Audit Commission, crime management units have developed.

These units attempt to combine the preventative (proactive) police roles with the detective (reactive) roles. In other words, they are cross functional units. At their very heart is crime information and their success ultimately rests on the effective use of such information. Both preventative and detective functions share the same crime information to take an integrated approach to dealing with crime problems. Unless there is a clear view of what information should be used, how it should be processed, managed and shared, the success of such units is questionable.

Information Sharing Between Organisations

While a formal information strategy will help to facilitate the effective sharing of information within and between police forces, increasingly, there is a need to share information with other agencies.

The publication of the Morgan report (1991) has required the police to enter into effective partnerships with other agencies in an attempt to take an integrated approach to dealing with crime and offenders. To assess the scope and nature of problems to be addressed clearly requires a sharing of information. This has several implications, not the least of which is the need for the multi agency group to identify its own information needs.

Individuals within organisations find this task difficult enough. To bring together a group of managers from a wide range of organisations and backgrounds and ask them to identify their collective information needs is quite clearly problematic. The need to share information in a multi agency environment raises several other issues.

There is the question of confidentiality. Organisations are often reticent about releasing certain information to other organisations for fear of its abuse. For example, the police may be wary of releasing crime and criminal data fearing that other agencies might use it in a way which could compromise police operations. Similarly, drug support agencies may be fearful of releasing client data to the police as it may identify drug users otherwise unknown to the police.

In many ways there is no simple solution to this problem. Such suspicion can only be addressed by the building of trust between the relevant agencies. The continued giving of assurances that the information will not be used for other, non-specified, purposes and the continued adherence to these assurances is the only way in which such trust can be firmly established.

A more practical problem is that of non coterminous boundaries between agencies. In trying to build up a profile of an area, it may be desirable perhaps to utilise crime and criminal data, census and other socio-demographic data and social services data. It is highly unlikely that the geographical base for such information is the same for each of the agencies providing the information. Police beat areas will probably not follow the same boundaries as census enumeration districts. It is equally doubtful whether either of those data sources will share common boundaries with social service departments.

It is therefore often difficult, if not impossible, to compare and share information between agencies. If there is a significant difference between boundaries, then the resulting pooling of information is effectively a meaningless exercise. Indeed, the use of such information to establish co-ordinated policies is likely to be dangerous as it may present a picture which is not representative of the true situation.

Information Technology

As noted at the start of the chapter, there is often an assumption that to make best use of the information within the organisation it must be stored, processed and communicated using information technology. This is clearly not the case and considerable benefit can be gained by making better use of information which is held and transmitted either verbally or in 'hard copy' format such as books, journals and reports. However, it has to be said that the monumental advances in computing and information technology in the last quarter of a century have enabled the latent value of information to an organisation to be exploited.

It is not the aim of this book to outline the basic concepts of information technology. The market is flooded with books which can provide explanations of the different types of systems and interpret some of the jargon surrounding the subject.

As a police management text this book concerns itself with the management implications of using technology in general in the police service. This is covered in chapter nine. However, it is recognised that information technology does present special opportunities and problems. The rest of this chapter, therefore, explores some of the issues specific to information technology.

The Benefits of Information Technology

When considering the use of information in police forces, police managers must be aware of the benefits offered by utilising information technology (IT) as a means of making best use of the information.

Speed of Data Processing

There have been remarkable increases in processing power in recent years with an inexorable trend towards more and more power being focused in smaller and smaller systems. Where there is a large amount of data to be processed, to gain full value from the information, IT can be of considerable assistance. Most personal computer systems now operate at several million instructions per second. This is almost impossible to comprehend.

Accuracy

Computers will consistently carry out instructions on data with perfect accuracy. The argument which begins 'it's the computers fault' is fundamentally flawed. Effectively, computers will only do what they are instructed to do through the software which they utilise. The only reason a computer will make a mistake is if it has been given erroneous instructions or data.

Storage

Computers offer clear opportunities for the storage of vast amounts of information and data. Even personal computers now come with immense storage capabilities.

This book was written using a portable personal computer the size of an A4 pad of paper (though slightly thicker). It has a storage capability of 400 megabytes or approximately 400 million characters, one character equating to a letter, a number or a symbol. That level of storage capability will quite easily deal with force standing orders and a few years weekly orders.

Data Search and Analysis

Using IT opens up an enormous range of data searching and analysis facilities. Raw data can easily be converted into useful information by using the data manipulation capabilities of computers. Vast amounts of data can be searched according to very specific criteria to identify certain records. Systems such as HOLMES and crime pattern analysis are well documented examples of how IT can help in this way. IT also allows users to change their search parameters very quickly and as such approach a single set of data from various directions.

For example, you may wish to search a list of burglary data to identify patterns . in method of entry. You may wish to then analyse the same data for place of entry and then link the two. To carry out this type of analysis on a large amount of data would be almost impossible without the use of IT . Such analyses, however, might hold the key to solving a series of burglaries.

Cost Effectiveness

The huge advances in processing power and storage capabilities in recent years through technological development have drastically reduced the cost of computing. With regard to large amounts of data, the cost per unit of data processed using IT has plummeted in recent years such that it is now far lower than data processed manually.

Ease of Use

Despite the presence of a considerable 'fear factor' which faces most first time users, it is generally accepted that IT is very easy to use. Increasingly user friendly software such as *Windows*, which interfaces with the user in plain English and not jargon, has helped to foster this feeling. Several training organisations now offer courses entitled 'Computing for the terrified' which lead the novice user very gently through the process of learning to come to terms with using IT. This, too, has helped to promote an acceptance of IT as a tool which is relatively easy to use.

The first cohort of students who have been taught computing through their school careers have recently reached higher education. This reflects the fact that there is now a higher level of IT literacy amongst the general population and as time passes, this can only increase.

Presentation

Much data analysis software now offers a range of excellent presentation facilities such as graphic representation. This, allied to the growth of desktop publishing packages available on many systems, means that it has never been easier to produce a professional presentation of information. This in turn ensures that the information being presented stands a far greater chance of being understood and hence its value is greater.

These are just some of the benefits that IT can bring to those tasked with making better use of the information within the police service. The role of IT can be summed up in the following quotation from a presenter at a recent technology management conference at Brussels:

> *'What is about to engulf society is an ocean of words, writings, pictures, books, codes and symbols. In other words there will be information pollution. Computers and communications technologies together with supporting software are the means by which we will navigate our way through.'*

Before we get carried away and all rush out and buy a system, not surprisingly there are a number of disadvantages to using IT which should not be taken lightly. The police manager seeking to make better use of the information at his or her disposal should take account of these, as much as the potential benefits, before considering whether or not IT can be of assistance.

The Disadvantages of Information Technology

Costs

Quite simply hardware and software costs money. This cost can be small, for example personal computers can come complete with relevant software for less than one thousand pounds. On the other hand, costs can be extremely high, for example a force wide mainframe supporting a network and literally hundreds of terminals can run into tens of millions of pounds.

At the top of the range this obviously reflects a major investment and needs to be managed and planned for carefully over a period of years. The police manager must ensure that the most cost effective solution is provided to meet his or her requirements if IT is being considered. To give a simplistic example, you do not need a force wide mainframe if all you want to do is set up a simple financial spreadsheet.

It is doubly important, therefore, to identify your information needs, as this will clearly have implications regarding whether IT will be used to meet them and, if so, the type and size of computer which will be most appropriate.

Accuracy

Under benefits, it was stated that computers will always accurately carry out the instructions given to them. This is quite so, but what if the instructions are wrong? There is a well accepted acronym in computing circles which is GIGO. This stands for Garbage In, Garbage Out. A computer will only do what you tell it to do, it cannot differentiate right from wrong. It is in essence a stupid machine which slavishly follows instructions without question. If you wish to add up the force overtime budget and divide it by your shoe size using IT, the computer will not tell you that the result will be nonsense. It will merely carry out instructions.

This should be borne in mind at all times when using or considering using IT. One should not expect IT to do that which it is not capable of doing. This has been a major problem in police forces (and for that matter other organisations) in recent years. With the greatest of respect some senior officers have entered crime data onto a computer and expected the machine to produce full and clear analyses showing where the crime hotspots are.

Quite obviously the computer is capable of doing this but it has to be told how to do it. In other words complex programmes need to be written which instruct the computer to first of all find the data in its storage facilities and then analyse it in certain ways. The writing of these instructions, or the programming, is both time consuming and costly but is unavoidable if any benefit at all is to accrue from using IT. Police managers must not lose sight of this fact when considering using IT.

Interestingly, the episode with faulty pentium chips a few years ago, threw doubt on the supreme accuracy of IT. Flaws in the chip technology caused mistakes in the processing of numerical data. Some of the errors caused were significant but were not immediately identified due to a general feeling that the computer technology was infallible. It has to be said, however, that this was an extremely rare occurrence caused by a specific fault and that one can be confident that, in the future, IT will carry out instructions with total accuracy.

Maintenance

Information systems are sadly not 100 per cent fault free and the larger the system, the greater the need for special maintenance arrangements. Computers are complex machines with numerous components. Whilst reliability has improved dramatically in recent years with the advancement of chip technologies, faults are still experienced. As computers play a more important part in police forces, so, any faults have more and more serious implications for the smooth running of the service.

While a simple fault in a word processor, though inconvenient, can be tolerated, a failure in the force wide command and control system affects the fundamental operation of the force. As a result, detailed contingency plans need to be put in place to cater for such an event and a very tight maintenance arrangement agreed with suppliers to ensure that downtime is kept to a minimum. Many suppliers offer a one hour call out which ensures that an engineer is on site within one hour of a fault being reported. Failure to meet this deadline causes the supplier to incur financial penalties.

Clearly, maintenance facilities are expensive especially if one starts to consider arrangements similar to those outlined above. Hardware components are increasingly cheaper to replace and also more fault tolerant. Computer downtime is increasingly caused by software faults, a subject which is returned to later in the chapter.

Specialist Support

Information systems do not run themselves. There is a need to recruit specialist support staff responsible for providing such services as programming, technical support and advice and simple fault rectification.

The larger the computer installation and number of remote terminal sites, the more extensive this team needs to be. Again, such support staff are not cheap and in recent years there has been a relative shortage of suitably qualified individuals to fill such posts. This in turn has further increased the costs of such staff.

Training

While IT is now relatively simple to use very few systems can be used straight away without some level of training for users. Unfortunately, if an IT project is close to its budget limit or overspent, the first thing to be cut is often the training.

Though this may meet short term financial objectives it is unlikely to enable the system to meet its long term objectives. A failure to carry out training will mean that the potential benefits to be gained from the IT will probably not be achieved through a simple lack of understanding of what the system can do and how it works.

It is clear that training does incur costs. There is not only the cost of the training itself but also the cost of having someone away from their job while they are being trained. In these days of pressures on resources and ever rising abstraction rates, it is tempting to forego IT training. In the long term this might be a counter productive strategy to employ.

Security

It is true that all technology within the force should be protected as far as is practically possible. However, the security of information technology resources should be given particular attention. Information is the lifeblood of any organisation. If the security of that information is in any way compromised then the very existence of the organisation is threatened.

With the growth of ever more powerful but smaller computer systems, the threat to organisations through the loss of their information is greater than ever before. The sheer financial investment in IT means that there is a considerable amount of corporate capital tied up in IT. For this reason alone, it should be protected.

Wider use is made of information technology and this means that greater amounts of organisations' information is stored in vulnerable formats. It is hardly surprising then that IT security has assumed great importance in recent years. This certainly holds true for the police service.

There are several threats to information and IT security which need to be taken into account. Firstly there is the physical security of the IT and the information which it contains. Risks to be protected against include fire, flood, building collapse and illegal access. It is easy to imagine the chaos that could be caused to police operations if the IT installation caught fire or was flooded. Care must be taken when siting computer installations, particularly force wide systems. For example, siting the command and control system in the basement of a building next to a river with a flood record is not a good idea.

More sinister is the threat of illegal access. Terrorist organisations across the world have publicly stated that they view IT installations in general as legitimate targets. Again, the impact of terrorist access to a police IT installation is obvious. The bombing of a command and control installation or illegal access to, and corruption of, police incident data would be disastrous for any force and the service as a whole. Many major IT installations therefore operate tight access control policies with a system of concentric controlled perimeters. The IT installation sits at the centre of a series of concentric rings with access controls between each ring. This means that several levels of physical security need to cleared before anyone can gain access to the hardware installation at the centre.

The second group of security risks are those of system integrity. Many threats are posed by the very nature of the media and method of storing data, that is electronically. Errors in the software and other system threats, such as systems crashes and problems caused by power supply variation, can be equally as damaging to the integrity of the data as the physical threats referred to earlier.

Once such system faults are encountered there is often little that can be done to rectify the situation, though there are now a range of devices to ensure a smooth and uninterrupted power supply to the computer. The only way that organisations can protect their information from such threats is through a rigorous system of data back ups. This ensures that several sets of data are saved and retained in separate locations on a regular basis, usually daily. If the systems fail then the saved data can be reloaded once the system is running again.

A prolonged period of system downtime is, however, unacceptable to certain organisations including the police. Command and control systems cannot lie idle for a few days whilst repairs are effected. To address this situation, special maintenance contracts are negotiated which often include instant call out. Another solution to this type of problem is the so called "hot start" facility which enables saved data to be used on compatible machines held by a licensing organisation. A fee is paid to allow access to these machines.

The third and most rapidly growing form of IT security threat is that of computer crime. The continuing miniaturisation of systems means that it is very easy to steal hardware and software. This threat must be countered as such theft could have dire consequences for the victim organisation. The theft of a personal computer containing localised crime records and crime pattern analysis could prove very damaging if it fell into the wrong hands. It would also be deeply embarrassing to the police. A clear example was the theft of a computer containing military operations relating to the Gulf War, from a car during the height of the campaign.

Computer crime can also take other forms however. There has been a widespread growth of computer fraud and 'hacking' in recent years. Computer fraud can be defined as 'the abuse of authorised access to IT', whereas hacking is defined as 'unauthorised access to IT'.

Films such as *War Games* have amply demonstrated the potential threats posed by individuals hacking into 'sensitive' systems. A hacker gaining illegal access to police computer facilities could be extremely popular with members of the criminal fraternity. Similarly, if those with authorised access to police systems, for example, those employed by the service, were to abuse that authority and make illicit use of confidential data, considerable damage could again be caused to police operations.

Any individual working within the police service who uses or has control of IT needs to be aware of the potential problems of fraud and hacking. Tight password and access control can go some way to restricting the opportunity for such illegal, or abuse of, access. This can be supported by rigorous recruitment procedures to ensure that those employed are trustworthy.

However, at the end of the day, there are ever more opportunities for individuals to make unauthorised use of information to which they have access. The most powerful security measure for police managers in this area is, therefore, continued vigilance.

Data Protection

To protect the abuse of certain kinds of data, the Data Protection Act became law in 1984. This Act relates to personal data and only such data which is 'automatically processed'. In other words, the Act only covers information recorded on a computer about living, identifiable individuals. It does not cover information held and processed manually or data which relates to a company or an organisation.

Those using and processing personal data must become a registered data user. In registering, the data users must state what personal data they will be gathering; why they will be using it; how they will gather and store it. All persons using that information must ensure that it is not passed on or used in any unauthorised way. Individuals found to have permitted the unauthorised use or disclosure of such information can face prosecution, together with their organisation.

The Data Protection Act also requires that an individual can demand to see what personal data relating to them is held on computer by any organisation. This might at first glance seem to compromise much of the data held on police systems, especially intelligence data. If the neighbourhood villain can demand to see what information the police have on him then he would clearly be able to modify his actions accordingly and perhaps not carry out a robbery which the police have been 'tipped off' about.

For this reason, certain types of data are exempt from the provisions of the Act. Data which, if disclosed, would materially affect the prevention or detection of crime and the apprehension or prosecution of offenders, is exempt from the provisions of data disclosure. In other words the neighbourhood villain cannot go into a police station and demand to see what computerised data is held by the police about him if its disclosure is likely to affect police operations. However, such data still has to be registered.

The Data Protection Act, while protecting individual rights, has placed a burden on those using IT to ensure that data which falls under the provisions of the Act is registered and used in an authorised way. This represents another potential disadvantage in using IT as similar data held manually does not need to be registered and controlled.

By listing both benefits and disadvantages of IT the point is reinforced that IT is not a panacea for information processing problems. Sometimes IT can create more problems than it solves and any introduction of IT into an organisation needs to be managed very carefully. Thought needs to be given to how information is to be used in police forces and whether or not IT can contribute to its use.

Too often police forces have been blinded by the jargon of the IT sales staff and have bought systems which, quite clearly with hindsight, make little contribution to the operations of the force.

Police IT phases

The development of IT in the police service has followed three distinct phases. The first phase was the implementation of force wide mainframe systems in the early to mid 1980s which underpinned force operations such as command and control or crime reporting systems.

The second phase corresponded with the growth of the personal computer which brought computing to the masses. Prior to the growth of the personal computer computing was very much the province of the expert but the personal computer meant that many people had access to systems. Computing as a concept began to be 'demystified' and individuals began to understand the vast potential that personal computers could offer. What emerged, therefore, in this second phase was the 'enthusiastic amateur' developing personal computer based systems at a local level. Examples include divisionally based false alarm activation systems, keyholder registers and duty rosters.

In many forces, this resulted in a mix of force wide systems and incompatible local systems, many of which were duplicated across divisions. In short a confused and less than effective use of IT.

The third phase has been characterised by a move towards the integration of force wide and divisional systems into a strategic approach to IT development in forces. The establishment, in 1995, of the National Strategy for Police Information Systems (NSPIS) has attempted to promote this by setting down national standard guidelines for forces to follow when developing IT.

Embracing thirty eight separate police data applications, it is the stated vision of NSPIS to move to a position where all forces in England and Wales under Home Office control work together to develop a service wide Information Systems (IS) strategy. That is, a strategy which takes account of information needs and delivers the systems which will meet those needs. It seeks to achieve this by controlling:

- The development of standard IS applications for forces
- The development and maintenance of hardware specifications
- The development and maintenance of software specifications

Whether this ambitious approach will achieve its stated aim is open to some conjecture. Previous attempts at service wide strategies have generally made little impact, and time will tell whether this latest development will be successful. Early indications suggest that there are concerns in some quarters that NSPIS is too centralised in its approach. This, allied to problems of resourcing and the sheer logistics of combining a large number of disparate projects, suggest that NSPIS might have a difficult future.

What is clear is that police managers must seek to develop a strategic approach to the use of IT in forces. The continued development of localised, incompatible systems which are not linked to any long term IT development plan will only serve to limit the effectiveness of IT within the police service. The subject of technology strategies in general will be covered in more detail in chapter nine.

Chapter Summary

- Information should not be confused with information technology.

- Data should not be confused with information.

- There are different categories of information which can be used at different levels in, and are of distinct value to, the organisation.

- Management information supports the decision making functions of managers.

- The emerging problem of information overload is primarily caused by confusion, or lack of understanding, regarding individual information requirements.

- There is a need to switch from resource driven to perception driven provision of information. Individual managers must identify their own information needs.

- Information professionals should support managers by providing and managing a strategic framework which ensures that individual and corporate information needs are met. This should include the establishment of a formal communications strategy.

- The sharing of information between agencies is fraught with potential problems which should be addressed before such information is used as a basis for decision making.

- The potential benefits and disadvantages of using IT to support the use of information should be fully considered before any decision is taken to use IT.

- A strategic and co-ordinated approach to the development of IT in police forces should be taken.

Chapter 9

Managing Technology

Introduction

'The science of muddling through.'

Lindblom

The shorter Oxford English Dictionary defines technology as:

'...mechanical arts and applied sciences and their application in industry.'

It is important to establish a definition for technology, as such an all embracing term means different things to different people.

In the police environment in recent years, technology has come to mean information technology or computers. However, technology covers other kinds of support aids to the police service which have little connection at all. These 'other' kinds of technological support also need to be managed.

This chapter outlines why technology should be managed and the role of police managers in doing so. It then identifies the range of technology in use within the police service today.

Having said that technology is more than computers, much of the chapter will use the management of information technology (IT) as an illustration. The main reason is that IT is becoming pervasive in the modern police service and as such needs to be managed more carefully. However, the principles outlined in relation to the management of IT apply equally to other aspects of technology.

Why Manage Technology?

Technology is another resource to be used in helping to achieve the aims and objectives of the organisation. As such, it needs to be managed, just like other resources available to the police service, notably people, finance and information. There are three additional reasons why technology needs to be managed.

Firstly, technology, in whatever form, is expensive and it must be managed carefully to ensure that the financial resources of the police service are utilised as effectively as possible. In other words, technology needs to be managed to maximise its cost effectiveness. For example, the service needs to ensure that it has the best deal in purchasing its patrol cars and it needs to ensure that the vehicles are regularly serviced in accordance with manufacturers' specifications in order that the technology performs as required. The process of ensuring that vehicles are serviced when required is part of making cost effective use of the investment in technology and needs to be managed.

Police managers therefore need to ensure that the process of procuring technology is controlled and that the best financial deal is agreed for the appropriate equipment. In addition, they must ensure that such equipment is used as cost effectively as possible within the force, once it has been procured.

Secondly, the police service, like any organisation, is there to meet the needs of its customers. The various forms of technology can be used to provide a better service to those customers. Police managers need to consider how technology can assist them in providing a better service to their customers.

To illustrate, consider whether patrol cars or bicycles provide a better service to the public. One might argue that there is a place for both forms of technology. A patrol car clearly provides a better service in responding quickly to incidents, but it could be held that an officer on a bicycle provides a better service in terms of strengthening links with the local community. Indeed several forces have now returned to using bicycles for precisely that reason.

These are exactly the issues which police managers need to consider; that is, ensuring that the appropriate form of technology is applied to the relevant area of work to maximise the benefits to customers, both internal and external.

Thirdly, technology in all of its guises changes so rapidly. It is important that the police service is aware of such changes and can take advantage of any benefits which may accrue to the service as a result. Who would have thought that IT in particular would have made such spectacular advances in the last ten years? When one considers that, less than twenty years ago, personal computers did not exist as such, the pace of technological development becomes very clear. Now many homes have computers considerably more powerful than the early mainframe type systems which took up large rooms and even whole buildings. It is the responsibility of police managers to ensure that the latest technological developments are taken account of.

What is Technology in a Police Environment?

We have already indicated that the term technology should embrace technical aids other than computers but what exactly does the term encompass? If one gave slavish adherence to the definition of technology, it could be argued that pens and pencil sharpeners, should be included and that they too should be managed. Whilst their use should be controlled, clearly, this is stretching the definition of technology somewhat.

A review of the police service indicates that there are perhaps four main categories of technology in use which individually comprise a significant component of the assets of forces. These are:

- Vehicle fleet
- Technical aids
- Operational communications technologies
- Information technology

Vehicle Fleet

The earliest introduction of technology into police forces in any significant way was through the adoption of vehicles to support police work. The vehicle fleet can vary from patrol motorcycles, through incident response vehicles, to top of the range saloons required for motorway patrol work. At the less glamorous end, however, the force vehicle fleet will also include pedal cycles (some forces now even use mountain bikes) and a number of vans for the transporting of various items around the force area.

Anyone who has recently bought a new car will realise just how expensive vehicles now are. Indeed, the purchase and maintenance of the police vehicle fleet now involves millions of pounds per year. The spend on new and replacement vehicles by police forces is now estimated to be in excess of £50 million per year. When one adds the costs of maintenance, it can be seen that a vast amount of police financial resources is used annually in maintaining and developing the vehicle fleet to ensure that it continues to provide effective support to the service. It is little wonder, then, that the police vehicle market is coveted by most of the major vehicle manufacturers. Not only is it high profile business, it also represents a considerable financial opportunity.

Technical Aids

This is something of a 'catch all' category but includes such technology as surveillance equipment, video and closed circuit television installations (CCTV) and intruder alarms owned by the police.

There have been major advances in the technological base in this area in recent years and accordingly there has been a significant increase in the amount and value of such technical aids used by police forces.

Many police installations, from individual stations to headquarters complexes, are now protected by comprehensive CCTV systems. These installations need to be managed and they are not cheap.

In addition, a wide range of technical aids are available to support proactive initiatives designed to prevent crimes and apprehend criminals, from the humble intruder alarm to the latest surveillance and eavesdropping equipment. Not surprisingly, it is difficult to identify the extent of utilisation of this latter category of equipment and the amount of spend on it. However, it is clear from reports of police operations in the media that state of the art technology is increasingly being used to support the work of the service. This clearly carries with it a cost and hence the procurement, maintenance and utilisation of these technical aids is something which needs to be managed very carefully.

Communications Technology

A long serving police officer was recently heard to say, 'whatever did we do without radios?' This illustrates that communications technology has become easily the most accepted and loved technical aid to the service over the years.

Communications technologies comprise primarily personal radios and other means of voice communication. Whilst there is an increasing convergence of communications technologies and information technologies, communications are still widely regarded as relating to the use of personal radios.

More than any other form of technical assistance to the service, personal radios have been accepted by all officers to be of considerable value. Given that all officers now go on patrol with a radio, it means that no officer is isolated from fellow officers and the control room in their station. This, in turn, means that an officer who encounters a dangerous situation can quickly call for help. This is clearly more reliable and more effective than the old police whistle or the shout for help.

Communications technology is the most pervasive form of technical help utilised in the police today. While all patrol officers are allocated a radio, they do not necessarily have free and open access to vehicles or computers for example.

However, as radio is so pervasive in the service, this again means that a considerable amount of force funding is tied up in the provision and maintenance of this technology.

This includes not only the actual radios themselves, but also the costs of control rooms and radio masts and the costs of staff to run the control rooms and support the use of the communications technologies. In 1999 a four year roll out programme will equip all forces in the UK with radio equipment which will, for the first time, provide them with a secure system, giving almost total geographical cover and a host of "value added" features. This new Public Safety Radio Communications Project (PSRCP) offers significant improvements on the current radio systems but the estimated costs for completion have varied between £800 million and £1.5 billion.

The role of the police manager is again crucial in ensuring that this form of technology is utilised as cost effectively as possible and that the latest developments (of which there are many in this field) are taken account of.

While considerable assistance in this particular field is given to forces by the Home Office, individual force managers still need to consider the most appropriate form of technology for the force and manage it accordingly.

Information Technology

Only perhaps fifteen years ago information technology in police forces, or computing as it was then referred to, was extremely limited. Those forces having any computing support at all either had a command and control system or a crime reporting and recording system. Very few forces had both (many still do not have, although most now have either one or the other).These systems were extremely expensive, large and resource hungry.

In the early 1980s the world entered the information age with the development, in a humble garage in Palo Alto, California, of the first personal computer. The police service, like most other organisations, was caught up in IT fever and during this period, there was an explosion in the use of IT to support the work of the service. The pace of technological change and the push for the adoption of information technology by police forces has been almost irresistible. Even now, forces are beginning to explore how the Internet can be used to their advantage. Strathclyde Police are now even advertising for recruits on the Internet, a strategy which has already generated phenomenal interest. Whether the use of IT in the service has been applied to the most important areas, or in a co-ordinated way, is open to question, and will be explored in greater detail.

What is not open to question is the fact that spending on IT in the police service has followed an almost exponential path during the last fifteen years. The estimated spending by police forces in England and Wales in 1996/7 is in excess of £65 million and, additionally, almost £30 million was spent on information services which include such central facilities as PNC.

Clearly vast sums of money are tied up in the provision of police IT systems. As a result, in this area of technology as opposed to any other, doubts are being expressed regarding whether value for money is being achieved. The potential benefits of IT to the service are clear. However, faced with a mind boggling array of systems, the breathless pace of technological change, technical jargon and persuasive sales teams, some police forces have adopted systems which have been seen to be less than cost effective.

In addition, the lack of a clear strategy for the development of IT has lead to the emergence of pockets of automation in many forces. This in turn has led to a duplication of similar applications, often running on incompatible systems within forces. This is certainly not a cost effective use of technology.

The role of the police manager is again very clear. In chapter 8, we saw the need to establish information requirements. This will help to identify the appropriate information system which then needs to be managed as do other technological aids to the service. Management issues relate not only to the hardware and software but also to the staff required to support the use of the IT and the infrastructure within which they operate.

The Technology Management Cycle

The management of technology follows a simple cycle. Obviously, each stage in the cycle comprises a complex set of processes and full use should be made of technical specialists wherever possible to complete each stage of the cycle. Figure 9.1 outlines the broad stages and police managers need to be clear about their roles and responsibilities at each stage of the cycle.

Fig 9.1: The technology management cycle

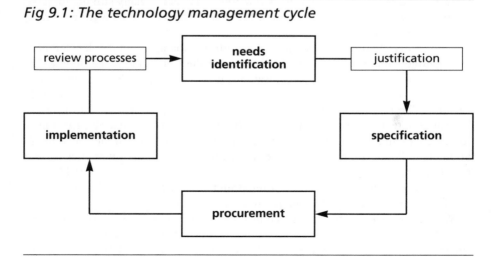

Identifying the Need

It is obvious that a need should be identified before the adoption of any technology into the force is actively considered. In the case of replacement of existing or obsolete technology, this process is relatively simple. When a model of existing patrol vehicle becomes obsolete, superseded by a more advanced model or simply life expired, the need to update the technology is clear. There is an acceptance that the force will use vehicles and therefore the only decisions which need to be taken relate to when to replace and with what.

In the case of new technology, the process becomes more complex. In the late 1980s, police forces across England and Wales were faced with an increasing mountain of paperwork which was threatening to swamp them. A lengthy study within West Midlands Police led to an administrative restructuring of part of the force and the development of Administrative Support Units or ASUs. These units centralised much of the post charge, pre court paperwork on division and provided a more streamlined service to the rest of the division. As a result of this work, ASUs began to spring up all over the country.

It became clear as ASUs developed, that there would have to be a level of IT support to enable the vast amounts of data to be processed effectively. In other words, the development of an ASU structure identified the need for IT support. If a force wished to adopt the ASU as a concept it was almost bound to take on the technology to support it.

The manager's role is therefore to identify the need for technological support and justify decisions for new and replacement technology. What criteria can police managers use to help them in this process?

In the late 1980s, Earl and Runge looked at the methods used in the private sector to justify spending on information technology. They argued that as the benefits accruing from IT were difficult to quantify, it was almost impossible to justify expenditure on IT in purely financial terms, using such criteria as return on capital employed.

A similar argument can be applied when considering the adoption of technology in the police service and even the public sector as a whole. When the organisation is non-profit making and non-sales based it is impossible to justify expenditure on technology in financial terms. Return on capital employed and increased sales and market share arguments cannot be used in organisations which do not make a profit or sell anything.

Managers in such organisations should not just shrug their shoulders and say "never mind". They need to be given some assistance in identifying a need for technological assistance. Several pieces of work have been produced to try to find a non-financial means of justifying expenditure on information technology. However, most of these relate to the private sector and include such factors as how technology can build competitive barriers and grow market share. These obviously do not apply in organisations such as the police service where effectively there are no competitors and the organisation already has total market domination.

A partial solution might be through adapting a piece of work carried out in 1984. Although relating to private sector organisations and looking only at information technology, some aspects of this work can help police managers to identify the need for, and hence justify, the use of technology in the service.

Two American management scientists, Ives and Learmonth suggested that the products that an organisation provides to its customers are, from the customers perspective, resources. In police terms, the services provided by the police are resources for the public to call on as and when they need them.

Ives and Learmonth went on to suggest that customers go through 13 stages in acquiring and using these services and they called this process the Customer Resource Life Cycle (CRLC).They concluded that, if an organisation could help the customer deal with all or some of these stages, then it would gain competitive advantage and hence grow its market share. They further stated that, if IT could be seen to support the organisation in doing so, then expenditure on the IT was justified.

Not all of the stages are appropriate for non-profit making, service based organisations, but some are. Modifying these arguments for the police service, it could be argued that if technology (not just information technology) can assist customers (both internal and external) at any stage in the CRLC, then its use can be justified. In other words, the need has been identified. Table 9.2 (below) outlines the stages of the Ives and Learmonth model appropriate to technology in the police service.

Table 9.2: Police resource life cycle applied to the justification of technology

Does the technology help the customer to:

- Establish the amount of service required?
- Establish the specific attributes and nature of the services required?
- Identify the specific source of the required services?
- Acquire the required services?
- Monitor the use and effectiveness of the services provided?
- Amend the level of services provided if conditions change?

It should be remembered that police customers can be both external, for example the general public, and internal, for example fellow officers. When viewed in this light it becomes clear that perhaps the arguments outlined in table 9.2 can be used to identify the need for, and justify the use of, technology. The more of these criteria which are relevant to the technology being considered, the more justified is the expenditure. This in turn helps to set some form of priority listing for technological applications competing for limited funds. Interestingly, all of these criteria relate in some way to the provision of services to customers, which is clearly the core business of the police service.

To illustrate, let us assume that an officer is attending an incident of public disorder late one night in a town centre. He is the customer. By using his radio he can establish the amount of requirement (I need five officers to help me) and the nature of the requirement (make one a dog handler). Control room staff, by using a command and control system, can identify the source of the services required (officers to attend from neighbouring beats and dog handler from headquarters). Vehicles can be used to transport the officers to the required location, assisting the customer to acquire the services. Through constant radio contact the provision of services can be monitored and the level of service amended as required (the situation is getting out of hand, send five more officers).

Communications, vehicle and information technology have supported the delivery of services in this example and in doing so have justified themselves.

Consider now the systems to support the development of Administrative Support Units. You may wish to consider who are the customers and what are the services being provided. This will help to identify whether or not some of the technology utilised in ASUs is justified. At the other end of the scale consider now the situation where a force might be considering the use of motorised unicycles as a fast pursuit vehicle on off-road terrain. Would this meet the justification criteria?

The role of the manager in justifying technology is clear. Given that the need for technology has been identified, what is the next stage?

Specification of the Required Technology

A clear specification needs to established for the technology required by the force. This can vary from a simple order for a clearly defined piece of equipment to a complex document which forms the basis of contractual arrangements, such as a specification for a crime reporting computer system.

The role of the police manager is crucial at this stage as is the ultimate user of the technology. For smaller pieces of technology specific users can be canvassed for their views regarding the precise specification. However, for larger specifications, it is likely that the views of a representative cross section of users will be gathered. For example, where a force is seeking to upgrade its motorcycle fleet a sample of motorcycle patrol officers should be approached and asked if they require any particular features to be built into the specification.

For very large specifications, such as a new force wide command and control system, it is likely that a project team will be assembled to specify, procure and implement the system. The team should either contain representatives of potential user groups or ensure that the views of such groups are taken into account.

The specification should state a number of factors which will assist potential providers of the technology to suggest products which will clearly meet needs. To enable this to happen the specifiers need to have a clear understanding of:

- The need for the technology
- The current situation in the area in which the technology will be sited
- The feasible technological solutions

This is particularly the case with respect to information technology and communications technologies. Before a specification can properly be prepared for a new IT system there needs to be clear justification for the system; a consideration of the feasible options; an analysis of current systems and a broad design which outlines the structure of the required system. Only then can a true specification be prepared.

This all sounds very logical but the police service is littered with examples of where technology failed to deliver what was expected of it. Whilst not always the case, many of the reasons arise from errors at the specification stage. Figure 9.3 illustrates succinctly some of the problems which can arise at this stage.

Fig 9.3: The dangers of a loosely managed specification process

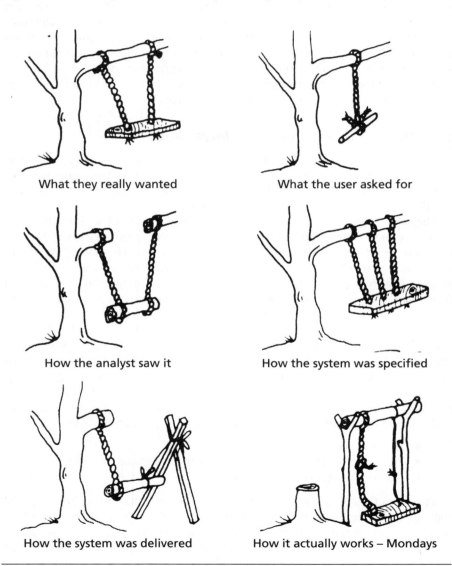

What they really wanted

What the user asked for

How the analyst saw it

How the system was specified

How the system was delivered

How it actually works – Mondays

The importance of the specification stage cannot be stressed too highly. Unless the needs of the user and the force are clearly identified and clearly documented and communicated, then it is highly likely that a less than optimal solution will ensue. One can hardly blame a supplier who provides what was specified if what was specified was not exactly what was required.

The specification process, therefore, needs to be managed and controlled extremely carefully. At the heart of the process is communication. Views of all interested parties need to be taken into account and reflected in the specification, which in turn should be clearly communicated to potential suppliers to minimise the potential for misinterpretation.

Each specification will be different, and as it is likely to be the only document which potential suppliers will use to assess your requirements, it needs to be as clear and detailed as possible. Specifications should, therefore, contain information regarding:

- The precise product or service required. *For example, the specification for a fast pursuit vehicle should not say we require a car, but rather a three litre saloon, with five gears and four doors.*

- The performance standard required. *For example, for the fast pursuit vehicle, the force may wish to state that the vehicle must be capable of 0 – 60 mph in four seconds.*

- Any special features required. *For example, all vehicles must be painted bright yellow.*

- The required support and maintenance to be provided to ensure that the technology continues to meet requirements. *For example, the specification may include the precise nature of maintenance required for its vehicles and suppliers may be asked to quote for providing such services.*

Police managers responsible for developing specifications must ensure that any documentation produced contains these items as a minimum. Police managers, as users, must ensure that their views and requirements are reflected in each of the areas listed above.

It should be noted that, in relation to information technology in particular, there has been the growth in recent years of what has come to be termed prototyping and end user computing. This means that IT systems can developed more cheaply, quickly and effectively by utilising special software. All that is required is a basic user requirement rather than a detailed specification. A specialist programmer then sits down with the prospective system user and, using the software, builds a prototype system which through test and modification, evolves into the required system.

While this is undoubtedly quick, its application is limited at present to relatively small, specialist computer applications. It is also relatively expensive and requires a knowledgeable user to be available for a considerable period of time whilst the prototype is developed and modified.

Police managers need to be aware that prototyping will significantly affect the scope and content of the specification document if it is to be used.

Once the technology required has been clearly specified then the next stage of the cycle is activated.

Technology Procurement

It is recommended that, if the force has a designated purchasing officer, then he or she should be consulted at this stage, irrespective of the size of the technology required, either in physical or financial terms. Alternatively the force finance officer might wish to be involved.

For major technological procurement it is recommended that a procurement strategy is adopted. This will invariably involve a formal tendering procedure.

There are two broad options under the tendering process. Either specific organisations can be invited to tender or a general advertisement can be placed and any interested parties can respond. Where specific organisations are to be invited, the first step is clearly to identify possible suppliers of the technology. In many cases these will be organisations already known to specific forces. The danger with this approach is that other organisations may provide a better product and solution but, as they may not be known to forces, they are prohibited from tendering.

At the heart of the tendering process is the formal invitation to tender (ITT) which is issued to potential suppliers. This document will vary in complexity, dependent upon the goods being tendered for. For example, the ITT for an administrative support unit computer system will be far more complex than an ITT for, say, 10 microwave ovens to re-equip all the force canteens.

Having said that, all ITTs should contain some information under the following headings:

- Current situation: *There should be a brief description of the current situation to which the technology relates.*

- Reasons for the technology: *A brief description should be provided which outlines the reasons behind the need for the technology. For example, the force requires twenty CD ROM personal computers to carry out crime pattern analysis which will support the move towards divisional crime management units.*

- Detailed specification: *The specification described earlier should then be provided. It is important that this is as detailed as possible as this is the primary document upon which suppliers will base their suggested product solutions.*

- Costing data: *The ITT should indicate to potential suppliers how the cost of the tendered product is to be recorded. Suppliers are usually encouraged to suggest at least two prices; one for the outright purchase of the product or service; one for the lease or rent of the product or the service. The ITT should in these cases require potential suppliers to supply details of the lease or hire arrangements being tendered.*

- Reference sites: *Where the ITT relates to a major procurement, the ITT should request that potential suppliers should suggest reference sites where the products tendered can be demonstrated. Where possible reference sites relate to product sites already existing in a similar environment. For example, if a force is looking for an electronic mail system it should ask in its ITT for names of other forces using the system proposed and contact names in those forces. These forces can then be contacted and their views sought regarding the system proposed and, if possible, a demonstration arranged. Where no live sites are available, the ITT should require potential suppliers to provide details of demonstrations which they can provide on their premises.*

- Financial details: *For a major procurement, potential suppliers should be asked to provide details of their financial position. This will usually require the previous two years annual financial reports to be incorporated in the response to tender. The reasons for this are clear. A force does not want to spend possibly millions of pounds with one organisation only for that organisation to go out of business, leaving the force without support. This is particularly pertinent with respect to the procurement of IT. There are several examples of forces purchasing IT only to be left a few months later with hardware and software which could not be supported and maintained due to the supplier going bankrupt.*

- Contractual arrangements: *The ITT should also contain any special contractual requirements which the potential supplier must meet. For example, there may be standard clauses in procurement contracts to which all suppliers will be expected to agree.*

- Supplier information: *The ITT should request that potential suppliers provide a range of material which outlines their range of activities and products or services.*

The invitation to tender, once agreed, can be issued to those organisations invited to tender, or to those responding to advertisements appearing in the press. Potential suppliers will be given a suitable period in which to respond to the tender. The exact period is dependent upon the complexity of the ITT but is commonly between two and four weeks.

A deadline is set for the responses to the ITT to be received and, strictly, any received after the deadline or not in the prescribed format, should be ignored.

Once the deadline has passed all of the responses should be reviewed against set criteria and either a decision taken regarding the preferred supplier, or a shortlist prepared, and those on the shortlist requested to provide further details. These details will then help to assess which supplier should be chosen.

The setting of criteria is crucial to the procurement process. If inappropriate criteria are chosen, then there is a strong possibility that the wrong supplier may be selected. Examples of selection criteria can include cost, performance, maintenance and support. Weights can also be applied to certain criteria and scores calculated for each response to the tender. The highest scoring response should then be the one which is chosen. For example, cost and maintenance may be important criteria but cost could be twice as important and hence would receive twice the score of any other factor.

For major procurements, project teams often identify criteria and select the winner from the tendering process over a weekend, often away from their place of work. This helps to focus minds on the issues in hand and facilitate the selection of the relevant supplier.

An emerging trend in procurement is that of consortia of buying organisations grouping together to get a better deal from suppliers. Using economies of scale arguments, some forces have come together to bulk purchase certain goods to gain a keen price and a superior specification. This type of arrangement is increasingly found with respect to the purchase of vehicles by forces.

A variation of this is the emergence of bodies such as ESPO (Eastern Shires Purchasing Organisation). This is a consortium of local authority departments (including police) in the shire counties of eastern England. All major items being purchased, technologically based or not, have to go through ESPO. In this way the best deals can be gained for members of the consortia. Forces facing a future of cash limited budgets should be increasingly looking to join with other forces to ensure that the best possible deals are achieved.

Once the technology has been procured then it needs to be brought into the organisation and incorporated in such a way that disturbance is minimised.

Implementation

Again, the nature of the technology and the size of the procurement will influence how it is implemented in the force. Our 10 microwave ovens can be implemented relatively easily but the introduction of a force-wide electronic mail system will need very careful planning. In addition, a full programme of training will need to be established to ensure that everyone in the force is aware of what electronic mail can do and how it can work.

Implementation planning should be considered as part of the overall project planning and this is dealt with more fully in chapter 10. However, certain potential problems can emerge when technology is implemented into an organisation (particularly when it is new to the organisation), which need to be anticipated and addressed. These problems are most commonly experienced during the implementation of communications and information technologies.

To many employees, such technologies are foreign. There is often much ignorance about IT and communications technology which in turn fuels fear. The two main fears of new technology are:

- A fear of failure, in other words a fear that individuals will not be able to cope with the new technology.
- A fear of the changes in the social environments and working practices brought about by the introduction of new technology.

These fears are also rooted in change and can be the cause of resistance to the introduction of new technologies. Kwiatkowski (1989) suggested that all individuals passed through a seven stage transition curve during the process of change. Levels of competence and acceptance of change vary with respect to the position of the individual on the curve. Figure 9.4 shows the transition curve for the introduction of technological change into an organisation.

Fig 9.4: Transition curve for acceptance of technological change

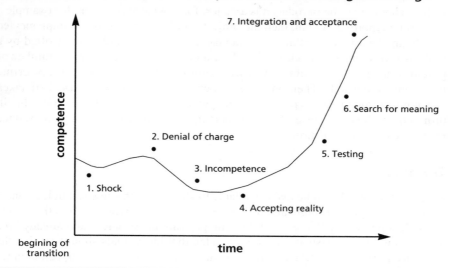

Kwiatkowski holds that individuals pass through the following stages. It might be interesting to consider whether you have experienced these stages to any degree when going through the introduction of new technologies into your force.

- Shock: *A sense of panic at the effects of the impending change.*

- Denial of change: *An illogical rejection of new technologies and a reversion to old methods of working.*

- Incompetence: *An acceptance that things must change but insecurity regarding how the changes will be successfully assimilated.*

- Accepting reality: *An acceptance that change is inevitable and new technologies must be tried.*

- Testing: *The trying and testing of new technologies.*

- Search for meaning: *A period of reflection to put new technologies and approaches into perspective.*

- Integration and acceptance: *The full acceptance of the technology and integration of it into working practices.*

Any plan to implement technologies into the force must address the fears and associated resistance of those tasked with using the technology. The implementation plan must therefore help individuals find their way smoothly along the transition curve. There are several ways of easing the introduction of technology, particularly new technology, into an organisation and these are equally valid in police forces.

179

Teams

If the technology to be introduced is a major, force wide application, for example a new crime reporting system, then the project should be managed and implemented by a team. That is, the technology management cycle should be controlled by a multi disciplinary team. This team should contain a representative number of potential users of the technology, for example CID, administration or crime management unit staff. Their presence will ensure that the views of users are taken account of throughout the process from specification to implementation. This in turn helps to foster a sense of user ownership of the new technology and reduce resistance to its introduction.

Training

Relevant training should be made available to all users of the new technology and a formal training plan established to ensure that everyone who requires training is given the opportunity to receive it. Despite pressure on resources and already high abstraction rates, it is strongly recommended that individuals should receive the appropriate training. Failure to receive such training is in the long run counter productive and restricts the full achievement of potential benefits offered by the technology.

Managing Expectations

Once there is an acceptance of change, individuals' expectations of the technology may be unrealistic. These need to be managed carefully as failure to do so may fuel dissatisfaction with the technology and, ultimately, rejection. This was the case with early crime pattern analysis systems. A lack of understanding of their purpose and capabilities led to unrealistic expectations of such systems. As the systems continued to fail to meet these expectations, so there emerged a disenchantment with such technology. Individuals need to be told throughout the implementation of technology what they can and cannot expect from it.

Support

Facilities must be made available for individuals to share problems which they are experiencing in the implementation of technology. These are not necessarily of a technical nature but may even represent a 'shoulder to cry on' for those struggling with the adoption of new technology.

Once the new technology is fully integrated into the force one might be forgiven for thinking that the technology management cycle was complete. This is not the case however.

Review Process

There should be a regular review of technology within the force which should address a number of issues, including:

- Whether the technology is still performing to standards set down in the contract with the supplier

- Whether the technology continues to meet the needs of the users and the force

- Whether the technology continues to give value for money

These reviews are likely to follow a standard format and take place at regular intervals, possibly half yearly. If the technology fails to meet any of the criteria of the review, then a need has been identified for either enhanced or new technology and the technology management cycle is triggered again as illustrated in figure 9.1.

Although perhaps simplistic, the stages of the technology management cycle are broadly experienced to varying degrees by all forces in the management of technology.

Before leaving the management of technology, there are two more issues which need to be considered.

The Role of Technical Specialists

There have been numerous works which have passed comment on the emergence of the 'omnicompetent' police officer. Whilst operationally this might be true, such is the complexity of new technologies that it is unfair and counter productive to expect police officers to 'have their fingers on the pulse' of technological developments.

Recent years have seen the emergence of technical specialists, responsible for the day to day management of the technological resources of the force. These individuals, usually civilian staff, are extremely knowledgeable in their own specialist field. We have therefore seen such roles as force IT managers, force vehicle fleet managers and force technical support managers begin to appear over the last 15 years.

This may imply that there could be some confusion in roles. How do the police manager and the technical specialist integrate? It would appear that the specialists provide technical support for police managers, indeed all officers in forces. The force vehicle fleet manager provides vehicles to meet the needs of police officers and manages that fleet. Police managers need to identify their requirements clearly and be guided by the specialists, who will often then take over the specification and procurement stages and heavily influence the implementation and review stages.

In line with points made earlier, for major projects such as force wide IT systems, police managers and technical specialists will work together as members of a project team though often a senior police officer will assume the role of project leader. These points are more fully explored in chapter 10.

As part of a continuing trend towards civilianisation, it is likely that greater use will be made of technical specialists to support the work of the police service. Ultimately this must be an effective use of police resources. It enables police officers to identify their needs and call on individuals with the relevant knowledge to assess how those needs can best be met.

Technology Strategies

It is clear from this and the preceding chapter that an enormous amount of force resources are tied up in technology. New technology is not always cheap; cars, computers and communications networks are definitely not cheap.

If forces bought individual items, for example a car or a computer, then the drain on force finances would not be too severe. Unfortunately in the real world this is not the case. When a force purchases vehicles, it usually does so in tens or even hundreds, usually once a year. When a force purchases a computer system it is often a cross force system and includes numerous terminals and the associated network.

The scale of such expenditure is well beyond the average annual budget of a force. Hence such technological developments have to be planned for in order to ensure that the required finance is available at the required time. In other words there needs to be a strategy for the development of technology within forces.

With respect to vehicles the situation is not too complex. It is generally accepted that the force needs cars (though how many may be open to question) and that these cars will have a limited life, say three years. There is, therefore, a rolling programme of vehicle replacement which is relatively stable and finance can be planned for, each year, to ensure that the required vehicles can be purchased.

What is the situation where the pace of technological change is rapid? How do forces set priorities on which computer systems they should buy? How do they decide between a new command and control system, or upgrades to the crime reporting system or a new electronic mail system or new word processors for the force? Clearly, finances do not stretch to purchasing all of these systems at once and clearly even if they did, it would be impossible to implement all of theses systems into the force at once.

Information technology and its development in the force, therefore, needs to be planned. A lucid but concise strategy needs to be developed which outlines what technologies will be implemented into the force and when. This strategy will also outline the financial implications of such developments and inform the budget planning process. In this way the large systems can be planned for over a period of years and their technology management cycle planned in advance.

It is easy to state that a strategy should be developed, but what does one look like and how do you write one? The development of IT strategies is one which is problematic across all organisations. The private sector are still grappling with IT strategies and how they should be developed. At the root cause of the problem is an issue raised at the start of the chapter, that of justification.

When the benefits of IT are so difficult to assess in quantifiable terms, how do you chose between different systems? What has more value to the force, a crime reporting system or a command and control system and which should come first? What has more value to the customer of police services?

It is these issues which IT theorists are continue to address. To help answer these questions, there have been several attempts at devising a national strategy for police information systems. The latest offering, the National Strategy for Police Information Systems or NSPIS, was launched in 1995 and referred to briefly in Chapter 8.

There are now several excellent texts on the subject of IT strategies, each taking a slightly different approach, though the work of Michael Earl (1989) in this area is particularly well respected. However, all texts seem to agree on two broad principles which underpin the development of IT strategies. Firstly, an information policy should be developed which will inform the IT strategy development process. Secondly, the IT strategy should be tied inextricably to the strategic aims and goals of the organisation. Any systems which support the achievement of those aims and goals should be pursued. This latter principle holds true for all technology. Only by keeping in mind at all times the long term aims of the force, and ensuring that technology helps the force meet those aims, can best value be achieved from the use of technology.

Chapter Summary

- Technology, in whatever form, needs to be managed within the police service as does any other resource.

- The management of technology in the police service broadly follows a simple cycle.

- Justification of the need for technology is often beset with problems.

- A clear specification is needed to identify the precise nature of the technology required.

- Forces should establish a procurement strategy to obtain technology, especially where major projects are involved.

- Forces should consider joining together as purchasing consortia to attain the benefits of economies of scale.

- Implementation of technology needs to be carefully planned to reduce the fear of, and resistance to, the new technology.

- A review process should be established to ensure that the technology continues to meet user needs and perform to specification.

- Technical specialists should be employed wherever possible to provide expert guidance in the use and management of technology.

- A strategy for the use of technology in forces should be encouraged which promotes the aligning of technological development with force strategic aims.

Chapter 10

Managing Projects

Introduction

> *'We must ask where we are and whither
> we are tending.'*
>
> Abraham Lincoln

Project style management is as much to do with corporate strategy, as it is to do with any of the many small projects undertaken within an organisation. It is a whole new culture which fosters a new style of more effective management and is turning some of the older traditional techniques on their heads.

It questions the effectiveness of the traditional hierarchical management structure, (figure 10.1) and offers a new constructive style of management in which many organisations who have adopted it, have found that it revolutionised their ability to compete and provide a better service at lower cost.

It is easy to see the difficulties that there can be in effective vertical communication with the traditional type of structure. It is questionable if the people at the top ever really know what is happening at the bottom level with any degree of certainty. Various levels of management filter out what they consider their superior does not need to know, not always with malice aforethought, but genuinely because they think it irrelevant to the main thrust of the communication. Imagine the distortion that can take place over seven or eight levels of management!

Fig 10.1: Traditional hierarchical management structure

Project Based Culture

'One of the greatest failings of todays executive
is his inability to do what he's supposed to do.'
Malcolm Kent

In the last few years, there has been a steady movement towards a project based culture in industry and commerce. At its most basic level, it has a structure in which a very flat management structure controls and directs teams of people who have specialist knowledge relevant to the project being undertaken. These teams change as the new projects occur and the requirements for different specialists are needed. The teams work under the direction of the team leader who is appointed for that particular project and may become only a team member on a subsequent project. This type of structure for a commercial organisation is shown in figure 10.2.

The managing of this type of organisation is complex and, if the managers are not given the training and expertise, the results can be disastrous. The organisation must have precisely designated objectives which are clearly understood by **all**

Fig 10.2: Basic project management structure in industry

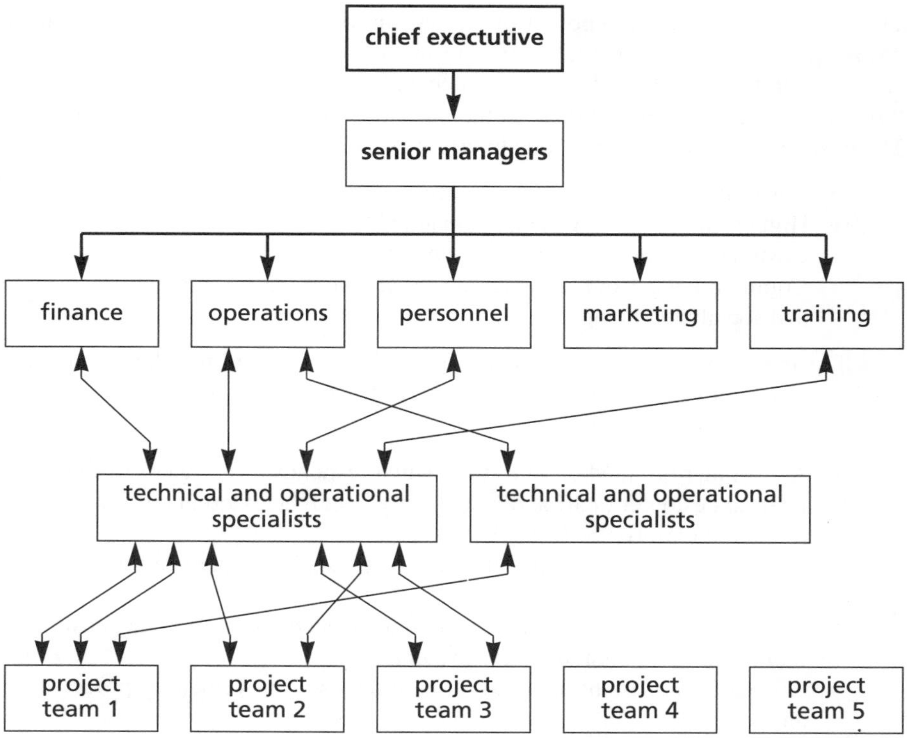

employees. Each team and project has exactly the same requirements of quantifiable objectives plus adequate performance indicators and a system for continuous monitoring of both cost and resource requirements in place.

At senior manager level, the posts are linked to specific areas of expertise. Communication with peers is activated daily with both formal (meetings) and informal interchange taking place and at least once daily with the chief executive.

The next level down of management is based on people who have skills in specific areas as well as the normal administrative and management skills required by a manager. The administrative skills are used to ensure that the routine daily processes of the organisation progress smoothly. This aspect of their work only occupies a part of their time, the rest of which is used to supply their technical and/or organisational skills to one of the project teams. This can be as team leader or as an ordinary member of the team whose leader has more pertinent skills to the particular project being undertaken. The remainder of the team is drawn from non-management staff who also have the varying but relevant skills required to realistically ensure the best chance for the achievement of the project objectives. Co-ordination and integration of the various projects is carried out by the senior management team.

Types of Organisation

There are two emerging types of organisation, one in which there is a hybrid environment in which projects and operations sit side by side, and a project environment in which all the functions and operations of the organisation are managed through projects. The first of these is the more relevant to the police environment. The reasons for the evolution of this hybrid type of organisation are:

- Customer demand for better service
- Higher satisfaction standards demanded
- Customer awareness of new technology
- Communities becoming more concerned about the environment and social well being

All of these above aspects are major forces in the demand for change and are driving organisations towards a more effective structure and use of resources. The benefits of this new structure are:

- A customer oriented organisation which responds to the needs of the internal customer (staff and management) and the external customer (the community)
- Greater individual responsibility and better self management for individuals and teams
- Integrated management (flatter, more manageable structure) and easier, more effective communication systems
- Greater awareness of the need for continuous improvement of processes and services

How are organisations (including the police), responding to these new driving forces? Some of the more important factors are:

- Achieving quicker response times
- Using resources more effectively
- Lowering costs
- Achieving flexibility from employees
- Committing resources to personal training and development
- Commitment to continuous improvement in all aspects of what they do

These organisations realise that the attainment of their strategic objectives depends on the abilities of their employees, their commitment to accepting responsibility, increasing involvement in the management process and awareness of the need for flexibility. The police are no different in this respect to any other commercial organisation.

Projects

There are many types of projects, from those with a major impact on the organisation such as the restructuring of the management and its individual responsibilities and authority, (the Police and Magistrates' Courts Act and its repercussions on the way in which police management is required to act is a typical example) possibly extending over a year or more, to smaller projects requiring much less in the way of resources, such as a typical small crime prevention project with a timescale of perhaps weeks.

What then is the feature that differentiates a project from any other activity? What is the definition of a project? M. Barnes (1989) described it as 'something which has a beginning and an end'. This is however scarcely adequate as it is sometimes difficult to quantify when a project actually started. The daily administration of a crime desk could qualify under this heading, but could hardly be described as a project. Other definitions have been tried, Clelland and King (1983: 1988) describe it as:

> *'A complex effort to achieve a specific objective within a schedule and budget target, which typically cuts across organisational lines, is unique and is usually not repetitive within the organisation.'*

Perhaps the best definition was that coined by Anderson, Grude, Haug and Turner (1987):

> *'A human endeavour which creates change; is limited in time and scope; has mixed goals and objectives; involves a variety of resources and is unique.'*

Projects often involve people from throughout the organisation and in some cases, people and other organisations external to the organisation. They always create change, they have mixed objectives and are evaluated on the basis of outcome, quality, cost and time. It is a unique operation which has been clearly defined at its outset. Routine operations do not qualify as projects, they are in the main repetitive tasks on which the day to day operations of the organisation depend and are not subject to time limitations, that is they are continuous, they do not bring about revolutionary change but rather evolve and bring about incremental change.

One of the more interesting aspects of projects is the way in which they bring about beneficial change. They upset the equilibrium of the force field referred to in chapter 7 and often change forever the way in which a particular series of actions is undertaken. It is however important to realise that change is only beneficial if it happens at the right time, in the right place and at the right cost, and it is therefore essential that it has a finite timescale. Value for money is a major criterion.

Objectives

Projects always have an objective, in the case of the police that may be the reduction or prevention of crime in any particular area, or the better and more effective use of resources, giving greater efficiency. They are undertaken because they achieve results which cannot be accomplished by the routine tasks which are carried out within the organisation. They are transient but may be repeated if the original need reasserts itself. The same measurement criteria would be applied but the tactics may change in light of previous experience.

The project objectives must be considered in light of the resources required, the time over which these resources would need to be allocated and the cost of the operation. These require to be balanced if the outcomes (objectives) are to be realistic and achievable (figure 10.3).

Fig 10.3: Balancing the objective(s)/resources/time triangle

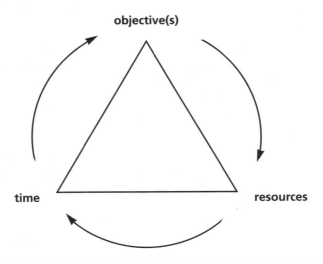

objective(s)

time

resources

An objective may be set which, when examined in detail has a requirement for resources over a given period of time which would prove impractical. A decision then has to be made as to which of these three should be modified. Can the original objective be achieved by running with the required resources for a shorter period of time or with reduced resources for a longer period of time, or does the objective need to be revised in light of the resources available and the time over which they will operate?

There are two additional factors which need to be considered if the project is to be successful. These are shown in figure 10.4 and are the scope of the project and the cost.

Cost

The cost of the operation must be weighed against the beneficial outcomes which it will achieve. The cost aspect as applied to the police was perhaps less important than it is to an industrial or commercial concern though this is now debatable in view of the requirement for better management of budgets, (forces now operate on cost limited budgets) and 'value for money' outcomes. Where the project is done in collaboration with other agencies, cost may assume an even greater degree of concern as local authorities and voluntary organisations come under increasing pressure to reduce costs.

Scope

The scope of a project can be broken down into three levels as defined by P. W. G. Morris (1979):

- Level 1: The unifying or integrating level (corporate strategy)
- Level 2: The strategic level (project strategy)
- Level 3: The tactical level

The project is integrated into the organisation at level 1 by defining how the purpose of the project is compatible with the organisation's objectives (very relevant where a BCU, or division is structuring a project which conflicts, or is certainly not compatible with one of the force objectives). This is discussed later in the chapter when we look at implementing corporate strategy. At level 2, a strategy is devised for the achievement of the objectives and at level 3, the tactics are developed which will achieve the elements which make up the strategic plan.

Projects are only effective when the task is isolatable, well defined and achievable within the time specified. They are an effective way of introducing change, showing what can be achieved by a well planned operation.

If projects are to be successful, they need the wholehearted support of senior management and a firm commitment to the achievement of the objectives. Management by a committee, (as can happen in the case of a multi-agency project) is not acceptable. There must be someone who has overall authority, to whom the project leader can turn to, if the need arises. Project leaders must be given the authority to manage, to act, to make decisions and to allocate the agreed resources. The project manager must be allowed to plan the project with clear sub-goals or

Fig 10.4

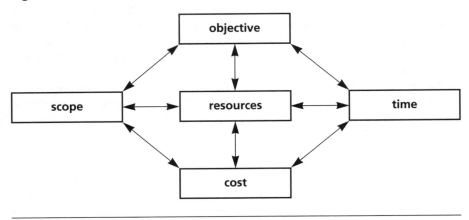

milestones to assign to his/her staff. Continuous monitoring and control procedures must be built in and the relevance of the project to its original objectives and the requirements of its end customers maintained. Managers who love order, stability and bureaucracy do not make good project managers.

Project Management

> *'So much of what we call management consists in making it difficult for people to work.'*
> Peter Drucker

Project management is the process by which a project is successfully completed, that is, it has achieved its objective(s). There are three aspects which need to be addressed if this process is to be successful:

- The objectives themselves
- The processes used to achieve the objectives
- The levels at which the processes are applied

The objectives cover the scope, the resources, the timescales and the cost. The processes include the planning of the operation, the implementation and the continuous monitoring and control. Projects bring momentary imbalance and people need time to readjust to the new situation. Staff can feel insecure and under pressure and tend to resist what they perceive may be a threat to their well being. In the constantly evolving environment in which we live, new requirements necessitate change. Projects have no 'steady state' but have identifiable 'phases'. Clear identification of these phases and their objectives can reduce the feeling of insecurity by allowing those participating to move forward in stages to achieve each stage or 'milestone'.

It is advantageous for the project manager to manage through a structured breakdown of the objectives (outcomes). Focus on results: What to achieve not how to achieve it. Balance results through task breakdown between people and systems. Clearly define roles, responsibilities and working relationships. Adopt a clear and simple reporting structure.

In the management of a project there are two clearly defined needs, that of the people involved, both as individuals and as a group, and that of the tasks that form the basis of action for the project. People needs are catered for by the project manager utilising his/her skills as a team builder to bind together what is essentially a transient coming together of the people involved and meeting individual needs by motivating, supporting and developing each person within the team, by communicating well, by making sure that each individual is properly briefed and understands what is required of them.

The task needs are catered for by the actions of planning, controlling and evaluating the project. These are interlinked as shown in figure 10.5 and highlight some problem areas where a clash of interests can occur. In problem area one, there is a potential clash of interest between the group and task needs. The project manager requires to be aware of the need to look after **all** of the group. If the task structure is such that it is incompatible with the group composition then there is a possible need to break up the existing group and restructure in order to gain greater efficiency.

Fig 10.5: Project management needs and problem areas

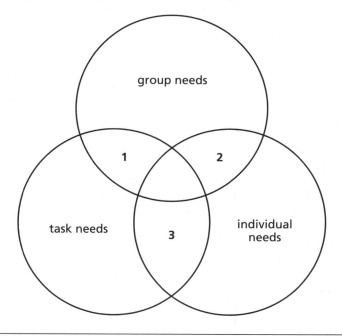

In problem area two, there could be a clash of interests between group and individual needs where the project manager needs to reinforce the group solidarity, but at the same time allowing for a degree of individuality in the participants and the opportunity for growth and development.

In the third of the problem areas, the clash of interest is between task and individual needs. In some cases a number of the individual's skills may not be relevant but he/she thinks they are. Job freedom will have to be removed and the individual made aware of the need to conform. At the same time the manager must ensure that the individual gains some degree of job satisfaction and the prospect for advancement by perhaps acquiring new skills during their participation in the project.

An illustration of these three areas might be found in the operation of a crime prevention initiative designed to:

- Increase awareness of the public to the incidence of domestic burglary so that they may take measures to ensure better security of their property and
- Reduce the number of burglaries occurring

The initiative is planned by the divisional crime prevention officer, and a group of officers, including CID, is brought together to implement the project. If the initiative is to be a success, the main thrust of the project must be directed at contacting the maximum number of people in the community and familiarising them with the best deterrents currently available.

It is proposed that the force crime prevention caravan will be located at strategic points in the division over a period of weeks, two lock manufacturers will supply sponsorship and there will be a communication sent to all neighbourhood watch co-ordinators advising them of the dates and locations of the caravan. The CID members of the team do not see this as any part of their duty and would be much happier investigating current burglaries, particularly where there has been repeat victimisation, this, they say would do more to reduce the number of burglaries than trying to educate the public. The first task need is to set up and staff the caravan and then to follow up on any queries, and/or intelligence, that might result from the contact with the community.

This scenario illustrates all three problem areas, the conflict between the group needs, (investigating) and the task needs, (setting up an information centre). There is also conflict between some of the group (CID) and uniform branch as to how the project should be run, whether by individuals in the group or by the task that requires to be done. These are potential problems of which the project leader must be aware and be able to take corrective action to avoid conflict of interest within the team.

It is more appropriate at senior management levels, to concentrate on what is delivered, its quality and value, rather than on defining the work required to achieve the outcomes. These processes are better left to those levels of management who are actually involved in the management and operation of the project.

It is important to focus on the purpose of the project and the quantitative and qualitative measures used to define the achievement of that purpose. This measures the quality of what has been attained during the execution of the project.

The Approach

*'Even if you're on the right track, you'll
get run over if you just sit there.'*
Will Rogers

Projects should only be undertaken to satisfy a need. This can be something generated within the organisation but can equally be addressed to a need voiced by the community or some of its representatives. As previously stated, projects must bring about beneficial change. That change can only happen if the project is delivered within certain cost restraints, within given timescales and meets previously agreed quality standards (outcomes). It should be established at the outset whether the cost of the initiative is not potentially greater than the cost of the problem itself and if it is, is it still worthwhile doing because of the public pressure in this particular area? Is the partial reduction of the problem a possible solution? There is always an element of risk management in managing projects.

Projects must be looked at in context, individual projects cannot be viewed in isolation, they must be compatible with, and be a means of assisting in the achievement of the goals and objectives set out in the corporate plan.

There are several parties who are involved in any project. There is the parent organisation, or organisations in the case of a multi-agency project, the operators, those who will be involved in the achievement of the objectives, the supporters who will supply the human and financial resources and the beneficiaries, (the organisation itself or the particular area of the community affected) who have to be satisfied that the outcome(s) have indeed been beneficial.

The standard measurement for the success of a project is that it is completed on time, to cost and to specification, but who judges these criteria? Different parties have different perceptions as to whether or not the project was a success. Individuals will judge a project to be a success if it fulfilled their own personal objectives. These may not be the same as the stated objectives and the time, cost and quality constraints imposed at the outset. The individual's personal objectives are very often part of the hidden agenda. These could be:

- Project managers aiming to enhance their career
- Managers hoping to widen their sphere of influence
- Staff wishing to protect their jobs
- People being generally resistant to change

The management of a project within its context requires a strategic management approach. This involves:

- The attitudes of the parties involved, at all levels of management
- The objectives of the project
- The means used to manage the project
- The context in which the project is undertaken
- The resources required

Appraising the Project

'The important thing is not to stop questioning.'
Albert Einstein

It is important when setting up a project, that all aspects are considered at an early stage. The originator must decide what information he/she requires in order to satisfy himself/herself that there is indeed a need – the people perception and investigation stages as shown in figure 10.6. There are two important aspects that need to be considered:

- The information required by the originator to ascertain that there is a need: *The possible solution(s), the aim or objective of the work which includes the benefits both to the organisation itself and to the community in general, the cost of implementing and running a project which will provide a solution, this must include the costs of the personnel involved, costs of any materials required and indirect costs, and the specific benefits that will accrue.*

- The information required by the organisation to determine the feasibility of the project: *What funds are required; what proportion of the costs might be met by other participating organisations and what, if any, 'strings' are attached such as interference by a management committee, bureaucracy and paperwork requirements. This is particularly relevant in the case of multi-agency projects where in many cases a committee composed of members of the various participating organisations will want a say and a degree of involvement in the running of the project. If central government want to use the idea, are they entitled to free use?*

It is important when submitting a project for approval that consideration is given to the 'selling aspects'. When it is submitted for approval, will it be seen to reinforce the force and/or Home Office strategy? Will it improve the performance of the force/division? Will it bring about improvement for the community and/or the environment and lastly will it benefit both the employer and the employees? These factors are seen as important by senior managers and will influence the decision to implement or not to implement.

The basic steps in the cycle of starting a project are given in figure 10.6. It starts with a perceived problem. This requires investigation in order to decide on the validity of the perception. If this is validated, the next step is to accurately define the problem. It is important here to draw a distinction between the symptom of a problem and the problem itself. In too many cases there is an attempt to define the symptom as the problem and to treat this instead of the problem. This may well be valid as a definition, but those involved must be aware that this is the case, and that they are about to treat the symptom.

The next stage is to hold a brainstorming session to generate some ideas on how the problem may be tackled. From this stage, evaluation of the various merits and demerits of the proposed solutions are discussed, out of which should come an agreed solution. Communication of the defined problem and the proposed method

Fig 10.6: The project cycle

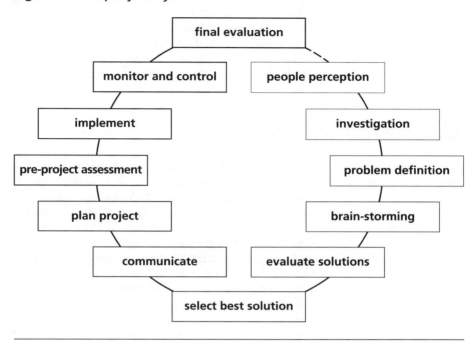

of its solution is communicated to interested parties. After consultation, a project plan is formulated with agreed objectives and outcomes, resource levels and timescales. Planning needs to be meticulous so that all resources are used as effectively as possible.

Operation 'Bumblebee', (a domestic burglary initiative which originated in the 'Met' and has since been copied in many other forces) is a good example. The problem was perceived as a dramatic increase in domestic burglary. The crime statistics confirmed that this was indeed the case and the problem definition was correct. A brainstorming session was held when ideas as to how best to tackle the problem were put forward. The proposed solutions were evaluated and the best solution decided upon. This was communicated to all interested parties and authorisation given to proceed on that basis. That was to target the known villains who were operating in this field. The pre-project assessment was, that by taking this action, the police would be able to find where the proceeds of their burglaries were located and by finding the goods, be able to relate them back to individual burglaries. Implementation was carried out and in every case the results have shown excellent reductions in the incidence of these burglaries.

Good planning can eliminate problems before they actually occur. It will identify key events during the running of the project and these will become the 'milestones' which will enable progress to be measured accurately. The planning stage is followed by the pre-project assessment stage, at which time any final changes or modifications are made prior to implementation. Continuous monitoring and control by the use of performance indicators is then undertaken, followed by a final evaluation of the degree of achievement and the close of the initiative. The framework for the management of initiatives and projects developed for the Home Office by the Centre for Police Management and Research at Staffordshire University sets out in a simple and easy format an effective approach to the whole process.

Setting the Milestones

The setting of milestones is often done on the arbitrary basis of 'we'll have a progress report every four weeks'. This does not take account of how the project is organised and the way in which the tasks are structured. It does not provide either the parent organisation or the project leader with meaningful data on which he/she can measure the progress of the project to plan. Milestones, if they are to be meaningful, must be related to what we will call 'work packages'. These will be related to actions, which when completed, will have a defined and measurable outcome and if successfully completed will have achieved a sub-objective or milestone.

It is perhaps convenient for senior managers to have meetings which correspond to a fixed time pattern, and which will allow them to keep free the first Tuesday of each month for a progress meeting. If, however, they do not provide hard evidence of measurable progress against target, then they are a waste of valuable time and resources. Progress meetings, if they are to be of any value must deal with 'chunks' of the project which achieve identifiable goals and are measurable.

Fig 10.7: Setting up of milestones and work packages

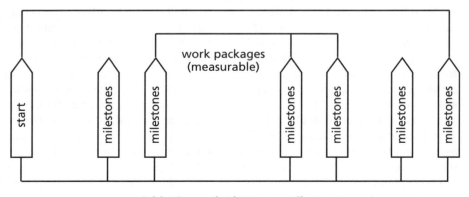

Figure 10.7 shows how this concept is applied. It may be that at the start of some projects, there are a number of measurable actions (work packages) that are of fairly short duration and will require a number of meetings in quick succession, others with actions of longer duration at the start may not require assessment for some weeks or even months, though the latter is unlikely. If the planning has been properly done and the work packages clearly defined, then the measurement of progress towards the final objective becomes fairly easy.

Corporate Strategic Planning

Earlier in the chapter we talked about a project's relevance to the overall corporate strategic plan. The purpose of the corporate strategic plan is to:

- Allocate the primary resources effectively
- Assist the organisation to adapt to its external environmental opportunities and threats
- Co-ordinate activities to reflect the organisation's strengths and weaknesses
- Build an organisation which learns from its past strategic decisions in order to improve on its decisions in the future

The term 'primary resources' covers such things as:

- Financial funding
- Allocation of central management skills
- Distribution and use of technological know-how

Secondary resources are less easily disposable discretionary resources, such as excess staffing, influential political contacts and specific human resources and expertise.

The Elements of Planning

The elements of strategic planning are:

- Adaptation: *Where is the organisation going? It is an outward looking activity which focuses on improving the organisation's chances to employ its resources for the best returns. It discourages extrapolation of past activities, such as central data banks held by forces and by central government, to be used as the sole guide to future activities and focuses on the emerging environmental opportunities and threats in order to determine the way forward. It sees the changing environment as an opportunity for change in the organisation and the ability to move ahead.*

- Integration: *How do we get there? This involves the orderly evaluation of the organisation's strengths and weaknesses which should lead to efficiency of operation. It is to do with identifying a strategic direction and programming to achieve its objectives.*

- Learning and development: *Learning from retrospective analysis of strategic decisions in order to improve future strategic decisions. Ideally this leads to a self-correcting planning system, in effect a closed loop process which monitors and updates plans. Development is concerned with the use of accumulated experience as a tool to develop a manager's capabilities and facilitates the transferability of strategic skills from one manager to another. This is not always true within the police service, where transfers (post tenure) are not always advantageous to either the organisation or the individual*

The corporate strategic plan of the organisation sets out the overall framework within which units must operate. It is essential that any projects which are undertaken by employees form part of this framework and contribute to the overall achievement of the organisation's objectives.

Project Lifecycle

It is often not appreciated that in common with material products which have a defined life cycle, projects are subject to the same basic rules that apply to the marketing of such a product. These are introduction, growth, maturity, saturation and decline. Relating these to the structuring and implementation of a project, the introductory phase is equivalent to the planning and pre-assessment phase when starting off a project. At this stage motivation and enthusiasm are high though nothing has as yet been achieved in the way of results. The growth phase starts after the implementation of the project, again motivation and enthusiasm can be at a high level and if the project has been properly planned and explained, expectations are that the project will be a success and achieve its objectives.

Maturity sets in after a while, enthusiasm has dwindled and there is perhaps not as much motivation as there was in the early stages. The results are thought to be acceptable, though no-one really knows because there were no meaningful milestones set out at the beginning. The project leader however, continues to be optimistic that everything will turn out well in the end. During the saturation stage, things start to stagnate. The participants have no real stimulus to push forward and their interest and their input decreases which leads to the final stage of decline and the project being wound up. The results are then analysed and the best case made out to at least indicate that it was not a failure, but if the final evaluation is properly carried out, this could be difficult, so the results are massaged slightly to try and show a better result.

All too often this is what actually happens, though it need not be the case if the project is properly planned and developed. It will still go through the same stages, but the final outcome will be entirely different. At the introductory phase, the project leader will have mapped out the forecast progress of the project with all the intermediate stages (milestones) defined and the times in which these have to be achieved clearly indicated. Participants are well briefed and again motivation and enthusiasm is high. Everyone knows what their part in the project involves and when it will have to be done.

The project is implemented and in a short space of time results start to accrue. These are measured against the relevant intermediate milestones and conclusions drawn as to the degree of success achieved. If the outcome is not satisfactory, action is taken immediately to put things back on track. The mature stage has now been reached, but this time there is not the same degree of loss of motivation and enthusiasm. The members of the project team know exactly where they are in relation to the planned outcome and because of the continuous monitoring of progress towards the interim objectives, are in a position to take positive action if things are not going exactly to plan. In this second scenario, there are no saturation and decline phases. The continuous monitoring against the milestones gives immediate indicators as to the progress of the initiative and allows the project leader to assess, on almost a day to day basis, the value of the project and the viability of letting it continue, or the decision that as it is not showing the promise that it should have done, it should be discontinued and the resources devoted to another and potentially worthwhile project.

Project Example

Figure 10.8 shows an example of a project designed to reduce crime in a particular area from a current reported value of 29% to 22% over a given period of months. The growth phase shows a healthy decrease which dips below the projected straight

Fig. 10.8: Typical project lifecycle

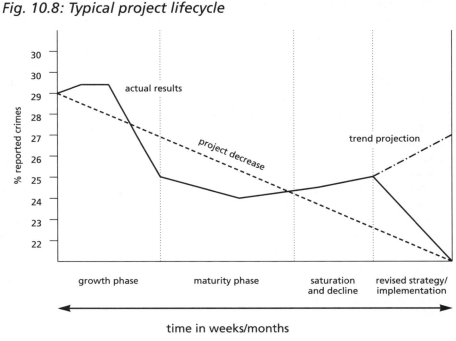

line decrease. During the next phase, the rate of decrease slows down and starts to level off. Continuous monitoring achieves even greater significance during this phase as it can give the indication that all is not well. The project then enters the saturation and decline phase when the rate of incidence of the crime starts to rise and the results are well below those predicted. If nothing is done at this stage, then the trend prediction shows that the percentage crime at the end of the timescale allocated to the project will have almost reached the level at which the project was started. Further allocation of the same resources are perceived as having little or no effect on the upward trend. A decision has to be taken during this latter stage as to whether or not to cut the project short and devote resources elsewhere, or to revise the strategy, perhaps introduce new resources and inject a new impetus into the project. It would be a matter of experience for the project leader to be able to judge which course of action was called for in each particular case.

Project Management and the Lean Machine

'So free we seem so fettered fast we are.'
Robert Browning

In chapter five the advent of the lean machine, its philosophy and its impact on current management thinking was discussed. The lean machine concept strips away all surplus labour and carries on until it hurts. It is said that it is not effective until it becomes painful. How does it fit with the concept of the structure required for project management?

There is no room for 'passengers' in such an organisation, every member of staff must contribute to the full both in expertise and input. The organisation should be so dependent on the performance of each individual that the non-performance of any manager, team leader or member of staff can seriously prejudice the quality of the outcome and jeopardise the full achievement of the strategic objectives .

If we relate this to the performance of a team, the similarities become immediately apparent. Here the successful outcome although on a smaller scale is equally dependent on each member of the team making the maximum contribution of which they are capable. If there were no restrictions on the number of people we could have in our team, human nature would ensure that we would have a considerable surplus – just in case. The restrictions imposed by international competition dictate that if we are to survive and maintain the standard of living which we equate with the western world, then we have to ensure that what we do is cost effective and contributes to the team effort of UK Ltd.

Benchmarking against good practice in other organisations both in the UK and abroad helps to maintain a standard which is competitive, will sustain momentum and stimulate ideas. There is nowhere to hide from benchmarking. Increasing pressures are constantly forcing organisations to concentrate on using their resources more effectively and on improving their policies and working practices. Benchmarking properly applied can be used to identify and secure opportunities which would not otherwise be apparent, but *caveat emptor* if it is not properly researched, resourced and interpreted, it will not only fail, but can lead organisations to a totally wrong conclusion.

Much has been written on the subject of team development and the forging of a cohesive unit in order to achieve the set objectives. Also on the subject of quality management there are considerable sources of information that can be tapped into. There is however, less on the combination of the two. This is surprising as the two form a holistic approach to achieving a higher level of commitment and achievement than could otherwise be done, they are totally interdependent.

Combining the best of the two concepts can arrive at a management style which will enhance people management practices and exploit the talents of the people concerned to best advantage. If maximisation of human input, and quality output and effectiveness is to be achieved, then an approach which stimulates and motivates participants and minimises the numbers of people involved must be used.

Any hopes of a letup of the pressures on organisations to increase output and decrease numbers is a forlorn hope with all western world and emergent countries striving to maintain their place in the world league. A review of Home Office spending (July 1997) is to look at the scope for achieving a leaner and more effective police service.

Concurrent with these demands is the absolute need not only to maintain existing standards and quality of products and services but to constantly strive to improve on them.

Organisations who implement project style management must be aware that if the project teams are to function well, the organisation must adopt an open policy where people are valued as individuals for reasons related to business interests as well as for moral and social reasons. The personal dynamics of the team must be in harmony, they need to be more task focused than behaviour focused. A properly integrated team operation can reduce individual pressure and reduce stress levels – an important factor in today's working environment. The organisation must operate an open workplace culture based on trust and mutual respect. People participating in a team operation must be empowered to express their ideas and to have a say in how the end objective should be achieved or a particular problem solved.

Teams operate as an integrated unit, each member being a key player in the achievement of their stated objectives. The standard of cohesion they achieve is dependent on the effectiveness of their organisation and structure. Tasks must be allocated on the basis of the expertise of the chosen team member(s), evaluation being carried out both during and after task completion, feedback given to the team leader who harmonises this within the overall progress being made towards the ultimate goal.

The question is often asked as to what makes people work better and harder. The old answer used to be pay them more. This has long been dismissed as the prime motivating factor, but the definitive answer remains as elusive as ever. A survey carried out by *People Management* magazine came up with some answers which are discussed in subsequent paragraphs and are extremely relevant in the context of team operation. Questions covered peoples perceptions of work climate and their awareness of job involvement, time commitment and work intensity.

Some work has been carried out on involvement by US academics Thomas Leigh and Stephen Brown. They reported in 1996 issue of the *Journal of Applied Psychology* that two key aspects of work climate for their sample were 'psychological safety' and 'job meaningfulness'. These factors they said seemed to

Fig 10.9: Improving team effectiveness

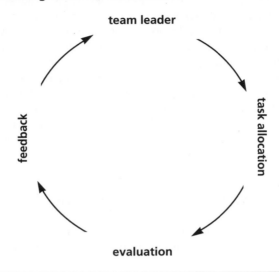

team leader

task allocation

feedback

evaluation

trigger greater job involvement. Job involved people say their work is one of the major satisfactions of life. The results of the survey showed that the factors influencing people to work better were:

- Employees are given authority and their decisions are endorsed by their boss. This is the support factor which is needed for effective working
- Employees know what is expected of them and what standards their work is measured against. Their roles are clearly defined
- Employees are given praise for what they do. The recognition factor

These three are classed under the heading of psychological safety which employees need if they are to feel a degree of security in what they are doing. The following three are classed under 'meaningfulness'. These supply the feeling that what they are doing is of value and strengthens the feel-good factor. They are:

- Employees are encouraged to express their personality at work and to be a person in their own right
- Employees can see that their individual effort makes a difference. They are contributing to the success of the organisation
- Employees are stretched by doing their job. It become a challenge and stimulates interest

If teams are required to function at maximum efficiency then the backup they receive must be of a very high order. It is an aspect of this type of structure whose importance can easily be underestimated by the organisation embarking on such a strategy. Too often the teams struggle to fulfil their tasks and fail because sufficient thought had not been given to the support management which was necessary for the effective completion of their objectives.

Team leaders must have the support of more senior management as and when required. Empowerment does not mean that teams are abandoned, left on their own struggling to achieve something for which they may lack some key piece of expertise and are loath to admit they are in difficulties. Because of the culture that exists in the organisation, the support and advice that they need to bring the project to a successful conclusion is lacking. It is a sure recipe for disillusionment and demotivation.

Multi-Agency Projects

The appreciation that crime was a community problem and not just a problem for the police has led to an upsurge in projects which are undertaken on a joint basis with other agencies, both statutory and voluntary. It seems a logical step in view of the emphasis now being placed on a greater integration of the police with the community, stemming from the Morgan Report (1993) which is mentioned in chapter 1. It has however, brought some unforeseen problems in its wake, not least of which is the different cultures which operate in agencies with widely different perceptions of the needs of the community.

The police, historically have been, and still are in many respects a highly reactive organisation, trained to react quickly to situations with little consideration given to the amount of resource employed but priority given to a swift outcome. Other agencies, particularly those in the public sector, have had to consider much more carefully as to how they would react to a particular situation, knowing that their actions would be subject to scrutiny at a later date and that they would have to show that they had considered all the options before deciding on the course of action taken. As a result, when a multi-agency project is proposed and a course of action decided upon, it is quite normal for the police to want to start almost immediately. Their culture and organisation allows them to be able to do this.

Most agencies other than the police, are normally obliged to consult at some length with other managers within their organisation, call meetings, obtain permission for resources, which in some organisations with a bureaucratic structure, can take weeks if not months. These organisations need time to react, and it has to be appreciated that unless consideration is given to the different operating procedures of the participating agencies, then friction will occur and it will be difficult to obtain an integrated approach with a start date which is agreeable to all concerned.

The Project Champion

> 'When the President says "jump!"
> they only ask, "How high?"'
>
> John Ehrlichman

A project champion needs to be appointed. He/she will be the motivating force which will ensure that the best effort is made to achieve the set objectives. In the authors' experience it has often been said that it always seems to devolve on the police to provide the project champion and to take the lead in virtually every project. This is perhaps natural as the police have more experience of, and more exposure to, crime than any of the other agencies. Providing there is ownership of the project by **all** the participating agencies and the project champion is aware of the differences between organisations in the speed with which they can react, then it is not a major drawback. Participating agencies should ensure that the person or persons sent to represent them on the planning committee, should have the sufficient authority to enable them to take decisions in line with the degree of participation to which they agree.

Where there are a number of agencies operating together on a project, it is essential to have a clearly defined reporting structure with well developed channels of communication. Very relevant to this aspect is the different terminologies used by organisations. It is essential that the project leader makes sure that 'police speak' or 'housing department speak' or any other particular terminology is either not used or that all participants understand its meaning and intent.

In multi-agency projects, it is very easy for some of the participating agencies to veer off in a direction which is not compatible with the overall objectives of the project. It is essential that there is a clear and understandable strategic plan, agreed by all concerned, and a clear task breakdown which defines the actions and timescales for each agency. The planning is of vital importance if the integration of the various actions by the participating agencies is to be effective, but this will not be so if they do not stick rigidly to the agreed timescales. For this reason if for no other, it is necessary that sufficient time is given to all the participating agencies to enable them to make all the necessary arrangements such as availability of personnel and any other resources that may be required to carry out their particular task(s) on time and in line with the planning.

If major projects are to be undertaken on a multi-agency basis, it may be prudent in the early stages to enlist the help of an experienced consultant who is aware of the complex issues involved and can provide the expertise which will provide a smooth passage through what can be a very troubled sea.

Multi-Agency Programme Management

If the management of a single multi-agency project can be difficult, the problems mount considerably when a number of multi-agency projects have to be run concurrently. There will be a number of agencies who will be participating in more than one of the projects and in some cases there will be an overlap of similar actions taken by the same agency for different objectives and which require different outcomes. If a number of such projects are to be undertaken, there has to be an overall co-ordinator who can look at the wider picture and who can ensure that any conflict of interests between the various projects are minimised. He/she should be involved with all the project leaders, meet with them on a regular basis and be a key recipient for any communications which might change the delicate balance between the various projects.

It is desirable that the project leaders of the various participating agencies should have management status within their own organisations that:

- Will give them sufficient authority to make the type of decision which will allow them to manage their project effectively. It is of little use to the co-ordinator if every decision has to be referred back to a more senior manager, and consequent delays seriously prejudice the agreed timescales.
- Will allow them the confidence to express their own opinions, enjoy a similar status to, and not be overawed by, more senior managers from the police or other agencies.

Chapter Summary

- The change to a project based culture is considered advantageous.

- A hybrid organisation which utilises a mixture of project and operations management set side by side is suggested as a suitable format for the police service. The benefits are outlined.

- A distinction is drawn between the normal operations of an organisation and the areas where a project needs to be undertaken in order to satisfy a need.

- The key aspects of a project are set out as:
  - the objectives
  - the resources employed
  - the scope
  - the time over which it will run, and
  - the cost.

- Managing the project is outlined as are the potential problem areas where the project manager will have to use his/her expertise to arrive at a solution.

- Projects are only undertaken to satisfy a need, either within the organisation itself or in the community.

- It is important to ensure projects are looked at in context and do not conflict with the organisation's aims and objectives.

- Pre-project appraisal or evaluation is stressed as of primary importance.

- Operation 'Bumblebee' is quoted as being a good example of a well planned project.

- Adequate milestones must be established if the project manager and those participating are to be able to measure their progress.

- The elements of corporate strategic planning and their importance when structuring a project are discussed.

- Project managers must realise that projects have a life cycle and the necessity for them to take requisite action if the project is to achieve its final objective.

- The lean machine and how it integrates with the requirements of a project management style is examined and the salient points brought out.

- The appointment of a project champion is considered essential for a successful outcome.

- Multi-agency programme management needs a different set of skills from the co-ordinator than are required for the project manager of a single project.

Chapter 11

Managing the Image

Introduction

> *'It is only shallow people who do*
> *not judge by appearances.'*
>
> Oscar Wilde

This chapter intends to examine management of image. This raises questions of what image is, why it needs to be managed, whose perception of image we are concerned with and how it is actually managed.

Management of image will be considered through the use of historical perspective and a case study, and an attempt will be made to track the changing image against the spirit and events of the times.

Once the background has been established, the need for market orientation in the late 1990s environment will be discussed, and the organisational implications of image management to the police service will be examined, including the roles of the press and public relations office and the community relations department.

Image? What Image?

An image is a representation in the mind. It embodies the character and attributes of an organisation. The image of the police service is the collective characteristics and attributes that together constitute the popular perception of what the police are and do. Managing image is concerned with developing that image, portraying its representation and transferring that image to a targeted audience, whether it is internally to an organisation or externally into the public domain. Projecting the image successfully concerns the effective management of external and internal communications channels, *(which is covered in greater detail in chapter 8)*. Within the police service a strong organisational and operational culture exists which impacts on the self image of police officers and their perception of the image of the service as a whole. The strength of this culture is such that it has transcended amalgamations, political and organisational changes. It has been a unifying factor and its relationship with image should not be underestimated. Nevertheless, the 1990s have seen numerous inquiries and reports concerning policing and the service has experienced an identity crisis concerning what it is and what it does. This in itself presents difficulties in portraying a clear and accurate image to the public.

Why does image need to be managed? Part of the answer lies in maintaining the confidence of the public – managing image is part of managing relations with the public. At the same time the confidence of the internal customers of an organisation must also be maintained. Therefore in terms of the targeted audience, the police service must look to manage its image both externally and internally. Externally the public have expectations as do central and local government. The police are accountable to the public and, as a service organisation representing law and order, are concerned to present a favourable image. This will be the case as long as policing by consent remains an underlying principle of our democratic system.

Internally, the importance of managing image should not be neglected nor overlooked. It has a role in projecting the mission of the service, changing aspects of its culture, and winning the hearts and minds of employees. If members of the organisation cannot believe in, or accept the image portrayed, there is little likelihood that it will be accepted externally.

The need to manage image also arises from the situation existing in the late 1990s in which the population are more news literate than ever before and there are cable, terrestrial and satellite television channels pumping out news, some twenty four hours per day. This is in addition to the expansive news coverage provided by the radio stations (some based on a 'rolling news' format) and the daily and weekend newspapers. This contrasts with the post war situation when access to televisions was limited and radio stations were fewer. In today's news hungry environment, law and order and the police are a staple ingredient, and consequently the police experience great scrutiny from the news media. For example, their tactics and behaviour are monitored at the increasing number of environmental protests at locations including the Newbury bypass and Manchester airport's proposed second runway. Police conduct is also scrutinised in detail by the media during increasingly frequent allegations of miscarriages of justice. Consequently, in this environment, there is a need for police forces to manage the way in which they are presented.

Having defined image and suggested reasons why it needs to be managed, the next section considers the police image from a historical perspective.

Historical Perspective

Fig 11.1: The changing image of the police service

Era	Dominant period images	Popular police image
1950s	The post war consensus Full employment Traditional class values dominate Respect for authority	Bobby on the Beat – dosing out the time and clips around the ear
1960s	Youth culture, Questioning of establishment and tradition Economic prosperity	Respect retained, *Dixon* and *Z Cars* on the TV, Big gang busts – Krays, Train Robbers – but whiffs of corruption
1970s	Recession, Industrial relations problems, race issues surfacing	Corruption scandals, popular image *The Sweeney* rather than *Dixon*
1980s	Recession deepens, unemployment, Society polarises, Thatcherism and strong government, greed, Union/Government showdown	Corruption e.g. W. Mids Serious Crime Squad. Public order peace keepers, Miners' strike, Non-partisan? Fallible
1990s	Fear of crime and obsession with crime rates. Stop/go economic recovery and recession, unemployment. Worries of drug culture and 'the youth of today'	Miscarriages of justice: Birminham 6, Guildford 4, Bridgewater 4. TV: *Between the Lines, The Bill* More technology, more remote, less able to cope? Quality of Service

From the enactment of the Metropolitan Police Act in 1829 to the present day, the image of the police has changed, the police have changed – not least in terms of their organisation. Writing in 1997 there are 43 forces in England and Wales, in 1940 there were four times as many, and the society which the police serve has experienced great and unprecedented change. Consider some of the events of the last 160 years – two world wars, universal suffrage, the rise (and fall) of a politicised labour movement, an increasingly educated public, the creation (and part dismantling) of the welfare state, and cycles of economic recession and growth.

Figure 11.1 shows at a glance the changing period images and the changing police image from the 1950s through to the 1990s. In the following sections each decade is considered in turn in relation to police image and pressures on the image.

It should not be surprising that as society has changed public relations with the police have ebbed and flowed. To all these trends the police have had to react and maintain their traditional role embodied by such characteristics as non-partisanship, preventive policing, a strategy of minimum force, and image management has played a part in this. Throughout the period an integral police task has been the winning of public trust whilst at the same time facing the difficulty of acting for the public against the public. Faced with changing times and these difficulties the police image has changed. Reiner (1992) charts the period 1856-1959 as one in which the police overcame initial opposition to their formation, until by the 1950s the police service had established an image of authority rather than power. The 1950s have been referred to as a 'golden age' during which the stock of the police service in the eyes of the public was at its highest – reaching a pinnacle that is still aspired to, but not achieved. However it will be argued in the case study which follows that those regarding this period as a golden age for law and order are possibly suffering from rose tinted glasses syndrome.

Policeman of the 1920s

A Case Study of Image Management

The Blue Lamp, The Sweeney, The Bill – different police, different worlds, same problems?

*London: a car chase and a police siren, a crash, a man
jumps out holding a gun, a bystander tries to stop him
– a shot rings out and the good citizen falls slowly and
dramatically to the ground as the pursuing police arrive
and restrain the gun-man.*

Consider, is the foregoing scenario from an acclaimed film which is widely referred to as representing a peaceable time when there was respect for law and order and the citizens of Britain slept soundly in their beds secure in the knowledge that the Constabulary were out there keeping the streets safe? Or is it from a more cynical era during which armed robberies and car chases are every day occurrences and the police may have to break the rules to secure justice? Read on as the narrator interjects, referring to the shot man...

*'To this man until today the crime wave was nothing
but a newspaper headline. What stands between the
ordinary public and this outbreak of crime? What
protection has the man in the street against this armed
threat to his life and property? At the Old Bailey Mr
Justice Finneymore in passing sentence for a crime of
robbery with violence gave this plain answer – 'This is
perhaps another illustration of the disaster caused by
insufficient numbers of police. I have no doubt that one
of the best preventives of crime is the regular uniform
police officer on the beat' – veterans like **George Dixon**...'*

All is revealed, our saviour on this occasion is not DCI Meadows of the 1980/90s The Bill, not even sneering Jack Regan of the 1970s Sweeney (Flying Squad), but George Dixon, though this is not obvious from the opening sequence with its portrayal of lawless times. However, an element of cosiness is restored as PC Dixon is seen directing a Scotsman to Paddington railway station, then admonishing with humour a street urchin who has kidded a probationer that he is lost, before enforcing the law by firmly but fairly moving on a street trader. The epitome of the British Bobby – providing service to the public, guidance to inexperienced colleagues and enforcing the law of the land.

And so was George Dixon introduced to the British public in the 1950 film *The Blue Lamp*. An enduring image of the police service was portrayed. The police officers were fine upstanding family men or young dedicated innocents sitting at the feet of respected elder statesman such as Dixon. Speaking fluent jargon in the correct Queen's English or with an 'amusing' regional accent (for example 'Taffy', who naturally enough was the choir master, and 'Jock' the shrewd CID man), these officers contrasted with the lower class accented villains – both the tight knit traditional underworld figures, the honourable thieves against whom the police had always pitted their wits, and the loose cannon young pretenders – again the narrator describing the young girl gone bad...

> *'...typical of many, the effects of a childhood spent in a home broken and demoralised by war. These restless and ill-adjusted youngsters have produced a type of delinquent which is partly responsible for the post war increase in crime.'*

Although *The Blue Lamp* was made almost 50 years ago, it has importance to popular perceptions of the police, or what the public would like the police to be. Such was Dixon's popularity that although he was murdered in the film he was not allowed to rest heroically in his grave, but was resurrected, promoted and served out eighteen years in Dock Green, beaming in monochrome into the houses of impressionable youngsters as televisions became household essentials in the sixties and early seventies.

It is accepted that Sgt Dixon did become an anachronism before he bade his last 'Evening All' in 1974 - Cashmore (1994) believes that this was the case even in the 1960s and that by the seventies the series (and by implication its portrayal of the police) was irrelevant. Reiner (1992) notes with some regret that 'PC George Dixon was not the norm for the British Bobby, but their finest hour'.

The Blue Lamp was dedicated to the Metropolitan Police and is obviously firmly in the establishment camp for projecting 'the right image'. However, whilst the film portrays a positive image of the police themselves, it is worth noting that the opening sequence described above does not appear to be the post war consensual golden age which is harked back to by those who periodically decry the current breakdown of law and order and wish things were like the good old days. On the contrary the opening of the film depicts a breakdown of the established order of cops and robbers as the existing relationships are threatened by young 'delinquents' with no respect but much ambition. Ironically, this film, rather than glorifying a consensual society, portrays a changing society, traumatised by the war and with its traditions under threat.

One purpose of discussing *The Blue Lamp* has been to show that the 1950s 'golden age' of peaceable policing was fictional, fuelled by nostalgic but inaccurate recollections of concerned sections of society, who yearn for more orderly times. There has always been concern about law and order, and the police must act within this environment and manage their image within it. *The Blue Lamp* is an illustration of positive management projecting a well regarded police service despite hard times and rising crime. The representation of the police was widely accepted, such that the film is remembered for the creation of the archetypal Dixon, rather than as an expression of the concern with the post war crime wave. In answer to the question posed in this section's heading it could be argued that the world has moved on, as has the police service, but the problems it faces are familiar including, for example, – public fear of increasing crime, worry about the 'youth of today' and the collapse of law and order. It is in this context that the police service has had to maintain its image.

One last remark on *The Blue Lamp* – Mr. Justice Finneymore's comments on the lack of police resources and Bobbies on the beat go to show that the nineties do not have a monopoly on such views.

A Faltering Image – the 1960s and 1970s

As the 1960s unfolded, the police image was characterised by the glamorous gang busting successes of such characters as 'Nipper' and Slipper of the Yard, though at the same time, and worryingly, allegations of police corruption, particularly in Scotland Yard, became regular news items. In the 1970s years of recession and polarisation, the police image was further tarnished as the service was deployed in public order situations, such as during disturbances at the Notting Hill Carnival in 1976 and 1977, and policing picket lines in the growing number of confrontational industrial disputes including miners' strikes (1972, 1974) and disturbances at the Grunwick film processing laboratory in 1977. The image faltered as the nation politicised and the traditional police image of being non-political was questioned. A crisis loomed and duly materialised as the decade turned and Britain rioted.

The 1980s: Lord Scarman and the need for a Change of Police Image

Riots are not alien to the British tradition, but the riots on mainland Britain in 1981 genuinely shocked both commentators and the public. Special attention was paid to the disturbances in Brixton during the weekend of April 10-12, 1981, and Lord Scarman was asked to undertake an inquiry into the causes. By the time he reported in November 1981, further riots had occurred in London and in other UK locations, including Manchester and Liverpool. Criticisms of the role of the police were made and it was suggested that the attitude and role of the police, and the state of police relations with certain sections of society had been a contributory factor in the causes of the riots. It appeared that the traditional image of the police as non-partisan was being questioned and that the implicit contract (between the police and the public) of policing by consent was in danger.

The greatest part of the Scarman report concerns policing issues and as such it crystallised the state of policing and the popular police image in 1981. Policing had become more technologically based, evidenced by the presence of panda cars rather than beat officers. Remoteness of the police from the community was one consequence. Sensing a police service losing touch with the community, the report returned to the founding tenets of the police quoting the function of the police service from Sir Richard Mayne's instructions to the 'New Police of the Metropolis' (1829)

*'The prevention of crime... the protection of life
and property, the preservation of public tranquillity.'*

This three fold function requires consent and balance i.e. the police must strike a balance between them if they are to secure the assent of the community which they need to support their operations (Scarman (1981) paragraphs 4.55 - 4.58). As these may conflict, Scarman stressed that in the case of conflict the maintenance of order should be given priority over the enforcement of the law – he advocated the common sense use of discretion.

Scarman made recommendations on police accountability, on police methods and on training. These comments on methods, advocating foot patrols, community based beat officers, consultation and accountability, were put forward not just as an antidote to the riots but 'necessary as a response to modern social developments'. This was a recognition of the failing image of the police, and a suggested response to regain the confidence of the community – to rebuild the police image.

Hard and Soft Policing

Scarman's comments brought into the public domain the debate concerning so called 'hard' and 'soft' policing. The former is associated with the enforcement of the law and in its late 1990s incarnation is seen in the 'zero tolerance' approach, popularised in New York under (ex) Commissioner Bratton, and which has made some inroads on this side of the Atlantic, for example in Cleveland. On the other hand the latter approach is associated with the maintenance of order, the use of discretion and the general notion of 'community policing'. Obviously policing practice based entirely on either one or the other of these approaches will present very different images to the public. Changes were implemented in the wake of Scarman – Reiner has argued that in the decade following the report most chief officers acknowledged the broader service oriented role of policing in practice, and there have been concerted attempts to change the rank and file culture by developing the service ethic (Reiner 1994). Nevertheless throughout the 1980s, as Thatcher's Britain polarised and the unions confronted the Government, the police were again thrust into political disputes, most memorably during the 1984 miners' strike in which police crossed territorial borders (as did miners), raising fears of a national police force and creating wounds which are yet to heal in the close knit coalfield communities. Further confrontational situations were experienced with revived rioting in 1985 in Handsworth, Brixton, Toxteth and Broadwater Farm, and during the second half of the 1980s the dominant police image was their presence in conflictual situations such as Wapping and the Notting Hill Carnival.

During the 1980s then the police were obliged to manage their image in a context in which they often occupied a confrontational position, attempting to uphold the law in angry, disturbing televised circumstances, whilst at the same time performing their traditional roles, endeavouring to maintain the confidence of the public, and with it their image.

The Influence of Equipment on Image

During this period the police found it necessary to adopt protective clothing, doing away with the trusty dustbin lid in favour of NATO helmets, body armour and shields. CS gas was also made available and used for the first time on mainland Britain during the Toxteth disturbances in July 1981.

Whilst necessary for the protection of officers, the adoption of such equipment was not without some regret amidst feelings that the police were taking on a paramilitary appearance and resembling continental police (which was not a compliment). Although an image of professionalism was conveyed, something of the traditional image was lost as the police shed their appearance of vulnerability.

Similarly in the 1990s as forces have adopted batons in favour of truncheons, and officers are being equipped more commonly with CS sprays following controlled trials during 1996, there is an argument that the traditional image of the British police officer is being eroded by following such policies. The media coverage afforded to the recurring debate on routinely arming police officers is one strand of this argument, and the sensitivity which ACPO has been showing in its evaluation of the patrol officers uniform is another.

The 1990s Image

To date during the 1990s, though urban rioting has diminished, the police have had to maintain their image in the face of further confrontational situations including clashes with Poll Tax protesters (very violently in Trafalgar Square in 1990) and Criminal Justice and Public Order Bill (subsequently Act) protesters (violently in Hyde Park in 1994 which generated much adverse press coverage). There have also been increasing numbers of clashes arising from environmental protests and demonstrations, most notably at road building sites, e.g. Twyford Down, the Newbury bypass and the A30 widening scheme at Fairmile, east of Exeter. The demonstrations against live animal exports from Sussex and Essex ports during 1995 also presented the police with the challenge of maintaining their image whilst facilitating the passage of a trade that few within the local communities supported.

Arguably throughout the 1990s, the most damaging challenge to the police image has been the allegations of police misconduct in the securing of convictions. The most memorable cases are those of the Birmingham Six, the Guildford Four and the Bridgewater Four, which had already been reviewed on two occasions. Such appeals against conviction and the media interest they create do not help to maintain the confidence of the public, whatever their ultimate outcome, and public knowledge that corruption does exist has been popularly exploited by the success of the television series *Between The Lines*, the first two series of which featured a team of CIB officers investigating police corruption.[1]

In addition the 1990s has seen a growth in fear for community safety. During a period when official statistics have shown a decrease in recorded crime – police figures recorded a 10% decrease in crime between 1993 and 1996 – other surveys suggest that the public is not reassured and that fear of crime is considerable. The 1996 International Crime Vicitimisation Survey which compared people's experiences of crime across eleven industrialised countries shows that people in England and Wales are more likely to expect to be burgled. England and Wales come out as the most security conscious of the surveyed countries. This puts additional pressure on the Police to 'do something about it', with an insatiable media creating bandwagons and fuelling very real fears, leading to demands for increased effectiveness from the police.

The foregoing historical perspective has illustrated some of the pressures on the police, and the threats to the revered impartial 'British Bobby' image. The characteristic of this history appears to be that there has been little proactive management of image (*The Blue Lamp* is an outstanding exception). In contrast, on the face of it, the emphasis has been to maintain the image despite the difficulties, using strategies of damage limitation, of making the best of a bad situation – in essence it has been reactive. Nevertheless this analysis is to some extent simplistic. Histories of the police service, whether presenting the service as a great British institution or as a coercive force of the ruling elite used to suppress the masses, have portrayed different images. Indeed the founders of the police could not have been ignorant of the importance of image. How else could the new, widely opposed institution have become accepted and later even revered without some clever strategic thinking concerning how such a force could be sold to the public in such a way that it was accepted (hence the founding principles of non-partisanship and a preventive policing policy)? In this respect there has always been a need for market orientation.

Market Orientation

From the late 1980s and throughout the 1990s there has been moves by the police service to look at commercial organisations and to consider whether the service can benefit from adopting business and commercial practices. Examples of this are corporate image management marketing practices and policies, quality of service initiatives including high profile campaigns such as the Charter Mark and Investors In People (IIP) initiatives. Indeed even the promotion of equal opportunity programmes, and recruitment campaigns aimed at ethnic minority groups, though worthy and necessary in their own right, can be seen in the context of image management.

---

[1] It is interesting to contrast *Between the Lines* with the unashamedly nostalgic *Heartbeat* (music of our youth and cars we wish we had owned) which features the 'golden age' policing of a mainly rural community (probably James Herriot's). *Heartbeat* is far removed from the realalities of modern day policing but can be seen in the context of redressing the balance and like *Between the Lines* it clearly has great appeal to television viewers.

Notably the Metropolitan Police have followed the practices of commercial organisations in their commissioning of consultants to assist with image promotion and public relations. Saatchi and Saatchi have been used to develop advertising campaigns at no little cost. The same force has used Wolf Olins, corporate image specialists, who suggested changes that would improve not only the public perception of the police, but also the self image of employees. For example one recommendation was to improve the appearance of police stations both on the front desk and behind the scenes (Wolf Olins 1988). Other forces have followed suit judging by the improved decorations and layouts of stations that the authors have had the pleasure of visiting in the course of their research.

Whilst there has always been a need for market orientation, it can be argued that in the recent trend towards adopting private sector techniques, there has been a change of emphasis from the service using advertising campaigns to send specific safety (worn car tyres kill) or danger (drink driving kills) messages to more subtle types of campaign which are aimed at sending messages promoting the service or changing public perceptions. These days there is more to police advertising campaigns than simply stated public information messages.

Fig 11.2:
The Metropolitan
Police's Operation
Bumblebee poster

An example is the extensive marketing which the Metropolitan Police apply to Operation Bumblebee. The campaign is planned by the Public Relations Branch of the Met.s Directorate of Public Affairs (DPA). They produce a Publicity Plan which details the aim of each campaign, the target audiences and the tactics. One enduring image of Operation Bumblebee is the distinctive poster (figure 11.2) showing a number of bees in flight over the city and the caption 'How to sting a burglar'. This poster sends messages of reassurance to the good citizen, of warning to the burglars and of a job well done to police officers themselves. Since its inception in the mid-1990s, the Bumblebee campaign has promoted confidence in the ability of the police to target and catch persistent offenders, i.e. confidence in the ability of the police to perform the function most commonly associated with them, that of combating crime. Similar high profile coverage has been subsequently afforded to variants of Bumblebee in the provinces.

In addition to advertising campaigns which may involve television coverage, press items, posters and possibly videos, other commercial techniques are available for exploitation by the police service, for example direct marketing. This technique is useful for single message campaigns aimed at a distinct group, to which leaflets or mail can then be directed, for instance it may be an appropriate technique to target groups who are suffering repeat victimisation.

A further technique, which is particularly appropriate in these days of 'partnership' is that of joint marketing initiatives, for example a divisional crime prevention initiative might benefit from the joint input of crime prevention officers, Neighbourhood Watch co-ordinators and a local installer of home security products. Such a symbiotic relationship would benefit the image of the police locally, whilst the police support for the initiative should give it authority and instil confidence in the targeted community. Strategic alliances of this nature are discussed in further detail in chapter 10. Such alliances have become more commonplace and broader based with the advent of sponsorship and the appointment of force sponsorship officers, often civilian professionals with specific expertise. This is a growing trend and the post is sometimes combined with a marketing function. Clearly if joint initiatives are contemplated, the choice of partner should be beyond reproach. Police forces are rightfully aware of the potential negative image implications which might arise from aligning with partners or sponsors whose integrity might later be questioned. This raises further management challenges.

With the possibility of privatisation a recurring theme in the nineties and influential senior officers such as the Metropolitan Police Commissioner Sir Paul Condon relishing the opportunity to compete on equal market terms as the privateers in his 1994 IPEC Conference address, whether the old guard like it or not they may have little option but to consider the benefits of such commercial techniques.

A Model Image for the Nineties?

To return to first principles, what image is the police service attempting to put across in the 1990s? It could be argued that their preferred image is:

- Efficient and Effective: *In these days of value for money (VFM),there is a need for the police to convince the public that their money is being wisely spent.*

- Accountable: *To the communities which forces serve.*

- Non-partisan: *Another traditional attribute which came under question during the 1970s and 1980s.*

- Service oriented: *The 'softer' service provider image is taking precedence over the 'enforcer' image. This presents a more sympathetic image in a polarised society. It also reflects internal changes in management and organisational matters. The hierarchic rank based structures are being eroded by a movement towards flatter, more consultative structures (encouraged by such ACPO and Home Office initiatives as 'Getting Things Right'). This has not come easy to all forces and a battle of wits and attrition is being played out between 'dinosaurs' and progressives. IIP and the Charter Mark initiatives can both be seen in the context of an emphasis on the service aspect.*

- A partner in the community: *Throughout the 1990s the belief has been maintained that the police alone can not solve the crime problem, and that there is a need to pull in other groups in society to use collective skills and resources to solve problems in communities. This has resulted in 'multi agency' and 'partnership' projects and the police service has often been the facilitator of such initiatives. The language of partnership remains dominant at police – public consultation meetings.*

Having discussed the historical perspective of the police image, and its management, and noted the current 'model' image and recent moves towards market orientation, it is now appropriate to consider how the image is managed from an organisational point of view.

Organising the Management of Image

As mentioned earlier in the chapter, the police service has begun to move towards utilisation of commercial marketing practices to promote the desired image. In addition there has been greater emphasis on developing media and public relations policies. At the forefront has been the Metropolitan Police. The pioneer of change in the Met. was Sir Robert Mark, Commissioner from 1972 to 1977, whose determined objective was to improve the force's media relations as a means of creating a 'better understanding on their part and **that of the public** of the force's problems' (Mark 1978 – the emphasis is the authors).

Sir Robert coined the phrase 'Winning whilst appearing to lose', in his opinion this being the true art of policing in a free society. It is particularly apt in relation to maintaining the image of the police. The enduring image from the 1977 Grunwick industrial dispute (which saw daily public order problems) is that of an unarmed traditionally uniformed police officer lying bleeding in the gutter, having been felled by a flying bottle. This image, shown on television news and in the following day's newspapers, caught the public imagination and won some sympathy for the police. It was picked up on and used for a subsequent Police Federation publicity campaign. Here the police won whilst appearing to lose. In contrast, during the 1984 Miners' strike, at the disturbances around the Orgreave coking plant, by using heavy handed tactics – thousands of officers, horses, cavalry charges against picketing miners, the police lost whilst appearing to win. The images of heavily protected police officers charging into miners, broadcast to the nation through the national news did the police image no favours. A similar image was put across following police clashes with Criminal Justice Bill (subsequently Act) protesters in Hyde Park in October 1994. Many column inches were devoted to personal accounts of police brutality and TV coverage to doubts over the competence with which the police operation was managed. In Mark's maxim, this was again losing whilst appearing to win.

Sir Robert Mark then was acutely aware of the importance of image management and the need to court and manage the media. Successive commissioners have re-emphasised the importance of openness with the media and the use of publicity to help the public understand the problems and issues facing the police, thus helping to maintain good police/public relations. As a result the Met has developed a large organisational infrastructure to support its media and public relations policies. At Scotland Yard there is a Directorate of Public Affairs and Internal Communication which in 1997 has almost 100 staff and a budget of approximately £9 million. The directorate has, *inter alia*, News, Public Relations, Public Order and Internal Communications and Performance Evaluation branches, together with a Business Unit. The news branch includes a 24 hour press office and the HQ Press Office. The five Met. Area Press Offices are also included in the structure of the DPA. These various branches and offices are responsible for maintaining media relations, developing policy, promoting good news stories about the force, and monitoring and responding to media stories relating to the force. The Public Relations branch is responsible for publicity campaigns, such as those mentioned earlier in relation to Operation Bumblebee.

This simplified description of the resource allocated towards image management by the Met. illustrates the commitment of one force, and a force with unmatched financial resources. The Metropolitan Police Service, with its high profile and central position, has often been a model for practice which has subsequently been adapted and used in provincial forces. In terms of media and public relations management, few other forces are subject to the same media scrutiny and pressure as the Met., they do not have such financial resources available and cannot justify or support such an organisational commitment. Indeed the different forces have varying needs and the Met. model would not be appropriate in any event for most provincial forces, for example a number of press offices run with two press officers, and a survey has shown that the most common staffing level in press offices is four people (Mawby 1997). Each force therefore must make management decisions in terms of balancing its particular need for image promotion with the predicted impact and the costs involved, especially in the prevalent climate of financial restraint and cash limited budgets.

No Home Office or ACPO press and public relations policy exists nationally. However, ACPO does have a Media Advisory Group (since 1993) which has a co-ordinating role and is instrumental in disseminating advice on policy and practice, for example circulars are distributed to forces on such subjects as naming crime victims in press statements and on the releasing of details of old cases to the media. Circulars may also result from specific high profile instances; one such example on media coverage followed the James Bulger murder investigation and trial. Therefore although there are national links, and a trend towards presenting more of a corporate image, there is no uniform way in which each force organises for media and public relations, allowing each force to develop flexibly to suit local needs and conditions. Nevertheless due to the circumstances described, all forces have become more conscious of their image and consequently of the need to manage media and public relations.

Larger forces which like the Met. are faced with dealing with national as well as local media on a daily basis have recognised the need to professionalise and demonstrate innovative approaches to media relations. Though not copying the practice of the Met., they have sometimes drawn on the experiences of senior officers who have served within the Met. and recognised the benefits of such policies. One such example is the West Midlands Police, who under the then chief constable (and former Met man), Geoffrey Dear, developed a proactive approach to media relations after undertaking research observing police/media relations in operation in Europe and New York. The proactive approach promoted positive stories and focused on issues the police felt were important. This contrasted with the previous practice of merely reacting to enquiries from the media. It was an opportunity for West Midlands Police to be instrumental in the portrayal of their media image. This approach is embodied in the Press and Public Relations Department's Business Plan which includes environmental scanning, stakeholder analysis and consultation, aims, deliverables and performance measurement.

Smaller forces, notwithstanding unusual and unexpected events in their area (for example the local, national, and international media siege of Gloucester during the Fred and Rosemary West investigation and subsequent trial), do not have the same scale requirements for a media and public relations organisation. However there remains the need to manage local public and press relations and the importance of a proactive press office and the development of trusting local press/ police relations should not be underestimated. Whilst research shows that most forces now appreciate the need for a proactive press office (Mawby 1997), practical experience suggests that staffing levels often limit the level of resources allocated to proactive work.

Civilian or Uniformed Press Officers?

One aspect of the management of media relations is the question of whether press and public relations offices need to be staffed by police officers or by civilians who can contribute specific skills in journalism, marketing or communications.

The Home Office Circular 114/83 'Manpower, Effectiveness and Efficiency in the Police Service' created central pressure to appoint civilians to posts for which they are specifically suited. Initially, as in other departments there was some resistance to movements towards civilianisation. It was felt that although civilians could contribute specialist journalistic or communications skills, they would encounter some difficulties that arise out of not being a police officer. One difficulty is that the media like to speak to an officer, particularly a senior officer in certain circumstances, for example, the coverage of murder investigations. Historically there is also a credibility problem within the force faced by civilians. If civilian press officers have to negotiate with officers to obtain information, resources etc., they are negotiating from a position of relative weakness. The strong operational culture is such that a no more knowledgeable, but uniformed, officer is more likely to be successful in such negotiations.

For a period press offices tended to comprise a blend of civilians with their specific skills, headed by an officer of possibly chief inspector rank. This was thought to provide the optimum situation, retaining journalistic ability and uniformed authority and credibility. However, a national survey undertaken in 1997 suggests that press offices have broken the convention that force departments need to be managed by police officers (Mawby 1997). Whilst there is a view that police officers can add value – an operational perspective – to press offices, there is a trend towards civilianised, professional offices. The survey showed that in 82% of forces the head of press and PR is a civilian. In addition 83% of staff working in press offices are civilians, and in 52% of forces all press office staff are civilians.

Towards a Media Policy

Irrespective of its size and organisational structure, each force needs to manage its image to some extent and the development of a media policy is a positive management aid. This might comprise a sophisticated and complex strategy, as is the case with the Met. and West Midlands Police. It may be more streamline, for example consisting of a force press and public relations office with specific functions, backed up in some forces by media related training courses and the development of guides for employees on the subject of dealing with the media. For example the good practice and practical tips guides produced by South Yorkshire Police. At a minimum the specific functions undertaken by the press office should include:

- Daily media liaison (whether press liaison is controlled by the Press Office or directly from BCU's/Divisions is a matter of individual force policy). This includes both reactive work, e.g. responding to media queries, and also proactive work, e.g. promoting initiatives and issuing police good news stories and information to the media
- Promoting and projecting the reputation and work of the force by clearly informing the public of the force's activities
- Co-ordinating media and public relations activities across the force
- Providing a media consultancy and support service to all force employees
- Monitoring of media news items – television, radio and newspaper, local and national
- Preparing press releases
- Organising press conferences
- Liaising with the media and senior investigating officers during serious crime investigations

- The development of emergency situation procedures
- Liaison with fire and ambulance services (and authorities and organisations) concerning press releases on specific incidents and issues

Other functions, if not undertaken by specific departments, might include the following, particularly in those forces which have created corporate communications departments with responsibility for all non-operational communications activities:

- Responsibility for developing and maintaining an internal non-operational communications policy
- Designing leaflets, brochures, promotional material. Producing audio-visual materials
- Designing and publishing a force (and possibly divisional) newspaper/newsletter
- Providing input to media training courses/seminars
- Development and maintenance of corporate image
- A role in the force sponsorship activities

These functions will be discharged to best effect if they are integrated within a media policy. This should specifically address:

- The aims and objectives of the policy
- The press office's terms of reference and where appropriate the specification of service levels
- The target audience(s), both external and internal
- The processes by which the objectives will be achieved and the audiences reached
- Monitoring of performance against the stated objectives. For example, this might be accomplished through periodically surveying regular users of the press office, in combination with the evaluation of media coverage obtained
- Guidance to all employees concerning liaison with the press office and with the media, i.e. clarification of who does what, where, when and how in terms of media relations.

In line with the development of media policies, there is a need to equip those personnel who liaise with the media, with the appropriate skills to discharge their responsibilities. There are a number of training courses (for all ranks) focusing on how to use and manage the media. These courses are run both within the larger forces and also at the Police Staff College at Bramshill. One aim of the courses is to encourage the breakdown of police suspicion of the media in order that the media can be used to positive effect, to the advantage of the police. The best of these courses include the active participation of media professionals.

The Contribution of the Community Relations Department

The force press office helps to manage and promote the police image in the media and to convey a positive image to the public generally, but operationally the image must be backed up, acted out and enhanced, if the promoted image is to achieve credibility with the public. Whilst the image of all organisations depends upon the conduct of its workforce, the police service has more pressures than most as officers must police society and conflict is endemic to this role.

The role of each officer whether answering the telephone to a member of the public or patrolling the beat is crucial, but none more so than those officers which serve in the units which fall within the department variously known as Community Affairs, Community Relations, and Community Services. This department commonly is responsible for, and co-ordinates the activities of, the press and public relations office, a community involvement unit, crime prevention (including the various 'Watch' schemes), schools and youth liaison, race relations, victim support and the lay visitors scheme. Clearly these are all areas where there are opportunities for the police image to be enhanced (or damaged if mismanaged). The department usually also employs more overt methods of promoting the police image by organising police open days, providing displays and exhibition stands at carnivals and festivals, and arranging visits to stations.

Officers heading in the direction of community relations may be put off by its comparatively low status, and once in community relations they may be derided by colleagues for not performing real policing. The operational culture within the service is partly responsible for such perceptions, and there is currently much debate in policing and political circles concerning issues of community policing in general. The police role in the community has always been valued – the bobby on the beat, keeping in touch with the community, has been a cornerstone of the legitimacy and authority of the police, so it is nothing new for the police to promote this image. Its current pre-eminence may be attributable to the ongoing debate concerning core police roles and the level of police resources. The image of the service cannot be seen independently of its role. The role and functions of the police will influence the image which needs to be projected – image management is an instrument used to facilitate the discharge of such functions.

Whatever the outcome of the recurring debates on core roles and community policing, the role of community relations departments and their officers are important to the police image. These officers present a side of the police which many members of the public are not familiar with. To many of us, police officers are encountered at the roadside for speeding lectures or accident statements, at the home following burglaries, or at public demonstrations. The antidote is the crime prevention officer who provides free security advice, the community relations officer who turns up at schools to befriend our kids, attends public meetings to provide the police perspective and participates in community based initiatives such as the myriad partnership schemes across the country which have been generated by such financial programmes as Safer Cities and the Single Regeneration Budget. The police are often the initiative takers in such projects whether by design or because nobody else will do it. The involvement of police forces in community, partnership based, projects is a powerful weapon in projecting a positive image providing that the officers involved are equipped with the appropriate skills and also take account of effective exit strategies.

It is notable that the police service is taking its role as a partner in the community extremely seriously. A review of the annual force reports over recent years reveals that most forces now stress the importance of working in partnership with the community. Indeed successive Met. reports and annual policing plans have placed particular emphasis on partnership activities.

One management aspect to ponder is that the community relations department is commonly based at force headquarters. The irony of this situation was noted by one borough council chief executive, who found himself being visited by the headquarters based community relations chief superintendent on the eve of a partnership initiative. The chief executive remarked that he had never met the officer before and suggested that those officers responsible for community affairs would make a greater impression if they were based within that community. Whilst there is an organisational argument for basing the department centrally to co-ordinate activities throughout the force area, the number and rank of the central staff does not need to be top heavy.

Chapter Summary

- The need for image management arises out of the position occupied by the police service in society. Whilst acting for the public, at times against sections of that public, the consent of the public must be maintained.

- Historically the police service has not managed its image proactively, although the founders of the service did create an image for the service which was designed to win public support and co-operation. Founding principles such as non-partisanship, accountability and the use of preventive policing methods are still regarded as important.

- A more proactive approach to image management can be traced from the appointment of Sir Robert Mark as Metropolitan Police Commissioner in 1972, though twenty-five years on force practice varies with no established national policy.

- Individual forces are moving towards a more strategic approach to image management. An emphasis is being placed on proactive work; media, public relations and marketing policies are being developed; press offices are integrating their traditional function of media liaison with others such as internal communications, marketing and corporate image.

- Image management can be approached from several directions and this chapter has looked at the application of commercial marketing practices together with organisational approaches based on the activities of press and PR offices and the community focused departments.

- Whatever approach is adopted towards image management, it is a subject which forces cannot afford to ignore in these days of efficiency, effectiveness and quality of service.

Chapter 12

Managing Civilians

Introduction

Arguably, one section of the police service workforce has consistently been overlooked, under-paid and underestimated and this may be the point where the reader thinks 'this must be the chapter about my section'. The group in question is the civilians, who present a management challenge as they occupy a unique position within the service. They work alongside police officers and yet have different terms and conditions, different pay scales and career structures. Only under the 1996 Police Act did they become answerable, ultimately to the Chief Constable. They have not always been welcomed by the prevalent operational culture and internal surveys suggest that many civilians feel that, as a group, they are treated as second class citizens. The management issues presented by this situation include how to manage civilians, how to approach the management of police officers by civilians and vice versa, and how to motivate and integrate civilians into the organisation and its culture in such a way that they are used effectively.

This chapter will explore the role of civilians in the police service and how they fit into the existing management structures and processes. It will explain how the numbers and deployment of civilians has expanded, but not in any strategic way, and will highlight the obstacles which exist to prevent their most effective use. Proposals will be put forward concerning the effective management of this group of employees who now constitute one third of the strength of the police service in England and Wales.

The Role of Civilians and Historical Perspective

The police service in 1997 employs greater numbers of civilians than hitherto in wide-ranging functions and with differing status and levels of responsibility. In addition to the obvious example of traffic wardens, civilians are deployed in manual posts as cleaners and mechanics, in administrative and clerical posts within headquarters and divisions, in managerial posts as heads of departments, press officers and sub-divisional administrative officers, and in a few, but increasing number of cases in executive posts such as financial director. They are used in technical posts as computer programmers and data analysts, and have broken into (quasi) operational posts as scenes of crimes officers (SOCO), crime prevention officers and also as information analysts attached to serious crime investigations. Thus civilians now pervade the service though they do not possess the influence or policy making responsibility that arguably their numbers and functions deserve. This situation contrasts, ironically, with an earlier age (pre 1945) when few civilians were employed by the service, but those that were occupied executive positions of great influence. For example, HMI's and Metropolitan Police commissioners, historically, have often been appointed without previous police service and other provincial forces have followed suit, albeit the appointee has often come from a military background. Nevertheless, as late as 1945 a senior civil servant was appointed Met. commissioner and, to this day, the commissioner is appointed as a magistrate, a Crown servant rather than a police officer. As Loveday (1993) has observed, this is an 'interesting commitment to civilian control'.

The increasing number of civilians employed on a 'bottom up' basis and the decreasing practice of recruiting chief officers from outside the service characterises the nature of civilian employment from the Second World War to the present day. Prior to 1939 when few police service employees were civilians, police officers were not particularly well paid and were as cost effective as civilians to employ. Consequently they were used for all functions from cleaning police stations to preventative patrolling, and it is from this environment no doubt that the culture developed engendering the belief (amongst officers) that all police functions are best performed by police officers, whether the function is detective work, foot patrol or custody control. However during the Second World War civilians helped the police, occupying support roles as clerks and telephonists. After the war the trend towards professionalising the service reversed the practice of appointing outsiders as chief officers, and, at the same time, there were pressures to utilise the potential of civilians to relieve the administrative burden on police officers, and thus release officers for operational duties. For example the Oaksey Committee in 1949 recommended the reviewing of police establishments:

> 'with a view to releasing policemen for police duty,
> wherever possible by the employment of civilians.'

and in 1966 the Taverne Report recommended the use of civilians in posts not requiring:

> 'police training, the exercise of police powers or
> the special qualifications or personal qualities of
> a police officer.'

The Taverne Report also addressed issues that remain pertinent today by suggesting that civilians should be used in technical posts such as photography and scenes of crime to provide a broader career structure for civilians. As will be discussed later, the absence of a formal career structure remains a barrier to the effective management of civilians.

Together with the pressure from Home Office committees to utilise civilians, improved conditions and pay for police officers created a financial environment in which civilians were more cost effective to employ in certain functions and civilian strengths grew – from less than 1300 in 1945 (England and Wales) to 8,500 in 1966, until by 1970 the Met. alone employed over 15,000 civilians. Between 1976 and 1978 the total number of civilian employees in fact declined, but this was due to the reduction in numbers of traffic wardens and cadets, and the numbers of manual, clerical and administrative staff remained fairly constant.

Civilianisation was given further impetus by the Edmund Davies pay award of 1978 and ensuing police pay awards during the 1980s which made civilians much less expensive to employ than police officers. In addition Home Office Circular 114/83 'Manpower, Effectiveness and Efficiency in the Police Service' encouraged civilianisation by stating that:

> 'the Home Secretary will not normally be prepared
> to approve increases in establishment if police
> officers are occupying posts which could properly,
> and more economically, be filled by civilians.'

Further Home Office circulars reinforced this position – 105/88 and 106/88 with the former including an attempt to broaden the civilian role by encouraging the use of civilians in specific roles such as coroners officers and detention officers.

Thus forces embraced civilianisation during the 1980s as it was a means of increasing establishment and by the early 1990s civilians made up over 30 per cent of the police service workforce in England and Wales. Home Office statistics for 1995/6 show a civilian strength of almost 57,000 employees including civilian grades and traffic wardens, but excluding special constables. The push for civilianisation has continued into the 1990s both as a means of promoting quality of service and also as a means of achieving value for money. The specialist skills of civilians have also been tapped into as the police service (reflecting society in general) has become more technological and has required the presence of specialist skills within the workforce, such as information technology and in a different area, journalism.

In his final report as Her Majesty's Chief Inspector of Constabulary (HMCIC) in October 1996, Sir Trefor Morris stated that almost 5,000 police officer posts had been "freed up" for operational duty in the preceding five years, through civilianisation. Despite this, he went on to criticise forces for delays in the pace of civilianisation and his successor, David O'Dowd has indicated that there is the potential to civilianise a further 6,000 posts, across the country.

Fig 12.1: Comparative numbers of police officers and civilians 1945 and 1994

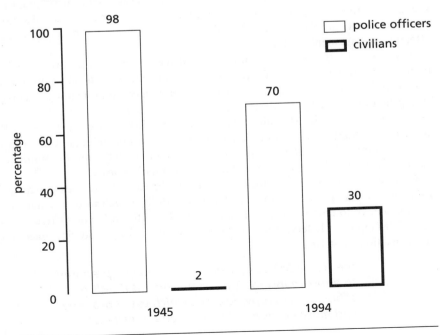

Highmore (1993) has traced civilianisation through four phases:

- Phase 1: *Manual* functions such as cleaning and catering (pre 1939)
- Phase 2: *Administrative/clerical support* functions (1939-66)
- Phase 3: *Administrative and specialist* such as SOCO, fingerprinting functions (1966 onwards)
- Phase 4: *Professional* functions such as financial/accounting, IT, personnel specialists (1988 onwards).

Highmore observes that in phase four a new class of civilian employee has emerged...

'A body of men and women with the necessary managerial and specialist skills to ensure a professional civilian support function for the police service of the twenty-first century.'

However, it could be argued that, in the 1990s, civilianisation has entered a fifth phase. This is the phase in which civilians are appointed to senior management positions more regularly. There are, already, increasing numbers of civilians being appointed to the senior management team. Merseyside were the first force to appoint a civilian as an ACC equivalent Force Administrative Officer, and as Police Authorities have taken control of their own finances, more have followed suit. This has led to the appointment of more and more civilians with financial, corporate or strategic management skills to executive positions. The characteristic of this phase has been the move of civilians, from technical and support roles, to truly senior managerial roles.

One could further argue that we are on the verge of entering a sixth phase with civilians now taking on roles which have perhaps previously been regarded as the sole province of a police officer. Devon & Cornwall caused considerable controversy when they considered the use of civilians as custody officers, giving them limited powers to enable them to do the job. More recently, Kent have "raised a few eyebrows" by advertising for civilian staff with "investigative skills" to support investigation teams and crime desks. The implication from this was this civilian staff would be used in a minor interviewing role, primarily in relation to cautioning.

Not surprisingly, this drew an angry response from the Police Federation who saw this move as civilians making further inroads into core policing skills. The force, however, saw this move as a means of reducing administrative burdens on officers and argued that the public were only worried about receiving the best service possible, irrespective of who carries out the work. These two instances indicate that perhaps we are entering a new phase, and one which will bring the divergence of police officers and civilians into even sharper focus.

This historical perspective suggests that there has been, and is, a centrally driven Home Office policy aimed at increasing the numbers, and indeed the roles, of civilians. However, despite this central encouragement of civilianisation, and the positive reaction of police forces, which has given rise to the situation in which forces are dependent on civilians for support and could not successfully operate without them, 'very little consideration, thought or planning had been given to the consequences of such recruitment in terms of civilian status, function or career structure' (Loveday (1993)).

As the numbers and roles of civilians have expanded, the difficulty of their position has increased. There has been pressure and incentives to recruit civilians, but no strategic plan or supportive infrastructure to induct, train and guide their careers – their role has been essentially one of support and, arguably secondary, and they have been treated as such by the police service.

Managing Civilians: The Issues

The problems manifested by the lack of strategic planning and a supportive infrastructure for civilian staff are obstacles to effective management and include:

The Ownership and Control of Civilians

Until recently, there has been a problem of ownership of, and responsibility for, civilians, which as a group left them in limbo, occupying an ambivalent position where little responsibility is taken for their careers and development. Section 15 of the Police Act 1996 states that:

> '*A police authority... may employ persons to assist the police force maintained by it.*'

It further states that:

> '*...any person employed by the authority under this section is under the direction and control of the chief constable...*'

This legislation meant that, for the first time, civilian staff were ultimately responsible to the chief constable and employed by the police authority and not the first tier local authority. While this may go some way to addressing issues of ownership, it is clear that many forces have not yet established appropriate structures and processes to support their own support staff.

Under the previous arrangements, Loveday (1993) argued that the Home Office had encouraged civilianisation but abdicated responsibility for its consequences and, that as a result, a policy vacuum resulted as local authorities were 'unwilling or unable to finance career structures and training programmes commensurate with the expansion of civilian employment'. The practical effect of this situation was that civilians were graded in accordance with local authority scales, but due to financial pressures, the grades were not always equal to local authority employees undertaking similar functions outside of the police service.

The Sheehy Report recognised this and was in favour of bringing civilians formally under the responsibility of chief officers in an integrated civilian/police management structure. This was formally enacted in the Police Act 1996 as noted above. However, there are fears amongst civilians that it may lead to the *de facto* situation of civilians being officially second class employees and that such a change will still not affect some of the arguments outlined below.

Contrasting Police/Civilian Pay Scales and Terms of Employment

Contracts of employment, pay scales, and terms and conditions of service differ greatly between civilians and police officers. Police officers are trained and inducted into a disciplined and hierarchical environment which provides them with a life long career. They accept that there must be immediate compliance with the order of a superior officer and they observe a disciplinary code. Civilians in contrast are not uniformed, at least not the same uniform, though some do now wear a form of uniform, such as some front desk staff. They are not subject to the same disciplinary code and are not required to offer the same degree of unquestioning obedience as their uniformed colleagues. They are unlikely only to work within the police service during their employment career and there is no civilian equivalent of the career officer. Management issues and challenges arise from the situation in which these vary different types of staff often sit side by side and work under the same line manager.

One problem that results concerns the motivation of civilians who see officers doing similar or lesser tasks for greater rewards. Although it has been determined by numerous writers on motivation that monetary reward is fairly low on the scale of priorities of most people, there are obvious frustrations inherent in this situation. It should be noted, however, that not all civilians share this frustration. Many have recognised that the police have a multi-functional role, while many civilians have single functions and that if a major incident "cracks off", only the police officers will be sent to deal with it.

Civilian support is becoming more organised, however. UNISON, the trades union responsible for looking after the interests of police civilian staff have now succeeded in standardising the conditions for police white collar and manual civilian workers. Building on this, they have stated that they will now consider bringing equal pay cases against forces where police officers and civilians are doing the same job for different pay.

Frustration often mounts within departments staffed by specialist civilians, for example journalists in the press office and computing professionals in the IT departments, as a succession of generalist police officers spend a relatively short time as manager of the department (partly due to the policy of tenure which applies to police officers but not civilians). During their tenure as manager, keen to make an impression, officers often embark on a worthy change of policy, which may never be implemented or which they may not still be in post to appreciate (or suffer) the consequences of. This so called 'butterfly effect' is observed with a 'seen it all before' weariness by civilian staff who often provide the only element of continuity in some departments.

In addition to considering the motivation of civilians in the circumstances described above, the manager must utilise his/her resources effectively, taking into account the different working practices of civilians and officers. Police managers are used to giving orders and expecting them to be obeyed. If, for example, a report has to be submitted to a tight deadline which requires individuals to work late, the police manager can order a subordinate officer to do so.

This is not necessarily the case with civilians. There are numerous examples of situations where requests to civilians to work late have met with flat refusal. In this situation the police manager is effectively powerless though the impact of the new legislation under the Police Act 1996, referred to above has yet to be tested in this area. This leads to the discipline aspect – if a police officer refuses to respond to an order, a disciplinary charge may result, while failure by a civilian to respond to the same order may go unpunished, especially if the order requires the civilian to go beyond their conditions of employment.

In this area, however, the situation may also be changing. In its' annual report for 1996, the Police Complaints Authority (PCA) recognised that:

> *'A number of sensitive police tasks are now being carried out by civilians who, although subject to their own disciplinary procedures, are divorced from the police complaints system.'*

They have suggested that their powers should be extended to cover civilian support staff and Specials and in so doing:

> *'Provide an element of reassurance to the complainant without unduly interfering in civilian personnel management.'*

Developments in this area are awaited with some interest.

Civilian Career Development

The growth of the civilian workforce without recourse to any strategic plan has resulted in the lack of a formal career structure for civilian employees. While police officers join the force as cadets or constables, can set their ambition at rising to chief constable and have a comprehensive career development and training structure to help them realise their potential, it is unlikely that a civilian will join the force as a junior clerk with the ambition of achieving a senior civilian position.

In general there is less opportunity for civilian promotion, and where it exists, it is usually to lower management levels in administrative or technical type posts. Prospects of career progression reduce considerably at office manager level (usually around scale 5/6 and SO1 grades). Indeed, civilians even face threats to their jobs as evidenced by the plans of the Metropolitan Police, announced in late 1996, to contract out over 2000 civilian posts such as pay and pensions administration, property services and central typing services, from 1998.

The result of this must in many cases be a loss of motivation as the employee sees no opportunity for future development. Ultimately this may lead to employees leaving the service to progress their careers, often in other parts of local government. The service may then be left with those who, for whatever reason, do not seek greater recognition, promotion and increased responsibility. In these circumstances it is questionable whether the service can attract the best in the field, or if they do, whether they can keep them. In this environment the civilian with transferable administrative and technical skills is likely to have less sense of loyalty to the service than the police officer whose skills, in most cases, are only really relevant in the police environment.

There is evidence that forces are recognising the need to develop the civilian workforce. Following a survey undertaken by Staffordshire University's Centre for Police Management and Research (CPMR) in October 1993 of management training provision within forces, Mawby (1994) suggested that structures were being developed for civilian career development. Some forces have created bespoke departments to attend to civilians whilst others have extended their existing career development departments to accommodate civilians. Nevertheless there is some way to go before a state of equality is reached, as the financial resources dedicated towards the development of police officers far outweighs the provision for civilians. This is equitable, taking into account the main business of the service – operational policing, but there is room for further development before a state of equilibrium is attained.

While there are long term opportunities for police strategic managers to improve the lot of civilians through further adoption of career development policies and encouragement of integration, the middle manager acting pragmatically on a day to day basis has no control over pay scales, career structures or working conditions. The factors outlined, which can lead to demotivation, are factors which they should be aware of as potentially disruptive influences in the workplace.

The Civilian Relationship with the Corporate Culture

Much has been written on the subject of the operational culture within the police service. It is sufficient in this context to acknowledge the existence of the culture and to observe that civilians must manage and be managed within the existing environment and must develop strategies to cope with the culture if that culture is unwilling to accept them. In time, with enlightened management, with organisational and personnel changes, the culture will develop further, possibly into one that accepts the position of civilians.

Part of the operational culture comprises a mistrust of civilians by many police officers. This presents an obstacle to the integration of police officers and civilians. The mistrust of civilians and the tensions which exist between police officers and civilians arise from several causes. Some officers feel that civilians are threatening their jobs, are taking those posts that in earlier days were used as sinecures for ageing or injured officers, others feel that all police functions are discharged more effectively by officers and the use of civilians, particularly in quasi operational roles, undermines the professional status of the police officer. Yet others refuse to accept civilians other than as support staff and resent their seepage into potentially influential positions.

The outcome on the civilian psyche appears to be a collective lack of confidence in the status of the group. Two surveys undertaken by the CPMR in very different forces in 1993 and 1994 suggested that civilians did perceive that they were treated as second class citizens within the organisation. Interestingly this contrasts with the findings of a study conducted by Hampshire Constabulary in 1993, which in a survey of three forces – Merseyside, Derbyshire and Hampshire – found that the majority of responding civilians agreed that theirs was a supporting role, but an important one and that their status was not any lower than that of police colleagues. However, almost half of the officers who responded did feel that the role of the civilian was less important than their own (Highmore 1993). Evidence from more recent conversations with civilians in other forces seems to indicate that the acceptance and integration of civilians varies from force to force. Without wishing to embarrass any force it would appear that some are far better than others in integrating police and civilian staff.

The dominant culture together with the disparities in pay and terms and conditions of employment have created an 'us and them' attitude. This presents difficulties of management, for example will police officers respect and work effectively for a civilian departmental manager? Will civilian specialists perform for their police manager who has little knowledge of the department he has been brought in to manage? Clearly greater acceptance by each group of the strengths of the other is required before true integration of the civilian workforce into the organisation can be achieved.

Out of the Impasse?

These issues all create difficulties of effective management – of how to use civilians most effectively to meet the objectives of the force, rather than merely to use their number as a performance indicator in its own right. Possible solutions may rest in proposals in the following areas.

A Clear Civilian Structure

The establishment of ownership and control of civilians should allow for the creation of a clear infrastructure to support civilians. From this should follow fertile conditions in which civilians feel valued, rewarded and able to satisfy their ambitions.

Career development structures have not been a priority for forces due to the ownership issues and also the nature of civilian employment, i.e. in generalist administrative posts with little chance of progression or in specialist technical posts lacking an obvious development path and lacking transferable skills (a factor which has never impeded the progress of police officers).

Clearer and more formal career development planning would improve the motivation of employees by allowing employees to match their ambitions to a career in the service and by allowing them to set personal goals.

The gradual implementation of career development planning within forces for civilians indicates that generally more thought and attention is being given to civilian career development. The introduction of appraisal systems for civilian staff is also a positive move.

It has been suggested that a clearer rank or status structure for civilian staff would help both police and civilian staff to understand each others roles and places in the organisation. This may facilitate the integration of civilians into the service and render officers more amenable to accepting civilian managers. Work place shadow schemes could also go some way to reducing mutual suspicion.

Increased (and Integrated) Training

The moves towards career planning cannot be sustained without the provision of increased training and development opportunities for civilians, and recent evidence suggests that forces are attempting to address this. However, in times of value for money efficiency drives, training is often the first area to feel the butcher's knife, which is ironic taking account of the possibility that training may make all levels of personnel more effective in their posts and hence provide better value for money. It is also a fact of police life that training will always be accentuated towards police officers, and civilians probably have to accept this as inevitable. Nevertheless the promotion of integrated training is to be encouraged as a means of further promoting the integration of officers and civilians and breaking down the 'us and them' attitude where it exists.

Continued Progress into Senior Management Positions

It is difficult to envisage significant change unless the fundamentals of control and improved conditions are clarified, and although civilians are already being appointed to senior posts, it is questionable as to the actual influence they have, i.e. are there civilians in roles which allow them to look after civilians' interests in policy making committees?

Nevertheless the appointment of civilians to senior positions is a breakthrough and is a positive trend as, for the first time, civilians are being allowed to hold positions which may allow access to policymaking groups. Previously, heads of departments, for example computing managers, might have been asked advice on policy matters or to head working groups but the ultimate policy decisions would be made by the exclusively uniformed executive team. Thus the presence of senior civilian managers on such executive teams is a talisman for all civilians, illustrating the potential for progress.

Quality of Service Initiatives

Quality of service has been forced onto the police service agenda by the Home Office in the form of performance indicators, and it is being pursued by some forces through quality initiatives such as the Charter Mark, 'Getting Things Right' and Investors in People (IIP).

These are good news for civilians as these initiatives encourage personal development and can be used as vehicles for the more effective management of civilians. Taking IIP as an example, this has the objective of realising the organisation's aims and objectives through the training and development of all its personnel. 'Getting Things Right', with its emphasis on doing the right things and consultation, is similarly progressive. Many of these quality initiatives utilise principles from total quality management (TQM) including the recognition that internal customer relationships exist as well as external customer relationships. These relationships need to be identified, monitored and improved where they are found to be lacking. Accordingly, to succeed with initiatives of this nature, forces are being compelled to address the effective management of civilians – to provide them with positive direction and to implement structures for effective management including career development policies and appraisal processes.

Motivation

Motivation of civilians in the current environment can be a problem, and one which is hard to alleviate without competitive pay, training and development, and career structures which allow employees to achieve and to satisfy their ambitions.

One of the more important motivating factors is recognition of employees as people and not as ciphers or insignificant cogs in the organisation. It is important for the police manager to recognise this fact and to realise its importance when ensuring maximum participation and co-operation from civilians working in the police environment.

Before we leave the subject of civilianisation, it is worth considering the fact that the original catalyst for civilianisation was that such staff could carry out tasks, otherwise done by police officers, at a lower cost. As civilian staff become more organised and UNISON considers taking forces to court over equal pay for equal jobs issues, there is a school of thought which suggests that this financial argument is less and less valid. Perhaps the justification for the continuing push for civilianisation is not now a financial one but a quality of service one. Civilians are effectively, highly skilled, single tasking specialists who can provide a very high quality of service in their particular area. By utilising them in the most appropriate roles, the police service is trying to provide the optimum mix of skills and expertise which will in turn provide the best quality of service to its customers. In so doing, it must recognise that these skills come at a cost and that the primary aim of any future civilianisation programme will not be to reduce the wage bill, but to provide a better quality of service.

Managing the Special Constabulary

Although civilians, the special constabulary are a sub group of the police civilian strength, in that they are a voluntary group providing an operational support function to regular police officers. Unpaid, these 'hobby bobbies' are motivated to attend for duty as a public service and are not subject to the terms and conditions and pay scale issues relating to full time civilian employees of the service (though civilians may also be specials of course).

The special constabulary has its own management structure based on rank, with section officers, sub divisional officers and an executive team headed by a chief commandant. The discipline of the regular officers is mirrored in the emphasis placed by the special constabulary on obeying superior officers and respect for rank and uniform. The chief commandant fulfils a key role in the effective management of the special constabulary by providing a focus for force policy; the post holder is an agent for promulgating the philosophy of the organisation.

Whilst members of the special constabulary do not face all of the issues which confront salaried civilians, there is an argument that specials are not utilised to their full potential, and more effective management could maximise their value to the service. The problems which they encounter include:

- Integration: *with, and gaining the acceptance of, regular officers. This issue has been highlighted as common to all civilians, and it is related to the prevalent operational culture. It can be addressed by educating and encouraging regular officers as to the valuable service which the special constabulary can provide.*

- Communication: *with regular officers. The part time nature of the role of special constables means that they are on duty irregularly and there can be difficulties of effective communication, which hinders effective management. Communications between special constables and regular officers can be facilitated and monitored by the (regular) liaison officer, by the use of specials' notice-boards, and their inclusion on circulation lists. However most importantly, the force communications strategy (see chapter 8 Managing Information) should acknowledge and plan for the utilisation of the resource offered by the special constabulary, thus creating an environment conducive to effective management.*

Some of the management issues concerning specials were crystallised in a Channel 4 television documentary shown in 1996 which featured the activities of a number of Derbyshire special constables. This programme generated exchanges in the letters column of the *Police Review* raising issues of professionalism and training. Derbyshire's ACC, Don Dovaston, emphasised that in an underfunded force, his managers had become adept at managing all resources to achieve optimum output and he reinforced that trained specials are 'seen as an essential part of supporting the operational requirements of the force.' (*Police Review*, 10 May 1996) Other correspondents were somewhat dismissive of the professionalism and training of the specials and argued that policing should not be carried out on the cheap, but should be the preserve of fully trained career professionals.

As the above example illustrates, senior police managers have undoubtedly recognised that in these times of pressured resources and limited budgets, the special constabulary are potentially a large and willing resource. In this respect, forces are running continuous recruitment campaigns to attract specials. The Home Office initiated and financed a national recruitment campaign (at a cost of £2 million) between April 1995 and March 1996. During this period 4,500 specials were recruited, but this figure only slightly exceeded the number of specials that left during the same period. The strength of the volunteer force remained at approximately 19,700 over this period (source: HMIC). One partial explanation for the wastage is that increasing numbers of potential full time officers are serving as specials until they succeed in joining the service on a permanent basis.

The Home Office recruitment initiative mentioned above was part of a programme through which £6 million became available for which forces could bid to fund the recruitment, training and equipping of specials. At force level there are signs that forces are planning their training more thoroughly. For example, Staffordshire Police has a training programme which runs over 26 weeks and includes examinations. The training is practical and up-to-date, including training in the use of CS spray.

Central government commitment to professionalising the specials is also evidenced by a report published in 1996 by the Home Office Working Group on the Special Constabulary. This group made recommendations that would place specials on a similar footing to regulars and civilians in terms of:

- Training based on the probationer training programme
- A more formal complaints and discipline procedure
- Access to the grievance procedures already available to regulars and civilians
- Compensation for injuries

These positive trends are reinforced by some evidence (particularly from HMIC sources) that during the last few years there has been more effective communication between regulars and specials. If such trends continue, they will contribute towards the more effective utilisation of the services offered by the special constabulary.

Chapter Summary

- The police service has a tradition of employing civilian staff. In earlier days civilians were appointed to senior posts but this practice declined as professionalisation of the service was pursued. The trend has reversed since World War Two from which time civilians have been appointed to predominantly lower management levels.

- Civilianisation has moved through phases of types of function. The civilianisation of manual posts was followed by administrative and then technical posts and in the 1990s there has been a breakthrough into professional posts.

- Civilians are finally breaking through into truly senior management positions, though the numbers of civilians in senior policy making posts are disproportionately low considering civilians now represent one third of the police service workforce.

- There are inherent problems in achieving the effective management of civilians. These include issues of control, of a lack of a career structure, of inferior pay and terms and conditions compared not only to police officers but to other local government employees.

- The strong operational police culture is a barrier to the integration of civilians and thus to the realising of their full potential.

- Despite the highlighted issues, there are indications that conditions are being created which will be conducive to the effective management of civilians. These include the development and implementation of career development structures and progressive quality of service initiatives.

Chapter 13

Managing the Future: Whither Police Management?

Managing the Future: Whither Police Management?

'And in today already walks tomorrow.'
Samuel Taylor Coleridge

It is at this juncture that the authors are hostages to fortune, gazing into the crystal ball and speculating on the developing trends in, and challenges to, police management for the late 1990s and into the twenty first century.

The previous chapters have examined different, but interlinking, spheres of management and the changing environment in which the police are operating. This environment and external factors including legislation, government policy and the public's expectations, will influence police managers as much as internal force policies and pressure from such agencies as the Home Office and HMIC.

Figure. 13.1 shows the factors which will play an increasingly more important part in the influencing of the strategy of police forces. The greatest of these will be the environmental influences which include the reaction of central government to public opinion nationally and the changing of the law as a result, local needs and perceptions as portrayed by local government, industry and commerce, and local voluntary and community groups. Work carried out during 1997 by the Centre for Public Services Management and Research at Staffordshire University for the West Mercia Police has highlighted the potential effect of the following 'top-ten' environmental influences at both the national and (West Midlands) regional level:

- Issues which derive from the development of new technologies
- Economic development and the decline of manufacturing industry
- Economic pressures on police funding
- The regionalisation of government and the increasing role of Europe
- Further development of local and regional partnerships
- Increasing regional and local corporatism
- Continuing problems of the criminal justice system
- Population shifts resulting from employment change and urban decay
- Transport changes and pressures of traffic on the environment
- Social and economic pressures which will continue to radically change the rural and urban environments.

Factors such as these will generate an ever increasing need for the police to have a positive reaction and to modify their strategy where this is required to meet the changing policing environment. In addition, the increased emphasis on monitoring and control of all operations will continue to place a greater burden of accountability on police managers for their day-to-day management tasks.

Continued cash limited budgets will mean that much more care will be required in the type, quantity and timescales required to meet particular strategies and to optimise their outcomes. Managers will have to plan more effectively in order to meet their objectives within these resource limitations.

Changing performance requirements have become a way of life. Sometimes the wheel turns full circle. In the earlier part of the twentieth century the 'local bobby' was an essential part of policing. This has been gradually phased out over the last

Fig 13.1

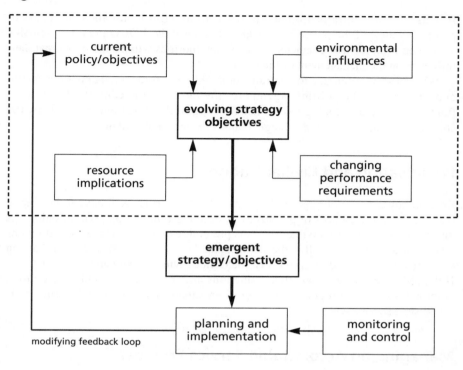

thirty years to be replaced by the police 'squad car', although the trend is currently being reversed with community policing coming back into favour. In a constantly evolving environment, changing performance requirements are a necessity if the incidence of crime is not only to be contained but also decreased. These and other factors are constantly acting on current policy and objectives, to modify them and to have an emergent strategy which will successfully meet these new criteria.

The immediate future will involve managing the implications of the 1994 Police and Magistrates' Courts Act, the Police Acts of 1996 and 1997 and other impending legislation. This in itself will require management skills in the areas covered in earlier chapters; **management of change** to cope with new relationships and accountabilities; **management of finance** as devolved budgets and their implications come on-line; **strategic management** as policing plans are developed; **project, information** and **technology management** as the plans are implemented; and overarching all these areas is the **management of people** and the **management of their professional conduct**, both **police officers** and **civilians**.

Other issues which are likely to continue to engage the attention of police managers include:

Centralisation and Politicisation

It is likely that centralisation and politicisation will remain an issue. Fears of political control of the police have been raised since the 1970s, and it still remains to be seen what the true character of the new authorities will be and how great their influence on the management of the service will be.

With specific reference to centralisation, although force amalgamations would appear to be off the political agenda for the moment, the central allocation of funding and the developing role of HMIC, suggest that this topic may occupy the speculations, and maybe the strategic plans, of senior police managers.

Privatisation and Civilianisation

Psychic powers are not required to predict that the service will have to be able to manage the consequences of privatisation, or at least increasing civilianisation. As discussed in chapter 12, civilianisation is preferable to police managers as it retains control of the functions within the service, and ACPO's successful rearguard action very effectively diluted the 1994-5 Home Office review of core and ancillary tasks. If the police are to retain ancillary functions and increase the number of civilian employees it is vital that a realistic civilian career and support infrastructure is established service wide.

Managing an Accountable Service Provider

The issue of accountability is likely to remain at the forefront of policing debates. In addition to financial accountability, accountability through the civil courts seems likely to be a likely trend. In addition, as a provider of services to the public in an increasingly customer oriented society, the pressure will remain on the service to manage customer service initiatives effectively, develop charters and standards and to monitor performance against published benchmarks. The diverse skills required to achieve objectives will include project management skills, and both technology and information management skills.

In these circumstances the importance of image management cannot be neglected. The service will need to develop strategies to promote and explain its activities in a proactive manner, and there is evidence that individual forces are becoming increasingly sophisticated in their media handling. This trend is likely to continue, particularly with the growing interest in police ethics and values. This interest is linked to accountability issues and image management will have a role to play as the statements of values are adopted and need to be publicised.

Information Technology

Like most organisations the police service has set off down the information highway and like many organisations reinvents the wheel and builds incompatible systems (has anybody noticed that continuing phenomena of the 90s – nomadic police officers roving the country observing computer systems in other forces and then going home and building (or employing somebody to build) the same but different system?) This may diminish with the implementation of the national IT strategy launched in November 1994, and it is the authors' firm belief as outlined in chapters 8 and 9 that 'information' must take pre-eminence over 'technology', the latter being the monkey to information's organ grinder and not *vice versa*.

People/Projects/Technology

If the drive for efficiency and effectiveness continues (and there is little reason to believe it will not) there will be the constant need to manage resources ever more effectively. This will necessitate skilful management of people, which may favour continued progression towards the flatter consultative management style which is currently growing in acceptance and popularity. This complements the project based culture explored in chapter 10, and will also encompass management of technology with all that it entails – from procurement to implementation and review.

... and Finally, Leadership

The police service is facing an uncertain future as it reels from new legislation and from reviews concerning its role, its functions and its rewards. Good leadership is a prerequisite of taking the service through the remaining years of this century and into the twenty-first, as an effective service capable of meeting the expectations of the public. There is evidence to suggest that the dinosaurs are becoming extinct and that an able generation of chief officers is assuming command. These senior managers will find succour in nurturing within their organisations good management principles and practices, by motivating all employees and allowing them the opportunities to realise their full potential.

Bibliography

Alderson, J (1984) *Human Rights and the Police*, Strasbourg: Council of Europe

ACPO (1990) *Strategic Policy Document*

ACPO (1990) *Through the Millennium*

Adair, J G (1984) 'The Hawthorne Effect', *Journal of Applied Psychology 69*

Ackoff, R C (1970) *A Concept of Corporate Planning*, Wiley

Andersen, E S *et al* (1987) *Goal Directed Project Management*, Kogan Page

Ansoff, HI (1968) *Corporate Strategy,* Pelican

Audit Commission:
   Reviewing the Organisation of Provincial Forces. Police Paper 9 (1991)
   Pounds and Coppers: Financial Delegation in Provincial Police Forces.
      Police Paper 10 (1991)
   Helping with Enquiries: Tackling Crime Effectively. Police Paper 12 (1993)
   *Cheques and Balances: A Management Handbook on Police planning and
      Financial Delegation.* Police Paper 13 (1994).

Barnes, M (1989) *Have Project, Will Manage*, BBC

Belbin, R M (1976) 'Building Effective Management Teams', *Journal of General Management*, 2, 1976

Belbin, R M (1981) *Management Teams: Why they Succeed or Fail*, Butterworth Heineman

Benyon, J (ed.) (1984) *Scarman and After*, Pergamon Press

Berry, G D (1994) 'Civilians in the Police Force', *Parliamentary Brief*, Summer Recess, 1994

Berry, G D and Carter, M P (1991) *Assessing Crime Prevention Initiatives: The First Steps*, Home Office Crime Prevention Unit, Paper 31

Berry, GD and Izat, JG (1995) *Framework for the Effective Management of Initiatives,* Home Office PRG

Bradley, D *et al* (1986) *Law, Organisation and Democracy*, Harvester Press

Brogden, M (1982) *The Police: Autonomy and Consent*, Academic Press

Burgstaller and Forsyth (1973) 'The Key-result Approach to Designing Information Systems', *Management Advisor*, May/June 1973)

Butler, A J P (1992) *Police Management*, Dartmouth

Cashmore, E (1994) *'...and there was Television'*, Routledge

Clelland, D I and King W R (1983) *Systems Analysis and Project Management*, McGraw-Hill

Clelland, D I and King, W R (1988) *The Project Management Handbook*, Van Nostrand Reinhold

Clutterbuck, D and Snow, D (1990) *Working with the Community*, Weidenfeld and Nicholson

Clutterbuck, R (1980) *Britain in Agony: The Growth of Political Violence*, Penguin.

Critchley, T A (1978) *A History of Police in England and Wales*, Constable

Diebold, J (1980) *Managing Information: The Challenge and the Opportunity*

Drucker, P F (1955) *The Practice of Management*, Heinemann

Drucker, P F (1988) *'The Coming of the New Organisation'*, Harvard Business Review

Earl, M J (1989) *Management Strategies for Information Technology*, Prentice Hall

Emsley, C (1996) *The English Police – A Political and Social History*, 2nd Edition, Longman

Fiedler, F E (1967) *A Theory of Leadership Effectiveness*, McGraw-Hill

Fiedler, F E and Chemers, M M (1974) *Leadership and Effective Management*, Scott Foresman and Co

Force Annual Reports 1993-7, including:
    Gloucestershire Constabulary
    Greater Manchester Police
    Kent Constabulary
    Leicestershire Constabulary
    Metropolitan Police
    Merseyside Police
    Northamptonshire Police
    Nottinghamshire Constabulary
    Staffordshire Police
    South Yorkshire Police
    Suffolk Constabulary
    West Midlands Police

Graef, R (1989) *Talking Blues*, London: Fontana

Harrington, J (1991) *Organisational Structure and Information Technology*, Prentice Hall

Herzberg, F, Mausner, B and Snyderman B (1959) *The Motivation to Work*, John Wiley

Highmore, S (1993) 'Pulling Together', *Police Review*, 12 November 1993

Highmore, S (1993) *The Integration of Police Officers and Civilian Staff*, Home Office, Police Research Group

Holloway, S (1988) *Data Administration*, Gower Technical Press

Home Office and Scottish Home Department (1949) *Oaksey Report: Report of the Committee on Police Conditions of Service*, Part I

Home Office: Police Advisory Board (1966) *Taverne Report: Report of the Working Party on Police Manpower*

Home Office (1983) Home Office Circular 114/83: *Manpower, Effectiveness and Efficiency in the Police Service*

Home Office (1988) Home Office Circular 105/88: *Civilian Staff in the Police Service*

Home Office (1988) Home Office Circular 106/88: *Applications for Increases in Police Force Establishments*

Home Office (1993) *Police Reform: A Police Service for the Twenty-first Century*, Cm 2281, London, HMSO

Home Office (1994) *Review of Police Core and Ancilliary Tasks*, (The Posen Report), London, Home Office

Houghton, G R and Willis, K (1986) Data Analysis Techniques and their Use in Providing Information to Police Management, Home Office SRDB, Appendices to 23/86

Hussey, D E (1979) *Corporate Planning: Theory and Practice*, Pergamon

Irving, B, Faulkner, D, Topping, P and Frosdick, S (1996) *Reacting to non-major crime: the management of police resources*, London: Home Office

Ives, B and Learmonth, G P (1984) 'The Information System as a Competitive Weapon', *Communications of the ACM*, Vol. 27, No. 12

Johnson, G and Scholes, K (1993) *Exploring Corporate Strategy: Text and Cases*, 3rd Edition, Prentice Hall

Joint Consultative Committee (1990) *Operational Policing Review*

Kleinig, J (1995) 'Ethical questions facing Law-enforcement Agents' in Almond, B (Ed) (1995) *Introducing Applied Ethics*, Oxford: Blackwell

Kleinig, J (1996) *The Ethics of Policing*, Cambridge: Cambridge University Press

Klockars, C B (1980) 'The Dirty Harry Problem' in *The Annals*, 452, pp. 33-47, November, 1980

Kwiatkowski, W (1989) 'Managing the Introduction of New Technology', *Management Services*, September 1989

Landy, F J and Becker, W S (1987) *Motivation Theory Reconsidered*

Leishman, F et al (1996) *Core Issues in Policing*, Longmans

Loveday, B (1993) *Civilian Staff in the Police Force*, Research Paper 2, Centre for the Study of Public Order, University of Leicester

Loveday, B (1994) 'The Police and Magistrates' Court Act', *Policing*, Vol. 10, No. 4. Winter 1994

Lubans, V A and Edgar, J E (1979) *Policing by Objectives*, Social Development Corporation, Hartford, Conn

McGregor, D (1960) *The Human Side of Enterprise*, McGraw-Hill

McKenzie I (1995) 'A clip round the ear' in *Policing*, Vol. 11, No. 3. Autumn, 1995

McLelland, D C (1961) *The Achieving Society*, Van Nostrand

McLynn, F (1991) *Crime and Punishment in Eighteenth Century England*, Oxford

Maguire, M and Corbett, C (1991) *A Study of the Police Complaints System*, London, HMSO

Manning, P (1977) *Police Work: the Social Organisation of Policing*, MIT Press

Mark, R (1978) *In the Office of Constable*, London: Collins and Son

Maslow, A H (1970) *Motivation and Personality*, 2nd Edition, Harper and Row

Mawby, R C (1994) *Dinosaurs versus Subversives: Management Training and the Police Service*, Staffordshire University Business School Discussion Paper, No. 2

Mawby, R C (1997) *Survey of police service media and public relations offices* Stafford: CPSMR, Staffordshire University

Mintzberg, H (1973) *The Nature of Managerial Work*, Harper and Row

Morgan, J (Chairman) (1991) *Safer Communities: The Local Delivery of Crime Prevention through the Partnership Approach*, Home Office

Morgan, R and Newburn, T (1997) *The Future of Policing*, Oxford University Press

Morris, P W G (1992) *The Management of Projects: Lessons from the Last 50 years*, Thos. Telford

Newburn, T (1995) *Crime and Criminal Justice Policy*, Longman

Nicholls, J G (1984) 'Achievement, motivation, etc.', *Psychological Review* 91, No 3

Nino, C S (1991) *The Ethics of Human Rights*, Oxford: Oxford University Press

Oliver, I (1996) *Police, Government and Accountability*, 2nd Edition, Macmillan

Parker Follett, M (1981) *The New State*, Peter Smith

Pike, M (1985) *The Principles of Policing*, Macmillan

Police Foundation/Policy Studies Institute (1996) *Report of the Independent Committee of Enquiry into the Role and Responsibilities of the Police* (The Cassels Report), London: Police Foundation/Policy Studies Institute

Police and Magistrates' Courts Act, 1994: HMSO

Porter, L W and Steers, R M (1983) *Motivation and Work Behaviour*, 3rd Edition. McGraw Hill

Porter, M (1982) *Competitive Strategy,* Free Press

Reiner, R (1991) *Chief Constables*, Oxford: Oxford University Press

Reiner, R (1992) *The Politics of the Police*, 2nd Edition, Harvester Wheatsheaf

Reiner, R (1994) 'What should the police be doing?' *Policing* Vol. 10, No. 3

Richards, M (1978) *Organisational Goal Structures*

Rix, B (1993) 'Marketing the Police' *Focus*, December 1993, Home Office, PRG

Saulsbury, W, Mott, J and Newburn, T (eds) *Themes in Contemporary Policing*, London: Police Foundation/Policy Studies Institute

Scarman, Rt. Hon. The Lord OBE, (1981) *Report of an enquiry: The Brixton Disorders* 10-12 April 1981 Cmnd 8427 London: HMSO.

Schlesinger, P and Tumber, H (1994) *Reporting Crime*, Oxford University Press

Sheehy, Sir Patrick, (1993) *Committee of Enquiry into the Police Responsibilities and Rewards*, Cm2280.I: II: HMSO

Stephens, M and Becker, S (eds) (1994) *Police Force: Police Service*, Macmillan

Stoffels J D (1994) *Strategic Issues Management: A Comprehansive Guide to Environmental Scanning*, Elsivier/The Planning Forum

Stoner, J A F, and Wankel, C (1896) *Management*, 3rd edition, Prentice Hall

Thomas, J M. and Bennis, W G. (1972) *The Management of Change and Conflict*, Penguin

Vroom, V H. and Yetton, Pp W. (1973) *Leadership and Decision Making* University of Pittsburg Press

Wolf Olins (1988) *A Force for Change*, London:Wolf Olins

Wright, A and Irving, B (1996) 'Value Conflicts in Policing – Crisis into Opportunity, in *Policing and Society,* Vol. 6, pp. 199-211

Wright, A (1996) *Notes on Environmental Scanning and Forecasting*, Staffordshire University (Policing Futures Forum)

Making Critical use of Experience' in *Policing and Society.* Vol. 6, pp. 199-211

Zander M (1994) 'Ethics and Crime Investigation by the Police' in *Policing*, Vol. 10, No. 1, Spring 1994

Glossary

Glossary of Terms Found in this Book

Aims
The direction or guidance with respect to a particular course of action. See Objectives.

Appraisal
The process of assessing the worth, value or performance of something or someone. The 'appraiser' should be suitably authorised and qualified to be able to judge.

Assessment
The act of assessing. *See Evaluation.*

Assets
Anything of value or use owned by an individual or organisation. An accounting term for the book values of such items, appearing on the financial balance sheet of an organisation.

Audit
A thorough and comprehensive inspection of a particular task, role, department or organisation. In an accounting sense, an audit is an inspection of financial systems and books of account with a view to issuing a certificate of verification.

'Bottom up'
The process of developing strategies, activities or approaches to a particular problem, taking account of the views of the lower levels of an organisation

Brainstorming
A technique by which a group attempts to find a solution to a particular problem, by amassing all the ideas and thoughts of its members spontaneously.

Budget
A plan for the co-ordination of resources across an organisation. Primarily, budgets are of a financial nature, representing the activities and resources of an organisation in financial terms.

Budget holder
Individual or department responsible for managing a particular budget or set of budgets. The budget holder may not be responsible for developing the budget, though they should at least be consulted in its preparation.

Cash limited budgets
Budgets which show how resources are to be allocated, where there is a limit on the total amount of funding available to the organisation to carry out all of its activities.

Change management
The management of incremental (day to day) change and the planned programme of change which reacts to the changing environment.

Competence-based training
Qualifications which assess the competence of the participant (NVQ, GNVQ, SVQ) in their workplace.

Competitive advantage
The process of influencing the circumstances under which competition takes place in order to gain advantage. For example, the use of a computer-based ordering system may enable an organisation to provide its products to its customers quicker than its competitors, thus gaining an advantage over them.

Corporate
Relating to a corporation or any other organisation.

Corporation
A group of persons or objects treated by law as an individual, having rights and liabilities distinct from those of the persons comprising it.

Corporate appraisal
The systematic review of the performance and effectiveness of an organisation.

Cost centre
An accounting mechanism set up to identify the costs and revenues relating to a specific activity. For example, expenditure on patrol vehicle fuel might be charged against a particular cost centre to easily identify and monitor the amount of money spent on that item.

Customer – internal/external
External customers are those outside the service, eg the public. Internal customers are those people within the service who receive added value to the work that they do through the use of the product or service that you give them.

Data
A collection of unprocessed facts associated with a particular activity.

Database
An organised store of data which is often, though not always, in a computerised form.

Demographics
The statistical study of the quality of life and living conditions in communities.

Electronic mail
A computerised facility for sending messages between individuals.

Evaluation
The process of assessing the performance of something or someone against stated aims and objectives.

Human resource management
The process of managing and making best use of the management of human resources (people) available to an organisation. It invariably encompasses such functions as personnel, training, career planning and counselling.

Information
Data which has been processed into a form which is meaningful to the recipient.

Information technology (IT)
The technology which is used to process data and information. The term usually encompasses all forms of computers (hardware and software) and communications technologies such as networking hardware and software.

Infrastructure
The component parts or structures which form the basis of any organisation.

Leadership
A management skill used in an organisation/team environment by managers with the qualities to provide a motivating climate. It is externally focused contrasting with motivation which is primarily internally focused.

Management information
Data which has been processed into a form, meaningful to the recipient and of value in supporting the decision making process.

Management – bureaucratic style Management which depends largely on inflexible systems and inhibits the participation of lower management and staff.

Management – active (proactive) Management which plans and anticipates and which predicts future problems and generates actions to address them.

Management – passive (reactive) Management by reacting to situations; the extreme form is 'fire fighting' management.

Manager centred management development programmes Programmes designed to fit the actual requirements of the personnel attending.

Market An economic term for the total population of persons or organisations which other persons or organisations are trying to sell their products and services to.

Market share The proportion of the total market which a particular individual or organisation can claim to be the supplier to. An organisation which has a 10 per cent share of the UK car market has one tenth of the potential customers in its market buying its particular models of car.

Marketing A generic term for any business activity designed to support the selling of products and services. It encompasses such activities as sales, advertising and promotion, pricing and distribution. It is often referred to as resting on the four 'Ps' of Price, Performance, Promotion and Place.

Milestone Key events in the life of a project which are identified at the project inception and enable progress to be measured accurately.

Mission statement A very broad statement of the underlying objectives and philosophy of an organisation.

Monitoring The regular observation, testing and recording of the operation of something in order to control its effective and efficient execution.

Monopoly A market condition whereby there is only one supplier of the required product or service to the whole market. A monopolistic supplier therefore has a 100 per cent market share.

Motivation To managers a process to induce others to act in a certain way; to employees, encouragement towards particular goals.

Objectives Desired outcomes from a particular activity or set of activities. *See Aims.*

Organisation An organised system or group of people working together towards a shared set of objectives.

Outsourcing The process of sub contracting certain activities to a third party. For example, certain traffic duties, research and development.

Policy	A generic principle or agreed plan of action which determines the nature of particular activities.
Programme centred management development	Programmes which are not tailored to individual's needs but cover a range of activities in a 'scatter gun' approach.
Project based management	A management style in which there is a flatter management structure which controls and directs teams of people who have specialist knowledge relevant to the project being undertaken.
Project champion	The person appointed as the motivating force to ensure that the best effort is made to achieve the objectives of that particular project.
Pyramid management	A 'top down' management structure comprising several hierarchical layers.
Quality	The totality of features and characteristics of a product or service that bears on its ability to satisfy given needs. (American National Standards Institute 1978 and British Standards BS 4778).
Qualitative measures	Performance indicators which attempt to measure the quality of outcomes from a particular activity or activities.
Quantitative measures	Performance indicators which attempt to measure the quantity of outcomes from a particular activity or activities.
Resources	Items which can be used by an individual or organisation to help it achieve its objectives. These will include finance, people and technology.
Scenario	The sketch or outline of a particular situation.
Service level agreement (SLA)	An agreement between the service provider and service consumer relating to the level and quality of service to be provided in a variety of situations.
Simulation	A form of modelling designed to assist decision making by attempting to replicate a real life situation and all the factors influencing it.
Spreadsheet	A computerised set of rows and columns which can be used to analyse and manipulate numerical data quickly and easily and present it in a variety of forms.
Strategy	A longer term plan or course of action which gives direction to the activities of an organisation.
Systems	A set of orderly or regular methods of procedure by which management can control the overall sequence of operations within the organisation.
Top down approach	The process of developing strategies, activities or approaches to a particular problem from the highest levels of the organisation.

Total quality The acceptance of the fact that quality standards pervade every level in an organisation and are a necessary factor in the successful operation of the units within it.

TQM Management by the application of total quality and the concepts outlined by W Edwards Deming, usually recognised as the 'father' of TQM

Training An activity directed towards maintaining and improving current job performance.

Variance Accounting term for the difference between a budget figure and actual figure. For example, if overtime costs are £1,000 compared to a budget of £800 there is a variance of £200.

Vision *See Mission statement.*

Work package Within project management, a number of associated actions which have a defined and measurable outcome and, if successfully completed, will have achieved a sub-objective or milestone.

Index